ISLAMIC DEMOCRACY AND ITS LIMITS

Tawfiq Alsaif

ISLAMIC DEMOCRACY
AND ITS LIMITS

The Iranian Experience Since 1979

SAQI

London San Francisco Beirut

ISBN: 978–0–86356–650–9

This first edition published by Saqi Books

© Tawfiq Alsaif, 2007

A full CIP record for this book is available from the British Library.
A full CIP record for this book is available from the Library of Congress.

Manufactured in Lebanon

SAQI

26 Westbourne Grove, London W2 5RH
825 Page Street, Suite 203, Berkeley, California 94710
Tabet Building, Mneimneh Street, Hamra, Beirut
www.saqibooks.com

Contents

Contents

Acknowledgments

I wish to express my deep gratitude to my academic supervisor Dr Abdelwahab El-Affendi, without whose patience and guidance this study would not have been completed. My appreciation is also due to Dr Ali Paya and Professor John Keane, from whom I have learned a great deal. I thank also my uncle Dr Abdul-Jalil Alsaif for his constant encouragement and support. I am indebted to many friends and colleagues who generously supported me throughout the last four years. To them all I express my deep appreciation and gratitude.

A Note on Transliteration

I have tried my best to make the transliterations of Arabic and Farsi names, terms and places as approximate as possible to the phonetic pronunciation. Names of authors who chose certain spelling in their published works were put according to their preferences. In the endnotes, I have used the original titles of Farsi and Arabic books and articles to which I referred. The same rule is followed in the list of sources, however with an English translation.

Introduction

Since the Iranian revolution of 1979, so-called political Islam has been a point of contention among politicians and political theorists throughout the world. The phenomenal mobilisation under the banner of Islam challenged the common assumption among theorists of development that, with modernisation, religion gradually loses its influence in the public arena. In the early 1980s, some researchers predicted a short life for Islamic revivalism. After twenty-five years, that assumption seems far removed from the realities on the ground. The extraordinary eruption of religious sentiments during this period has gradually evolved into a trans-national movement featuring at least one common characteristic: the assertion of religion in national politics. Whether this presents a revival of national identity, a reaction to alleged humiliations at the hands of foreign powers or a renewed conviction in the viability of the religious cure for the grievances of Muslim societies, this phenomenon represents a provocative challenge to the study of politics.

The broad religious trend combines a variety of outlooks, including traditionalist, modernist, anarchist and others. Among these, one outlook seems to have attracted less attention: the one that argues for the possible formulation of a new discourse bringing together the major principles of democracy and Islam.

This study aims to investigate the viability of this discourse, particularly with regard to its capability for dealing with the religious, cultural and political barriers that have so far hindered the process of democratisation in Muslim societies. The study focuses on the discursive and doctrinal transformations within Shi'i Islam in Iran after the 1979 revolution in order to establish an empirical framework for the analysis of this possibility.

The Islamic Republic of Iran represents, as one scholar puts it, 'an evermore interesting laboratory for observing political Islam in practice'.[1] This is partially due to the country having already experienced some aspects of modernity, including a degree of industrialisation and constitutionalism, in addition to the fact that the Islamic regime was brought about by a popular revolution. In such cases, society becomes intensely politicised, and its desires profoundly influence the making of the new political system. The Islamic Republic has brought together a set of traditional and religious-oriented concepts with some modern ones, most of which were previously unfamiliar to the religious circles, including republicanism, elections, constitutional rights and so forth. It was assumed that such a combination would feature a profound and positive exchange between religious traditionalists and modern constituents, thus delivering a modern political order inspired by religious values.

The thesis argues that religious political thought, like every other aspect of life, does not exist in a vacuum. Its evolution is closely conditioned by its relations to other constituents of the surrounding environment. By the same token, the thesis argues that the political engagement of religion is likely to make it more appreciative of the imperative of the modern state. The direction towards which religious thought will evolve, whether by an embracing of democracy or the justification of autocracy, is likely to be determined by other factors, namely the influence of the forces within the social structure and the international atmosphere.

To advance the above argument, an eclectic approach will be employed. A special emphasis, however, is to be put on approaches developed by the theories of political development, particularly those that stress the role of political culture. The concept of development is based on the definition advanced by the UN Development Programme (UNDP), in which development is viewed as a comprehensive process aiming to enlarge people's choices. Democratisation is conceived with reference to the theories of political culture, where the vigour or otherwise of the process is ascribed to the hegemonic culture, whether it leans towards participation or self-alienation.

Although Iranian affairs continued to attract considerable interest among political researchers, the current debate over democracy and the general reconciliation between religion and modernity within the country has attracted less attention. In this regard, I would like to refer particularly to the insightful studies of Ansari (2000), Vahdat (2002) and Moslem (2002), which offer valuable information on and analysis of the course of change within the Islamic Republic. Nevertheless, their studies stop short of addressing many important questions in this regard. Thus, this study will try to cover some of the areas that, although crucial to an accurate treatment of the issues in question, remain in need of more investigation.

The Structure of the Study

The study covers the current debates over democratisation, its ideological background, the social forces involved and the way it affects the political process.

Chapter One charts the course of evolution of the Shi'i doctrine of authority since it took shape in the eighth century until the emergence of the Islamic Republic in 1979. This chapter presents a background to the questions arising through the ongoing debate over political authority, the sources of legitimacy and the role of the religious establishment. By locating the major developments of the above doctrine within their historical context, the chapter tries to explore the motives, potentials and limitations inherent in the established paradigm of authority and the chief concerns of its guardians. The argument is that the major revisions of the Shi'i conception of power have been instigated by the change of socio-political conditions for the Shi'a community, particularly after the emergence of Shi'i dynasties in the tenth century and after. To put it differently, religion's propensity for adapting to the living realities of its followers is largely contingent upon the existence of a helpful environment. This becomes even more likely if the religion gets directly involved in the political process.

Chapter Two discusses the extensive revision made by Ayatollah Khomeini to the established Shi'i doctrine of authority. Khomeini's contribution involves some essential adjustments to both the basic elements and function of the doctrine, amounting to a discursive shift within the established paradigm. Khomeini is presented as one of those charismatic leaders whose person and discourse have, in a certain epoch, bridged the gap between the ages of tradition and modernity. He helped his people to rethink their traditions and join the march of modernity without fearing the loss of their identity or cultural specificity, as was the case of the Shah's modernising programmes of the 1960s. By so doing, religion had the opportunity to shift from being a pretext for self-alienation on the part of the society into an agent for active participation in public affairs. The chapter also presents a new approach to Khomeini's notion of 'the jurist's absolute authority'. While his critics take it as evidence of his authoritarian tendencies, the chapter will argue that the notion is employed as a means of removing the mystical character from religious authority and reuniting the hitherto-divided religious and state authorities.

The discussion then focuses on the application of the principle of 'social justice' through the political and economic strategies of the post-revolutionary governments. The aspiration for justice is the axis of the Shiʻi political worldview. Chapter Three aims to explore the thread running through the constantly changing Iranian political environment. This process is regarded as a quest for identity on the part of the Islamic regime. Since this study is concerned in the first place with the type of transformations that feature durable and far-reaching effects, the emphasis here is on cultural and institutional changes. It has been quite a long time since the study of development in the Third World shifted from emphasising the role of the so-called modernising elites to focusing on the social structure as a whole as the pivot of development. In this light, the chapter goes through some of the major developments since the Islamic Revolution until the present day, trying to explore the landmarks that signify the advance of the democratic discourse. In other words, the chapter considers the totality of the political process during the last twenty-five years as a laboratory to explore whether the approximate direction of the Islamic regimes is leaning towards democracy or not. The chapter will use Thomas Kuhn's theory of paradigm shift as a conceptual framework to explain the emergence of the Reformist discourse. My aim is to highlight the wide gap between the model of ruling and socialisation which prevailed since the revolution and that advocated by the Reformist faction. I argue that the shift of public opinion towards the Reformist paradigm represents a definite disassociation from the established paradigm of religiosity and politics. The chapter outlines the deficits that brought the traditional-revolutionary paradigm to its knees and made the shift of paradigm inescapable. In addition to the authoritarian and populist dispositions of the Islamic regime, the chapter underlines its potential to develop from within.

Chapter Four illustrates the model of state advocated by the conservative faction, including its standpoints towards such issues as citizenship and political rights, legitimacy and the rule of law, republicanism and the role of people, as well as the grounding principles of the faction's political ideology. The discussion expands on the main thesis of this study, which regards the political involvement of religious ideology as the determinant factor behind its evolution.

The conservative camp represents mainly the traditional segment of Iranian society, including the clerical establishment and the leading Bazaar traders. It upholds traditional jurisprudence, together with the general jurisprudential perception of religion, as the defining framework for the questions arising within the political and social arena. Nevertheless, the conservative discourse shows a clear deviation from the earlier traditions of the Shiʻi seminaries. This is undoubtedly a consequence of the integration of religion into the state system and the constant expansion of modern patterns of administration, socialisation and politics.

Chapter Five aims to highlight the intrinsic incompatibility between the conservative and the Reformist discourses, which supports my assumption that the Reformist ascent to power in the late 1990s represents a paradigm shift in the sense advanced by Thomas Kuhn. The Reformist trend emerged through the Thermidorian phase of the Islamic Revolution. Thus it bore, at least partially, a reactionary feature with regard to the norms, values and patterns that prevailed during the first post-revolutionary decade. The Reformist discourse appeals mainly to the modern segment of Iranian society and leans towards liberal democracy. The chapter goes through the main themes of the Reformist discourse, including the notion of religious democracy, the theoretical ground of the discourse and its distinctive conception of secularism.

Chapter Six expands on the assumption that a democratic discourse can make no difference unless it is upheld by influential forces through whose agency the call for democracy shifts from an elitist aspiration to a mobilising appeal embraced by a considerable segment in society. The chapter thus aims to examine the viability of the course of democratisation with regard to the political forces that support it and those that oppose it. One of the main arguments of the study is that the evolution of religious thought towards democracy or otherwise depends to a large extent on the function of civil forces within the society that enlighten the people, mobilise them to exercise their rights and roles and hence enact their preferences. The chapter discusses briefly the relevance of party politics to the Iranian context and the social background of the major factions. Then, it introduces the main groups contending over power in the country.

Chapter Seven discusses the shift towards radicalism since the legislative elections of 2004. It provides a brief analysis of the elevation to power by the new conservative generation, the strategies embraced by the group and its implications to the national economy, political reforms, as well as the foreign relations of the country.

The concluding section includes a final assessment of such points as the possibility of reconciliation between religion and democracy, the role of the people within a religious-based political system, the capacity of religion to adapt to the modern patterns of politicisation and lifestyle, and so forth.

As stated earlier, the development of political thought in post-revolutionary Iran has attracted only slight attention among the large body of research focusing upon Iran and religious politics in general. This study therefore tries to offer an insight into that particular area. It focuses particularly on the Reformist trend, its ideology and performance, since it is assumed to be pioneering the modernist trend among the wide variety of Islamist groups in the Middle East. The trend can claim an exemplary role for many reasons, including its having a considerable number of well-trained politicians, activists and intellectuals, its open embracing of democracy as the ultimate goal and the centre of activity and its capacity to produce a relatively large and high-quality literature in support of its ideology and standpoints. Despite the failure of the trend to retain power, its eight-year rule has effectively changed the political environment of the country. When he stood down in August 2005, almost everyone felt that Iran after Muhammad Khatami, the Reformist president, was far different from what it had been on the eve of his election in 1997.

CHAPTER ONE

The Foundation of the Doctrine of Authority in Shi'ism

Shi'i political thought is undergoing a major shift. The theory of political authority as it is developing in the context of contemporary Iran is mainly concerned with the ruler's power, particularly his authority to use coercive power in cases that might result in taking an individual's life or limiting his right to property.[1] Established belief acknowledges that a divinely designated imam can enjoy such an immense power, and the debate thus concerns the delegation of the imam's authority to the fallible, i.e. non-divinely designated leaders. This explains why a good deal of the argument revolves around the source of the ruler's authority. Until recently the issue under question has been the nature of the delegation of authority from the imam to the leader, namely the qualified scholar. Since the early 1980s, however, the debate has come to be concerned with the relative weight of the authority delegated by the imam compared to that entrusted by the people. This shift in concern has been the result of the change of the doctrine's jurisdiction: from being the basis for a communal, mainly spiritual leadership to the major constituent of a state ideology.

With the emergence of Ayatollah Khomeini's version of *wilayat al-faqih* (guardianship of the jurist) in 1979, the ruler was authorised on both civil and religious grounds. The civil aspect is realised through general elections, while the religious one is secured through the conferment of the imam's authority onto the highest in rank among the religious scholars. The point of contention has thus been about the implications of that combination and the relative weight of political legitimacy secured by each of the two sources.

This chapter discusses the foundations of Shi'i political thought and the course of development through which the theory of wilayat al-faqih has emerged and become established as the major response to the question of political legitimacy in Twelver Shi'ism. This will provide for a better understanding of the background to many of the current debates. The chapter will start with a brief discussion of the factors responsible for the formation of the school's political thought. Then it will discuss how the first version of the doctrine of power has emerged and developed since the tenth century. This will help to understand the primary theoretical challenges to the doctrine of jurist guardianship.

The Foundations of Shi'ism

Shi'ism, the minor one of the two main branches of Islam, had shifted from being a mainly political to a mainly religious group to escape oppression at the hands of hostile rulers.[2] This transformation involved a review of the principles underpinning the group's leadership and its attitude towards the state. At the same time, there was a process aimed at driving the politically-minded and extremist trends out of the school's mainstream. Twelver Shi'ism emerged in the early tenth century,[3] the Usuli trend only establishing its dominance in the late eighteenth century. The more traditional Akhbari trend was driven to the margin at the hands of Wahid Behbehani (1705–1803), an influential scholar who challenged its dominance in the Shi'i school of jurisprudence.[4]

Shi'a religiosity and culture are dominated by three major themes: the tragedy of Karbala, the doctrine of Infallible Imamate as shaped by the sixth imam Ja'far al-Sadiq and the Occultation of the twelfth imam Muhammad al-Mahdi.

1. *The Karbala Tragedy*

Shi'a communities start the new year of the Islamic (*Hijri*) calendar with a ten-day mourning ritual, during which professional speakers and eulogists remind their audiences of what happened in Karbala over thirteen centuries ago. For some Shi'as, the communal service known as *'Ashura* is an expression of grief and mourning; for others, it is an indication of their readiness to make sacrifice for the cause of religion; and universally, it is the way in which Shi'a communities have maintained their distinct culture over centuries and generations.[5]

The town of Karbala, sixty miles south Baghdad, was the scene of a bloody showdown in which scores of the Prophet's family members and their supporters, led by his grandson Al-Husayn, were brutally massacred at the hands of the Umayyad forces in 680/60 ah. The impact of the massacre remains paramount. None of the many tragedies which Shi'as have endured in their history has been as influential as 'Ashura.[6] There are certain events, Welhausen suggests, which exercise an amazing effect, not because of the events themselves and their inevitable consequences, but because of their memory in men's hearts.[7] 'Ashura is undoubtedly one of these events, for it has been symbolised as a myth of heroism, purity and self-sacrifice in a worthy cause.[8]

Politically, 'Ashura was reproduced as the cultural foundation for renouncing the legitimacy of all forms of temporal rule. Soon, it would bring about an aspiration for an ideal form of justice that could only be realised by the Prophet's descendents taking over power.[9] Post-'Ashura Shi'ism has not consisted of a clearly definable group. It was the debates over leadership and the extent of political involvement that raised the need for definition and divided Shi'ias into many branches, including the Zaydis, the Isma'ilis and the Imami Shi'as.

The latter trend comprised the followers of the fourth imam Zayn al-'Abidin, the grandson of 'Ali bin Abi-Talib, the first Shi'i imam, and his successors. The trend would later evolve into the Twelver Shi'i sect, whose position was mainly apolitical.[10] The attribution of Twelver Imamis relates to the particular paradigm of religious leadership that became the chief feature of communal belonging. However, it had to wait for Ja'far al-Sadiq (702–65) to put the notion of the centrality of leadership into a definite religious form.

2. Al-Sadiq's Doctrine of Infallible Imamate

The sixth imam assumed the office of Imamate in 733 and retained it until his death in 765. This epoch was characterised by the decline of Umayyad power. In contrast, the move towards politicisation with the revolt of Zayd, the uncle of al-Sadiq, against Caliph Hisham in 739 gave rise to Shi'ism.[11] After the Umayyad dynasty collapsed in 750, the Islamic Caliphate was taken over by the 'Abbasids, a branch of the Hashim clan of the Prophet Muhammad. Many historians, such as Welhausen, believe that the 'Abbasids reaped the benefit of the struggles made by Shi'i factions to depose the Umayyads.[12] The last two decades of the Umayyad reign and the first decade of the 'Abbasid reign provided an interval during which the rulers were busily defending their power. Therefore, al-Sadiq and almost all other scholars of different schools in Islam had the opportunity to pursue without interruption their cultural and educational causes.[13]

Al-Sadiq was famous for his thorough and hard work. He is said to have had hundreds of disciples.[14] Such claims by Shi'i narrators are hard to verify since many of their written works are said to be lost.[15] However, the significance of al-Sadiq's work is evident by the sizeable body of traditions he left behind. According to some sources, the whole body of traditions of the twelve Shi'i imams was narrated by 5,415 actual witnesses among whom 3,217 narrated only al-Sadiq's teachings.[16] This indicates the amount of time he had dedicated to teaching and the variety of religious subjects with which he dealt. Today, almost two-thirds of jurisprudential rules common amongst Shi'as refer to al-Sadiq's traditions, which explains why the Shi'i legal school was named after him as the 'the Ja'afari School'.[17]

It was al-Sadiq's efforts which transformed the Shi'i faith from a sense of political or social affinity with the Prophet's family (*Ahl al-Bayt*) into a distinct religious school. In this regard, al-Sadiq has elevated the community leadership to a theological level. It was exclusively attached to the divinely designated persons whose role was regarded as an embodiment of God's grace and continuity of the Prophet's mission. Therefore, obedience to the leader would be, literally, linked to that of God and the Prophet, regardless of any political or social considerations.[18] Such an extremely high regard was necessary in order to distinguish the religious grouping under a God-ordained leadership (infallible Imamate) from the politically motivated groups that were widespread during this period.

Al-Sadiq's commitment to theological causes was evident in his renouncing of all revolutionary movements, including the Hashimite movement, which wanted to nominate him as caliph.[19] His approach was even tougher when it came to those who claimed a religious-based right to leadership.[20] Nonetheless, al-Sadiq welcomed with reservations those revolutionaries whose claim was limited to political leadership, as was evident in his treatment of Abu Muslim al-Khurasani, the 'Abbasid commander. According to Tabarsi, the Shi'i narrator, Abu Muslim, who helped the 'Abbasids to take over Persia, had sought the support of al-Sadiq against his rival 'Abbasid leaders. Al-Sadiq did not want to interfere; nevertheless, he gave him a warm welcome,[21] far different from his treatment of his own revolutionary relatives who claimed a divine right to leadership, including his cousin Muhammad bin 'Abdullah bin al-Hasan, known as al-Nafs al-Zakiyya (the Pure Soul).[22]

As Montgomery Watt rightly put it, up to the year 750, the proto-Shi'i idea of charisma was in an extremely fluid state.[23] The charismatic figures of the house of Hashim were popular among the Muslim masses during the period from 700 to 850.[24] The Shi'i community became the major source of recruitment for the militant groups struggling for power. Due to the political chaos, al-Sadiq concluded that the time was not right to engage in political activity. Given the revolutionary situation, his withdrawal could not have been easily accepted by the Shi'i community. Hence, he had to redefine the concept of leadership on a different basis. His new conception makes a clear-cut distinction between political leadership and religious Imamate with regard to the following principles:

Denouncing political leadership as lacking morality, compared with the religious Imamate, which is based on pure religious values. Religious sanctity was exclusively assigned to the special concept of Imamate, which was no longer associated with a political role.[25] This principle has brought about the dichotomy of Imamate-usurpation that dominated Shi'i political thought for quite a long time[26] and effectively hindered the apprehension of politics as a sphere of continuous change.

Ridiculing the struggle for power as futile. To advance this argument, al-Sadiq employed the doctrine of divine predestination (*qadar*), according to which the timing of the rise and collapse of dynasties is predetermined by God.[27] Its implication is that the size or strength of the opposition cannot determine the fate of dynasties and rulers whose deposition was not due. This notion was previously utilised by the Umayyad dynasty to frustrate their opponents. Here it is noteworthy that the doctrine of predestination was discredited by al-Hassan, the second Shi'i imam.[28] Goldziher suggests this tendency has been common among Muslims during most of the Umayyad and 'Abbasid eras, during which the rulers encouraged people to be indifferent towards politics.[29] Apparently al-Sadiq's argument intended to extract Shi'as out of the revolutionary groups without being obliged to offer a political alternative. It became, however, the basis for a wide range of anti-activist traditions in the Shi'i school.

Modifying the prerequisites for leadership and its outcomes. In the new concept of Imamate, the leadership is no longer a public office. The imam is designated by God through the words of the Prophet (*nass*), regardless of the will of the community members.[30] Accordingly, the authority is no longer given by contract (*bai'a*) nor is the imam accountable before the public.[31]

The tendency to differentiate political from religious leadership was apparently intended to break the linkage between religious-based legitimacy and the struggle for power. This revolutionary tendency was common amongst Shi'as, especially the revolutionary trends such as the Zaydis. The separation of the two scopes, although never plainly acknowledged as Sachedina argues,[32] became an established principle amongst Shi'i scholars. Similarly, the qualification for leadership was linked to the possession of infallible knowledge as distinguished from interpretive knowledge acquired by fallible scholars.[33] Al-Sadiq's special conception of leadership has served to change the Shi'a attitude from being in opposition to the state to being apathetic[34] as a means of consolidating the school and preserving its distinctiveness. As suggested by Hodgson, the emphasis on infallible knowledge and designated succession has crucially aided the consolidation of the school behind al-Sadiq and his line.[35]

3. The Occultation of the Twelfth Imam (260 ah/874)

According to Shi'i sources, the eleventh imam, al-Hassan al-'Askari, had a son, Muhammad, born in 869; but he was not allowed to appear in public in order to protect him from the 'Abbasid caliph al-Mutawakkel (847–61).[36] Only a few of the close members of the family had seen the heir of the Imamate before he went into hiding. Apparently, the earlier Shi'i scholars supposed that his seclusion would not last long.[37] Nevertheless, as the years went on, the hope for the early return of the imam gradually dimmed, and the community divided over the viability of Imamate.[38] This traumatic state of affairs went on for years. As the notable scholar 'Ali Ibn Babwayh, known as Shaykh al-Saduq, wrote in 979, people were still doubting the case of Occultation and seeking an explanation.[39]

The Occultation has symbolised the absence of the possibility of reinstating justice and legitimate government in the world.[40] One day, Twelver Shi'as believe, the saviour Mahdi will appear, summon the believers to arms, destroy all tyranny and fill the earth with justice even as it has been filled with injustice. No one can guess the time or place in which his triumphant reappearance will take place.[41] For Shi'a scholars the Occultation means that bidding for power is no longer legitimate since such an endeavour lacks the potential to succeed. If this were not the case, the imam would have reappeared:[42] hence, the religious rules whose enforcement requires that state power would be suspended[43] or entrusted to temporal rulers.[44] By so doing, the aspiration for social justice was given an idealistic character and dealt with as a theological rather than a practical concept.[45]

Post-Occultation Challenges

Despite the turmoil on the religious front, the Shi'a community saw an overall improvement in its fortunes, aided by the decline of the 'Abbasid power throughout the greater part of the tenth century.[46] In many regions, the 'Abbasid caliphate had its power taken over by local commanders, including Shi'i tribal lords. In North Africa, Isma'ili Shi'as established a counter-caliphate in 909. Northern Iraq and then Syria came under the control of the Hamdanids in 944. The Buyids were able to take control of Baghdad, the centre of the Islamic caliphate. It is not surprising, Kohlberg suggests, that the tenth century has come to be known as the Shi'i century.[47] The rule of the Buyids (945–1055) was characterised by tolerance and respect for all schools of thought. Their reign saw the emergence of some important theories regarding the relationship between religion and state in Islam, notably the theory proposed by Mawardi, the notable Shafi'i scholar, and the one proposed by Sharif al-Murtada, the Shi'a leader. Both scholars draw a clear line between the legitimacy acquired through public consent (*bai'a*) and the permissible obedience to the ruler who acquires power by the means of usurpation, as in the case of the Buyids.

During the first half of the eleventh century, religious scholars have emerged as a major force in the Shi'a community. The evolution of their role was aided by the recognition of relative knowledge, hence, independent judgement, or *ijtihad*, as a proper source for authoritative rulings in religious affairs.[48] Ijtihad gives a role to rational judgement (*'aql*) almost on par with the imams' traditions (*naql*) when giving religious rulings relevant to the realities of social life.[49] Through the process of ijtihad, the scholar abstracts the principle embedded in a contextual judgement previously made by an infallible imam and applies it to the other contexts which bear similarities to the previous one. In respect of political thought, ijtihad has helped to remove the limitations inherent in the traditional theology which effectively restricted Shi'i political thought to the narrow framework of the doctrine of Imamate. It must be recalled that the model of leadership adopted after al-Sadiq was tailored to fit exclusively the holders of divinely ordained knowledge, namely the infallible imams.[50] With relative knowledge being recognised, the office of communal leadership would be perceived impartially whereby every Shi'a could qualify for the office through the acquisition of fallible knowledge.

Ijtihad was first employed in the Shi'i school by Hassan al-'Umani and Ibn al-Junayd al-Iskafi. The two scholars lived in Baghdad in the late tenth century and were famed for pioneering the call to integrate reason as an independent source for religious rule.[51] The initiative of 'Umani and Iskafi was pursued by Mufid, Murtada, and Tusi, whose influential works have earned them the spiritual leadership of the community and signalled the emergence of the earliest form of religious establishment in Shi'ism.[52]

The First Approach to the Issue of Authority

The Shi'as rise to power was an upsetting blow to the dogma of passively awaiting the return of the Mahdi (*intizar al-faraj*), an integral principle of the belief in his Occultation. According to the doctrine of Mahdism, the possibility of just rule has disappeared from the world. Thus all forms of cooperation with temporal rulers were seen as an affirmation of injustice and usurpation, hence they were impermissible. The latter assumption was affirmed by the inherent tendency of the Imami Shi'as to dissociate themselves from all ruling powers as a result of the lack of any prospect of taking political power.[53] In contrast, new socio-political developments have made the dogma appear irrelevant. This challenge has prompted scholars to rethink the old doctrine of leadership.[54] The problem posed here was how to allow people to take part in state affairs without damaging the fundamental doctrine of Imamate, which has been so far the major agent of communal cohesion.

The approach of the three scholars, Mufid, Murtada and Tusi, involved a revision of the doctrine of Imamate whereby the office of ruler was differentiated from the person of the imam. Shaykh al-Mufid (d. 1022) was taught by 'Umani. Sharif al-Murtada (d. 1044) was the son of a notable family. Abu Ja'far al-Tusi (d. 1076) is known for establishing the religious school of Najaf. All three have assumed the leadership of the Shi'a community in Baghdad and were famed for being the fathers of the Shi'i jurisprudential school.

Theoretically, it was said that the imam in person is the appointee of God to care for the interests of the umma. If the imam is not available, the office of Imamate is to be suspended. On the other hand, the interests of the umma are to be administered in the best possible manner by other people. The focus here is on public order and other material interests rather than the righteousness and the quality of the ruler, which is the focus of the doctrine of Imamate.

To effect that change, the scholarly discussion over the state was transferred from the domain of theology to that of jurisprudence, where the formulation of religious rules follows reason-based criteria. The function of the state was attached to the conceptual framework of *al-amr bi'l-ma'ruf wa'al-nahy 'an al-munkar* (commanding good and prohibiting evil). In this framework, the focus is on the state's objectives and performance. On the same basis, the state institution came to be seen as being independent from the person of the ruler. Employing Plato's explanation of the emergence of the state, Tusi holds that:

> The presence of an obeyed ruler would effectively balance the relationship between people, by deterring heedlessness, punishing felons, and helping weaker people to recover the rights abused by stronger ones. Thereby the community would more likely be virtuous. In contrast, the absence of an effective leader would result in the spreading of corruption, indiscipline, disorder, and in general, a hardship of livelihood. This is an established and indisputable fact.[55]

Tusi concludes that the assumption of power, if helpful to achieve said objectives, is desired by God. Mufid outlines a set of norms to be observed by state officials in order to ensure the legitimacy of their rule. In his view, a legitimate official should commit himself to preventing injustice, helping powerless people attain their rights and ensuring the good of the community. Upon the observation of these norms, individuals are allowed to cooperate with temporal rulers.[56] Mufid's approach was enriched and methodologically reaffirmed by his two disciples Murtada and Tusi.[57] In his *Mas'alah fi'l-'amal ma'a al-Sultan* (A Treatise on Working for the Ruler) Murtada justifies political participation on an ethical basis, which is clearly distinguished from the normative principles legitimating political domination.[58] His thesis was written in 1025, but it still dominates Shi'i jurisprudential debates over the relationship with illegitimate rulers.[59]

This conciliatory approach was aided by the notion of *hisba* as conceptualised by Abu al-Hassan al-Mawardi, the notable Sunni scholar (d. 1058). Hisba provides an operational framework for carrying out the range of duties grouped under the category of the commanding of good and the prohibiting of evil. It aims mainly to maintain social order and general welfare.[60] In this view, the responsibility for fulfilling these duties is borne by society as a whole. An individual can undertake the responsibility within his capacity as a member of the society, i.e. an actor in the public sphere.[61] According to the prominent Iranian scholar Ayatollah Montazeri, most of the duties categorised as hisba are identical to the public services undertaken nowadays by the various branches of the modern state.[62]

The new approach has benefited Shi'a laymen and helped to enhance the role of the scholars. On the intellectual front, it was a remarkable step towards a new paradigm of authority in Shi'ism, concentrating on achievable and rationally defined objectives rather than idealistic ones. From then on, most of the debates over religious-based authority would revolve around the extent of correspondence or differentiation between this approach and the old one.

The Emergence of the Theory of Jurist's Guardianship

The rise to power of the Seljuq Sunni warlords in Baghdad in 1055 signalled a reversal in Shi'a interests in politics. Tusi, the community leader, moved from the capital to the outlying village of Najaf. His death in 1076 was followed by a century of decline in Shi'i educational institutions.[63] During the fourteenth century, a revivalist movement emerged among the students of the school of Hilla, twenty miles south of Baghdad, including al-Muhaqqiq al-Hilli (1205–77), 'Allama al-Hilli (1250–1325) and 'Amili, known as the First Martyr (1333–84). Their intellectual work made a significant breakthrough in religious studies and helped to revitalise the rationalistic methodology of Shi'i jurisprudence.[64] While keeping aloof from politics, the school of Hilla has made an important contribution to the religious debate over leadership, notably formulating the notion of deputyship of the imam.

The term *na'ib al-imam* (the 'imam's deputy') was first employed in a limited sense by Abu al-Salah al-Halabi (d. 1055), who permitted the qualified scholar to assume the office of judge under the usurper's rule. In his view, the judge acts on behalf of the absent imam and in the capacity of his deputy, notwithstanding his apparent submission to the usurper.[65] In contrast, the notion proposed by al-Muhaqqiq al-Hilli suggests that every qualified jurist is a potential deputy of the absent imam, hence authorised to oversee the tasks falling within the imam's competence.[66] Compared with the approach of Mufid and Murtada, which aimed to facilitate the participation in state affairs by the Shi'a laymen,[67] Hilli's approach aims to consolidate the position of *mujtahid* (qualified scholars) as the source for emulation and the responsibility for spiritual affairs of the community. Hilli's disinterest in politics is evident in his sceptical approach to political issues such as the enforcement of laws by fallible rulers.[68] Nevertheless, his work effectively helped the rise of mujtahid to the highest authority in Shi'a community.

The Rise of the Safavid Dynasty (1501–1722)

The rise of the Safavid dynasty in Iran marked the most significant event in the pre-modern history of Shi'ism since the Occultation. From 1501 onward, Iran and Shi'ism became inextricably associated. Shi'ism gave the new state its national identity and earned the political power it needed to forge a committed society.[69] Declaring Shi'ism as the official religion, and the decisive efforts which were made to incorporate the population within the school, aided the emergence of the school's spokesmen as a powerful force in the public sphere.[70]

Shaykh 'Ali al-Karaki (d. 1534) was the first eminent Shi'i mujtahid serving at the Safavid court. Politically minded, Karaki was keen to establish his status as a 'partner' in the king's authority. In his lengthy book *Jami' al-Maqasid* and other treatises, he asserts that the imam's deputy is the only holder of legitimate authority.[71] Enayat suggests that Karaki had a great conviction about the jurist's guardianship.[72] This suggestion is arguable. An analysis of his various works shows that he was not decisive when it came to the political aspect of the jurist's authority. Nevertheless, he empowered the imam's deputy with two important privileges, namely the endorsement of the ruler's authority and the assumption of all religious functions initially assigned to the infallible imam.[73] Karaki's proposals were initially disputed by his peers[74] but gradually gained wide currency in religious circles. Embracing a realistic view, Karaki has acknowledged the division of labour between state and clergy, yet he tended to redress the balance of power possessed by the two sides. For him, the imam's deputy was independent and his department was by no means subject to the rule of the king.[75] In Arjomand's account, the recognition of Karaki as the imam's deputy by Tahmasb, the second Safavid king, could be regarded as the milestone marking the creation of a Shi'i hierocracy in Iran.[76]

During the interval of chaos following the demise of the Safavids in 1722, the 'ulama lost their political influence but retained stronger positions at the local level. Shortly after the rise of the Qajar dynasty in 1794, the 'ulama recovered much of the influence they had lost[77] and were ready to play a wider role in national politics.[78] The Qajar era was characterised by state impotence and increasing foreign interference.[79] Both factors have contributed to the rise of the political role of the 'ulama, especially during the reign of Fath 'Ali Shah (1797–1834).[80] The decisive moment came in 1808 when the king sought the support of the 'ulama against Russian encroachment in the northern territory. Three of the eminent mujtahids wrote theses endorsing the authority of the king and asking people to stand by him.[81] Ja'far Kashif al-Ghita, the great mujtahid of the time, seized the opportunity to outline his proposal on legitimate authority. Kashif al-Ghita (d. 1813) was known for his great interest in reasoning and rationalistic derivation of religious rules. He was described by his biographers as politically minded and famed for his efforts to mobilise people to defend Najaf against the Saudi-Wahabi assaults (1801–6), as well as mediation between the Ottomans and the Qajars in 1812.[82]

In comparison with preceding scholars, Kashif al-Ghita dealt with the question of political authority in a relatively precise manner. He firstly defines the main point, namely the issue of political leadership 'which needs an effective, intelligent, and decisive ruler.'[83] Then he states the problem pertaining to rule, namely the state suppression of the individual, whereby he argues that: 'Initially all human beings are equal. No one is superior to any other, unless he is authorised by God, the master of all.'[84] His aim was to assert the legitimate objectives of state and its performance as a sufficient basis for claiming obedience. His proposals came through comparing obedience to the imam and to the king, whereby the former is ascribed to God's ordinance whereas the latter is linked to the legitimate objectives pursued by the state.[85] Kashif al-Ghita was among the few scholars who acknowledged the conventional basis of the state and set aside the theological dichotomy of Imamate-usurpation. For him, the best ruler is the imam or his appointee, including the qualified jurist.

Should they be unavailable, incapable or reluctant to undertake the responsibility, any fair-minded and skilful Muslim might take over. Accordingly people should give him full obedience. Insurrection is tantamount to opposition to God and the Prophet.

Finally he concludes that 'provided the authority of the king has to be endorsed by the imam's deputy, I hereby endorse the authority of king Fath 'Ali Shah'.[86]

In a sense, the assertion of Kashif al-Ghita has effectively extended the authority of the mujtahid into the political domain. While Hilli focuses on the religious aspect of the imam's deputyship, and Karaki employs this prerogative to claim a kind of partnership in power with the king, Kashif al-Ghita takes the matter to its logical conclusion by claiming the right of the religious leader to rule or otherwise endorse the authority of the incumbent ruler. Apparently, he was the first eminent mujtahid to claim such authority in plain words. In my opinion, his proposal is tantamount to the prototype of the theory of wilayat al-faqih (jurist's guardianship) without putting forward this particular term.

The doctrine of jurist guardianship was finalised and methodologically established by Ahmad Naraqi, the religious leader of Kashan, central Iran

(1771–1828). Unlike Kashif al-Ghita, the political application of the theory does not seem to have concerned Naraqi. In the preface to his thesis, he ascribes his concern with the issue to the irregularities committed by non-qualified judges who unlawfully claim the position of imam's deputyship, i.e. the authority to act independently.[87] He also gives numerous examples to illustrate the scope of the authority enjoyed by a qualified faqih, none of which relates to the political sphere.[88] Nevertheless, his formulation has provided later scholars with a ready-formed theory to be employed in the political sphere. The spectrum of the faqih's authority in the thesis of Naraqi falls into two categories:

> All functions attached to the office of Imamate unless they are assigned to the imam in person.
> The duties concerning public interest under the category of hisba. They are to be fulfilled by the faqih or other individuals with his consent.[89]

To establish his proposal theoretically, Naraqi referred to a number of narrations attributed to the imams, none of which is sufficient to support such a radical conclusion. Admitting this problem, he argues that they all voice the same idea, namely the authority of faqih, and that none of the preceding scholars have denied their authenticity.[90] In a previous work, I have made an extensive examination of the narrations adopted by Naraqi, focusing on their authenticity and reliability with reference to both the criteria of Shi'i jurisprudence and the opinions of a number of eminent scholars. My conclusion is that Naraqi's thesis cannot be firmly grounded on the imams' traditions.[91] However, it could be legitimised on a rationalistic basis, as Ayatollah Khomeini did later,[92] which effectively takes the theory into another territory but absolutely not the traditional platform.

Naraqi's proposal gained currency in the scholarly circles only after it was challenged by his disciple Murtada al-Ansari in 1862. Ansari (1799–1864) was probably the first leader recognised by Usuli Shi'as as *marji' al-taqlid* (universal exemplar).[93] His theoretical work enjoys considerable authority in the Shi'i school of jurisprudence. His work on the religious accommodation of worldly affairs, entitled *al-Makasib,* has been commented and elaborated upon by most of the later great mujtahids. Of these works, there are at least twenty published books. One of Ansari's most important legacies has been his review of the theoretical basis for the relationship between the religious leader and individual members of the community. After him, Cole argues, the office of exemplar introduced the possibility of a strong and centralised leadership.[94] Although Ansari refrained from political activity, the structure he helped to establish had a great potential for mobilising the Shi'as in political causes.[95]

Ansari was not satisfied with the extensive powers invested in the faqih by Naraqi's theory of jurist's guardianship. He fundamentally challenged its basis and applications and concluded that none of them could be safely established on the basis of the imams' traditions. Unlike his predecessors, Ansari took the doctrine of Imamate as the only criterion for correcting the delegation of power from the imam to fallible persons. He acknowledges the absolute authority of the imam but firmly rejects a fallible person's eligibility to hold such immense powers.[96] In his view, the powers of mujtahid are restricted to the instruction of religious laws (*fatwa*) and judgement (*qada*).[97] Here, it is noteworthy that Shi'a scholars are in agreement on the absolute nature of the imam's authority in the broad sense,[98] yet some of them are sceptical about its applicability in the cases that involve a clear curtailment of the basic rights of individuals. Bahr al-'Ulum, for instance, argues that it is almost impossible to find any indisputable evidence in the entire history of the imams proving that they have actually exercised the absolute authority they claimed.[99]

In Ansari's view, the powers of the imam cannot be delegated simply because they either stem from his infallibility or because infallibility is a prerequisite for exercising them.[100] He argues that there is no undisputable means to distinguish those particular powers that pertain to infallibility from the ones pertaining to his office as ruler. Therefore, the only practical way to avoid violating the imam's sanctity would be to restrict the faqih's authority to the scope of non-disputable cases. Having done so, Ansari says, we would not have the imam's authority invested in the mujtahid but rather a number of tasks that could be independently based upon general or specific principles available in Shari'a. Such a basis is different from the one upon which the imam's authority is based.[101]

One of Ansari's significant innovations was his differentiation between two aspects of the imam's authority. The first is the power based on infallibility or, as he puts it, 'power upon'. The second is the power attached to his office as ruler, or, as he puts it, 'power for'.[102] The former cannot be invested in a fallible person since it is of an absolute nature. The latter type of power is applied to meet 'the need for supervision' in particular cases where individuals such as orphans, people with a mental disability and so on need to be supervised. In such examples, Ansari suggests, the authority is a fostering one. The authorised guardian has the power to care for the dependent individual, including the management of his properties, but not the power over his person. This type of authority could be obtained by every trustworthy adult with the consent of mujtahid in his capacity as judge.[103]

Despite Ansari's discontent with the theory of jurist's guardianship, his profound argumentation with regard to its bases and applications has drawn the attention of the religious seminaries to the focal questions of authority and its implications. It could be said without reservation that almost all subsequent debates about authority in the Shi'i seminaries have, by and large, revolved around the assumptions and conclusions laid out by Ansari. On the other hand, the political developments during the following years have fuelled the debate about the political application of the theory. From the Tobacco Revolt on, the involvement of the 'ulama in politics intensified, which brought into question the nature of this involvement, its basis and limits.

Towards the Twentieth Century

The Tobacco Revolt of 1891 was the first opportunity to demonstrate the political potential of the exemplary institution established by Ansari. The revolt was triggered by a concession given by Nasir al-Din Shah, the fourth Qajar king (1848–96), to a British company, involving a monopoly of the local tobacco trade. Mirza Shirazi (d. 1895), the successor of Ansari, had protested and issued a religious decree (fatwa) prohibiting tobacco trade and usage. The decree was observed throughout the nation and forced the king to back down.[104] Despite its limited purpose, the Tobacco Revolt was the first mass mobilisation against the state. It has also facilitated a special role for the clergy, who appeared as the most likely candidate to represent the people and their interests.[105] In his correspondence with the king, Shirazi did not deny the king's authority but reminded him of its 'limits' as well as his duty to safeguard the national independence and the rights of the nation. Apparently Shirazi is the first Shi'i grand mujtahid to use the concept of 'nation' in the political sense. Before that, mujtahids tended to use the term 'subjects' rather than nation or people.[106]

Fifteen years later, there was another showdown with the state over the limits of the king's authority. On both sides, the Constitutionalist and the royalist, there were clerics, traders and secular intellectuals.[107] The Constitutional Revolution was the threshold that Iran crossed to join the modern world. Since 1906 the country had a constitution, a parliament and, above of all, a nation aware of its rights and role.

It is noteworthy that the doctrine of wilayat al-faqih was not a prominent issue during the Constitutional Revolution, despite the fact that many high-ranking clerics, including grand mujtahids, have played major roles in the revolution.[108] There are, however, various explanations for this. According to Mahallati, a Constitutionalist cleric, the question of a jurist's governorship had not been raised by the public. The 'ulama used to address questions only when they were raised by the public.[109] Na'ini, another Constitutionalist mujtahid, expressed doubts about the theory's efficacy in curbing state tyranny. Instead, he argued that only a well-defined set of institutions, rules and procedures could do that job.[110] Na'ini's treatise on the constitutional government is the earliest scholarly work of its kind from the religious seminaries.[111] The highest-ranking mujtahid of the time, Akhund Khurasani, rejects many of the arguments supporting the theory and suggests that the authority of the faqih is limited to religious affairs.[112] Fazlullah Nuri was the only eminent mujtahid to uphold the idea of the faqih's political authority. Unfortunately, he stood by the king against the constitution, which effectively invited accusations that his argument came from political, rather than purely religious, motives. With the Constitutional Revolution, the 'ulama gained more political power and their role was formally acknowledged in the constitution.[113]

Conclusion

Imami Shi'ism emerged as a political trend but developed into a religious school with mainly apolitical tendencies in the eighth century. Until the Occultation of the Twelfth Imam in 874, the Shi'i worldview was dominated by the dichotomy of Imamate / usurpation in which all forms of rule other than the Infallible Imamate were regarded as illegitimate. The improvement of the socio-political circumstances in the tenth century had incited a shift in the Shi'i thought and reflected on three aspects: fallible knowledge was established as an authoritative source of the religious ruling; religious scholars emerged as a communal leadership; and cooperation with temporal rulers was permitted.

A formal Shi'i religious establishment emerged in Iran during the Safavid reign and acquired more influence over public affairs by the late nineteenth century. With the Tobacco Revolt of 1891, the religious establishment emerged as a major political force and had its role recognised in the constitution of 1906. Although the doctrine of wilayat al-faqih has appeared since at least the early nineteenth century, the religious establishment did not seriously seek to establish an exclusively clerical government. It was the ripening of the general circumstances in the late twentieth century that enabled the doctrine and its major advocate, Ayatollah Khomeini, to emerge as the determinant force on the political arena in Iran, a development that led to the Islamic Revolution in 1979.

The long debate over religious authority has been centred on three points:

1. The source of authority, whether it is based on divine designation or objective considerations.
2. The extent of power wielded by a fallible person, particularly when it involves a curtailment of individual rights and property.
3. The role of the religious scholars as the source of religious teachings.

Successive modifications throughout a long history have culminated in a paradigm of authority different from the one fostered by the doctrine of Imamate. The two paradigms agree in some respects and differ in others, including:

Legitimacy: In both paradigms, Imamate is the only legitimate form of government. Nevertheless, the new one acknowledges a kind of provisional legitimacy based on the competence of the temporal ruler to promote the public interest. Thus, unlike the doctrine of Imamate, political participation within temporal rule is permitted.

Obedience: In the old paradigm, individuals were asked to obey their rulers in order to avert oppression, whereas in the new paradigm, conformity with state regulations was permitted on rational grounds, i.e. to enforce public order. This came through the acknowledgement of the secular nature of the state, which effectively took society-state relation out of the religious framework.

The role of people: Compared with Sunni scholars, Shi'i fiqh has largely ignored the contractual aspect of legitimacy, namely the bai'a. Murtada was among the few scholars who indicated the possible role of the people in generating legitimacy. He suggests that a usurper's rule can acquire legitimacy if it satisfies the public.[114] Along the same lines, 'Amili, the First Martyr (d. 1384) and Miqdad al-Sayuri (d. 1425) suggested that a legitimate ruler should step down if people are no longer satisfied with his rule. He rules on their behalf and must not impose himself upon them.[115] However, these ideas remain isolated in Shiʻi jurisprudence in general. During the Constitutional Revolution some scholars came to regard the people as an essential part of the political system and their participation as the guarantor of justice.

CHAPTER TWO

Ayatollah Khomeini's Project

The emergence of Ayatollah Khomeini's version of the doctrine of wilayat al-faqih (jurist guardianship) signifies a sharp discursive shift in Shi'i political thought. It involved an overhaul of the established paradigm of authority based upon the theology of infallible leadership (Imamate). By delegating the imam's political authority to the state, Khomeini put an end to the confusion in which Shi'i political thought had been caught up for centuries.

Khomeini undertook the challenge to politicise a doctrine that was never meant to work in real politics or, at least, that was not sufficiently equipped to do so. His treatise on Islamic government provided a unique approach, applying the principle of jurist guardianship to the broader political crisis over how to provide a religious-based solution in Muslim society. The short book entitled *al-Hukuma al-Islamiyah* (Islamic Government) was the only precise treatise on legitimate government that Khomeini wrote. It was delivered in January 1970 as a part of his study on the jurisprudential issue of authority.[1] Although the treatise was meant to address the jurisprudential aspects of the doctrine, it went far beyond this limit and dealt with some theological, political and cultural questions related to the subject. Later Khomeini elaborated on the jurisprudential aspect as part of his research on earning and contracts, in *Kitab al-Bay'*, first published in Najaf in 1971, in which he dealt with the various sources of earning and authority.

Most of Khomeini's views in this book resemble those common to the religious seminaries. In his argument regarding jurist political authority, Khomeini candidly observed his peers' reservations towards the technical weaknesses of the texts and the chains of narration of the imam's traditions.[2] He relied heavily on rational reasoning in his discussion of legitimate authority in order to skirt around the weak points that earned Ahmad Naraqi, the founder of the doctrine, a great deal of criticism. Khomeini attached his concept of religious leadership to the principle of the continuity of religion on the one hand, and to the rational justifications of state authority on the other. Apart from the two books mentioned above, Khomeini's political views were expressed mainly through his many speeches and letters, the majority of which were published in a twenty-two-volume compendium entitled *Sahifeh Nur*.[3] Khomeini's other works include forty books and treatises on various religious subjects, most of which remained unnoticed, except *Kashf al-Asrar* (1945), which was seen by some scholars as his first political proclamation.[4] Nevertheless, his arguments therein are hardly relevant to his later thought.[5]

Khomeini's thought has been carefully examined by many researchers. Hamid Enayat takes a comparative approach, aiming to locate Khomeini's views within the broader scope of Islamic political thought in the twentieth century.[6] Ervand Abrahamian, while a critic of Khomeini, challenges the common perception of him as a traditional fanatic or fundamentalist and argues that he was a populist leader representing the aspirations of Iran's petite bourgeoisie.[7] Mohsen Kadivar has examined the idea of the faqih's absolute authority and its claimed divine source, with reference to Shi'i jurisprudence and modern political thought. He has taken a normative approach and made an exhaustive critique on both ideas.[8]

In this chapter, I will outline the unique contribution made by Khomeini, namely his attempt to alter the role played by religion, from being an agent of alienation between the public and the state to an agent of association, which effectively facilitated the emergence of a consensual political system, probably for the first time in Iran's modern history. My assumption is that a lack of national consensus has been a symptom of a cultural split brought about by the ruler's disregard for the role of religion on the one hand, and by the theological limitations inherent in the religious worldview on the other. The reconciliation between religion and state is crucial for ensuring both the coherence and efficiency of the political system.

I will start by highlighting the relevance of consensus to the stability and development of the political system and the role of religion in this regard. After a brief account of the reflections of modern trends upon Khomeini's thought, I will highlight the theoretical barriers he had to negotiate in order to advance his arguments.

Consensus and Stability

Throughout the twentieth century, the dualism of authority – religion on the one side and state on the other – has made it difficult to reach a national consensus over the conceptual foundations of Iran's political order.

Consensus is essential for nation-building and political development. It serves to form the national will, remove tension from state-society relations and facilitate peaceful participation of the population in political activities. As Binder asserts, the developed political system is characterised by a historical-cultural consensus which lends stability and continuity to what would otherwise be a chaotic, characterless system which is always in flux.[9] Lack of consensus is partly a symptom of cultural fragmentation where the state and the majority of the population act politically with reference to different, even contradictory, conceptual frameworks.

For the state to perform in a smooth and consistent manner, there has to be a universally agreed normative structure to legitimise the political process. That is particularly important, for affairs of state represent a realm of conflict emanating from the incongruity between the public's expectations and the state's response.[10] Easton's 'input-output' model provides a practical method for examining the state's performance as the prime factor for maintaining legitimacy. He holds that the complexity and diversity of state affairs make the division of labour, and therefore structural differentiation, indispensable. This division could endanger the harmony within the political system unless there is a mechanism observed by both the state and society to ensure an orderly exchange of demand and response.[11] Consensus, according to Tsurutani, signifies the willing adherence on the part of both government and population to a mutually agreed set of procedures for decision-making which is recognised by both sides as necessary and appropriate for maintaining public order, general well-being, the resolution of issues and conflicts and the elicitation of social goals.[12] An agreement of this kind accredits the political system with legitimacy, which Almond likens to a thread running through the system's input-output process, endowing it with its special quality and coherence.[13]

Likewise, consensus is indispensable to sustainable development. Tension is seen as a concurrent associate of the process of modernisation in developing nations, mainly because of the constant change of structures, roles and procedures. Such a problem has been shown to be understood in classical studies of development, although it is perceived as a feature of a transitional stage whereby the traditional value system breaks up in order to pave the way for a new system that is relevant to modernity. In the period of conversion, says Apter, values of the community remain in a constant flux; the socialisation process becomes a tension-creating system, inciting all kinds of conflicts in respect of status, value and roles. He regards such tension as a key feature of the development process and a prelude to the prevalence of modern patterns of social behaviour. This shift involves status-based relations being supplanted by contractual forms, organic by mechanical solidarity, instrumental by conclusive ends, sacred by secular beliefs and traditional by legal-rational authority.[14]

The process of modernisation is said to be a success only if it breaks through the trenches of traditions. In this sense, the process has a two-fold function that is destructive in respect to the traditional elements of social institutions and constructive in respect to new ones. The classical assumption regarding the displacement of value systems seems to have ignored the contingent nature of such a process:

First: Since we are dealing with non-material objects, the process of replacement cannot be taken as an orderly and inevitable operation; indeed we are talking about the *degree of penetration* of modern values into the social-cultural web. New patterns can either touch the heart of a social system or be confined to the surface.

Second: The assumption that society undergoes a process of value-adaptation after it receives the shock of modernisation disguises the consecutive impact, i.e. the polarisation of the social system into pro-modern and pro-traditional spectrums. The extent and permanence of dissension depend upon the function of the penetration noted above. During the intervening period of polarisation, the old patterns of behaviour – that is, the norms, values, roles and institutions upon which political action is based – cease their legitimising function. The ability of the political system to shorten the period of polarisation and restore its legitimacy by relying on the modern classes or by integrating the traditional ones would be at stake.[15]

The actual experiences of modernisation in the Middle East show that fragmentation has persisted, and in some cases it has endangered the political system and the modernisation process altogether.[16] Such events as the Islamic Revolution in Iran prompted a number of researchers to question the assumption that industrialisation and social change would necessarily result in the traditional elites and belief systems giving way to the modern state elite, and in religion being relegated to the private realm.[17]

The idea of the degree of penetration indicated above suggests that the resilience on the part of traditional patterns is a determining factor in respect to the length of the transitional period and the level of social consciousness affected by the new patterns. To put it in a different order, the willingness of the population to adapt to modern patterns is determined by two factors: whether or not the people will perceive the new patterns as a worthy alternative to what they are asked to abandon; and whether or not the offer proves to conform to the people's common belief. Whereas the first point is directly related to the efficiency of the state's performance, the latter is related to the appeal of the offer to the cultural orientation of the population. For many researchers, this point partially explains why modernisation in the Middle East has stumbled and has caused many theorists in recent years to question the sharp division between tradition and modernity and the assumption that religion cannot help the process of development.[18]

Religion, State and Modernisation

After the rise of the Pahlavi regime in Iran, the social role of the clergy was perceived as the salient challenge to the coherence of the state, which calls to mind the assumption advanced by Max Weber regarding the inevitable clash over authority between state and hierocracy. The double function of religion is well acknowledged by sociologists: as an apology and legitimisation of the *status quo* and as a means of protest and liberation.[19] Reza Shah, the founder of the Pahlavi dynasty, was an admirer of the model established by Mustafa Kemal Atatürk of Turkey, which associates modernisation with consolidating the state structure and secularising the public sphere.[20] During the 1960s and 1970s, the government undertook a large-scale programme to modernise industry, education, transportation, communication systems and a land reform program, all of which aimed to bring about a new public order based upon secular principles.[21] The assumption was that the reconstruction of the economy, public services and the education system would necessarily help the hegemony of modern patterns of socialisation and eventually curtail the political power of traditional forces, notably the clergy.[22]

The modernising project has proven to be a relative success, resulting in a considerable improvement of state administration and public services, as well as the economy. Nevertheless, it has evidently failed to achieve its core objective, namely the assurance of long-term political stability. The relative stability felt in the 1970s was largely indebted to the strict policies implemented by the security apparatus, notably the secret police (SAVAK). This could not compensate for the lack of legitimacy and harmony between the state and society, reflected in the persistence of the feeling of insecurity among the ruling elite.[23]

According to Bashiriyeh, an Iranian sociologist, modernisation in the form adopted during the Pahlavi reign (1925–79) effectively worsened social fragmentation,[24] although it helped to improve the standard of living. Bashiriyeh's account is in line with the concerns expressed by many theorists regarding the impact of Western-modelled modernisation on Third World societies. As for Binder:

> The most conspicuous manifestation of the impact of the West has been the creation of gaps in social communication, in stratification, in values, in economic orientation, and in political techniques among the various sectors of society.[25]

The exacerbation of social divisions in the context of Iran suggests one of two possibilities: either the processes of nation-building and modernisation have actually failed to proceed from the first stage – i.e. the disintegration of the traditional structure into the final stage and the restructuring of a modern one – or the assumption of adaptation was not applicable in this particular context. In my opinion, both possibilities have some relevance, but the major problem appears to be the misconception of the role of religion and its relevance to national consensus.

The state's endeavours to contain the political influence of the religious establishment evolved into an indirect confrontation with religion itself, leading to determined efforts to manipulate religious activities. On their part, the 'ulama, who claim authoritative representation of the nation's culture, turned to their old means of confrontation: politicising religious symbols and mobilising the population against the state. The predisposition of religion to function for or against the state and its modernising policies is fairly understandable. After the sixteenth century, Shi'ism became a major part of Iran's national identity, therefore any national agreement over public order has to consider a satisfying role for religion and its representatives. However, the established Shi'i doctrine of authority lacked a definite and up-to-date formulation for the state-religion relation. The misconception of the nature and role of the state and the lack of a normative basis for political participation created a sense of alienation among the majority of the population. On the part of the state, the lack of public support gave rise to a sense of insecurity among the ruling elite, prompting it to rely on mainly coercive means to maintain the political system.

In brief, the function of religion throughout most of the twentieth century has been seen as more of a hindrance to the course of modernisation. On the other hand, the dual structure of religious and political power has provided the potential for destabilising the political system.[26] Therefore, reconciliation between religion and state is not only indispensable for ensuring stability and public order but also for forming the kind of consensual political order that allows the population to embrace the state and interact positively with its institutions, helping it to achieve its objectives. The role of Ayatollah Khomeini concerns this very point. He was the one who helped to transform the established Shi'i doctrine of authority so that it was able to interlink with the state, and by so doing he facilitated the integration of the masses into national politics.

The Effects of Social Change

Khomeini's discourse features a combination of traditional and modern political notions. His affirmation of religious principles alongside the modern notions of republicanism, the nation's right to self-determination, public liberties and so on, has earned him attention among both the modern and traditional spectra of the nation.

The traditional elements were, however, the original constituents of his thought and discourse. Ayatollah Khomeini started his learning career in Qum in 1920, an epoch characterised by a clerical withdrawal from politics due to the failure of the Constitutional Revolution of 1905–6. Until 1962, his circle was largely limited to the traditional clerical spectrum. His first master was 'Abdul-Kareem Hairi, an apolitical scholar who chose to distance himself from the clerical arguments over Constitutionalism. Professor Algar made a detailed survey of Khomeini's teachers,[27] none of whose names is familiar among the Constitutionalist clergy. The latter group was representative of the modern trend in the religious community in the early twentieth century. During the political fray of the 1950s, Khomeini's name did not appear among the clergy members allied with the liberal reformist group of the National Front against the Crown.

Generally speaking, the effective communication between Khomeini and the modern intellectual movement probably dates back to the period of his residency in Najaf (1965–78).[28] Although he continued to identify with the traditional spectrum, Khomeini had to consider the changing conditions in Iranian society since he had left the country. The change in social relations and realities was evident throughout the society, including the spectrum upon which he relied for political and material support. It is well known that Khomeini had no support among the traditional clergy, especially those belonging to the upper echelons.[29] His faithful followers came mainly from two major camps. The first included students, political activists and junior clerics who identified mainly with the Islamic left. The second included fragments of the modern Islamic intellectual trend represented mainly by

41

Nehzat-e Azadi (Iran Freedom Movement). Both camps were familiar with Constitutionalist ideas and deeply influenced by the anti-traditionalist views of 'Ali Shari'ati. Indeed, it was the supporters of Shari'ati, not the clergy, 'who took the somewhat blasphemous step of endowing him with the title of Imam'.[30] To this we have to add the fact that during the 1970s, the notion of human rights also gained currency in Iran with the election of Jimmy Carter as president of the United States in 1977 and his proposals concerning political reform in allied governments.[31] It is not an exaggeration to claim that up to the decade preceding the Revolution, the majority of Iranians, especially those who were expected to be active in any major political fray, were far from being acquainted with the traditional clergy, in the sense of both communal loyalty or intellectual affinity.

With the above considerations in mind, Ayatollah Khomeini would not have had such tremendous appeal if he had limited his discourse to traditional religious language. There is no doubt about the originality of his political approach; however, the issue in question is his modernist tendency, given his career in traditional learning. Therefore, his embracing of modern notions could be explained as a reflection of his alliance with the modernist trend. On the other hand, Khomeini's denunciation of religious apathy caused him to rethink a great deal of the principles and traditions established in the religious community. Here, it is worth noting that pragmatism and openness towards non-traditional notions were often seen among politically minded scholars. This leads to the conclusion that a greater involvement in public life is directly translated into a greater desire to ease the rigidity inherent in the traditional paradigm of authority. By the same token, it could be said that Khomeini's determination to achieve his objective, namely the establishment of an Islamic modern state, effectively put him face to face with the impediments that sprang from the conflict between the contextual considerations of the old paradigm and contemporary realities.

Compared with his peers among both Shi'a and Sunni scholars, Khomeini is in fact closer to the modernist trend, although in a broad sense he is hardly considered as a modernist. Unlike many of the Muslim scholars who considered a restored caliphate as the likely form of an Islamic state, Khomeini advocated a republican system. Within this form, he endorsed the legislative role of parliament, popular will as the source of authority, universal suffrage for all citizens and the priority of public interests over some fixed religious rules. These notions were previously rejected by most of the religious scholars for their Western orientation and incompatibility with the principles of Shari'a.[32]

Some analysts doubt the originality of Khomeini's advocacy of republicanism.[33] These doubts could be supported by the fact that he did not establish his proposals within the Shi'i theological framework, nor did he make sufficient effort to integrate them with the established jurisprudence. Apparently, Khomeini was aware of this theoretical weakness but did not seem to have had a solution other than his own assertion of their authenticity and compatibility with the ethos of religion. In his view, there was nothing wrong with religion or with the modern notions he advocated. The problem lay in the failure of the religious seminaries to grasp the changes in the surrounding world. Khomeini argued that the religious seminaries (*hawza*) had alienated themselves from the real world and consequently were no longer able to explore how religion could possibly interact with the realities of the time and society.[34] He often censured the traditional scholars for what he described as the failure to grasp the adaptability and all-embracing nature of religion, which enables modern notions to be accommodated fairly within a religious framework.[35]

Khomeini thus perceived the problem as methodological in the sense that a solution would be possible if an updated methodology was employed. In contrast, Ayatollah Shabestari, a Reformist scholar, saw the problem as being within the paradigm itself, rather than its methodology. He argued that the notion of republicanism and its related principles are impossible to establish within the traditional paradigm, simply because they pertain to a different discipline: namely, political philosophy. However, he insisted that they could be firmly grounded on the general principles of Islam.[36]

The Impediments of an Outdated Doctrine

I have already mentioned in Chapter One that, according to the established Shi'i doctrine of authority, the state was deprived of legitimacy in the sense that it could not be legitimised while the infallible imam was absent. Although, thanks to the establishment of Shi'i states, the rigid limitations in this regard were relatively eased, there remained in Shi'ism a strong tendency towards apathy, and participation in state affairs was never acknowledged as being fully appropriate for the community of believers.[37]

The exaggerated emphasis placed upon the office of leadership, especially its attachment to the person of the imam, made it impossible for the doctrine of Imamate to engage with political realities. This problem has been detected by many scholars throughout the history of Shi'ism. Only a few of them, however, have dared to address the key issues in relation to this. The majority have contented themselves with the established assumption which takes it for granted that no one is obliged to help with the establishment of a just government while the infallible imam was absent.

During the twentieth century, Iranian society saw the revival of Shi'i activism through the Constitutional Revolution and the movement for oil-nationalisation, neither of which achieved their goals, partly because the 'ulama stayed away from the fray. In Arjomand's account, the failure of the 'ulama to properly conceive the secular implications of constitutionalism led to that retreat.[38] I would like to see the problem from the other side: the absence of an alternative doctrine capable of embracing constitutionalism without infringing the religious basics could be seen as the reason for the withdrawal of the 'ulama from political arena in the early twentieth century. During the 1950s there was a similar cycle: a considerable segment of the 'ulama supported the reformist movement led by Mohammad Mosaddaq,[39] yet they failed to mobilise the clerical mainstream led by Ayatollah Burujerdi, the great exemplar of the time (d. 1961). The lack of a normative standpoint to justify political participation effectively resulted in the break-up of the clerical – and hence the public – support of the movement. In brief, it can be seen that the degree of public involvement in politics in Iran was directly affected by the behaviour of the 'ulama. In the meantime, there was no consensual framework for regulating the political behaviour of the 'ulama. As a result, there were different approaches, each of which refers to a distinct interpretation of the doctrine of Imamate.[40]

This is, however, an intrinsic problem within the traditional paradigm. The Shi'i doctrine of leadership emerged and evolved as a theological notion intending mainly to justify a communal type of leadership concerned with spiritual, rather than political, affairs. As suggested by Mo'men, while Sunni scholars were concerned with developing an applicable political theory, their Shi'i peers had an absent imam who could only be a subject of theological speculation, rather than of political theory.[41] Shi'a 'ulama addressed the question of leadership and authority within one of two frameworks. The first was theological, concerning the lives and qualities of the imams, obviously a restatement of what had been repeatedly said in the past, with no relevance whatsoever to any actual situation. The second was jurisprudential, focusing on the relationship between the exemplar and the follower with regard to spiritual, mainly personal, affairs.[42] Here too, politics was not a matter of concern. Khomeini's project to politicise the traditional doctrine came through a careful handling of the theoretical barriers residing in the two frameworks: the theological and the jurisprudential.

With regard to the first theoretical barrier, theological debates over authority were meant to address the question: is it possible for fallible people to bring about a just government? In the traditional paradigm, justice was conceived in an ideal sense that could be realised only under a divinely ordained ruler, i.e. an infallible imam.[43] All other forms of government were regarded as illegitimate. With the imam in hiding since 874, Shi'as were supposed to await his return when he would supposedly fill the earth with fairness and justice. 'Allama Na'ini, an eminent scholar, argued in 1908 that the stipulation of the imam's personal leadership, while beyond the reach of the people, endows the idea with hope.[44]

Khomeini's project started by denouncing the applicability to the political realm of the theological notion of passively waiting for the absent imam (*intizar al-faraj*). His revivalist interpretation of the notion implies a separation between the duties and rights of the imam, which can be addressed in theological terms, and those of ordinary Muslims, whose rights and obligations are understood in regard to the actual requirements of their lives. He argued that passively awaiting the imam conflicts with the ethos of religious teachings. While the imam is expected to return some time in the future to bring about ideal justice in a global context, Khomeini maintained, a faithful follower would rather struggle to help realise the objectives of the religion, namely a just government, wherever possible.[45] He strongly criticised the linkage between the two aspects as it inevitably facilitated the suspension of the sacred law and frustrated the people's desire to improve their lives. His main argument suggests that sacred law was prescribed by the Prophet to accommodate the life of the Muslims. Since religion transcends time and place, none of its rules can be arbitrarily suspended.[46] Khomeini dismissed the idea that the absence of the imam justifies the suspension of the ordinances concerning or requiring state power[47] and insisted that the obligatory nature of those rules places a responsibility upon the Muslims, the religious leaders in particular, to do their utmost to have them realised, i.e. to help the establishment of a religious state.[48] The suspension of those rules, he argued, was the fruit of indifference on the part of the Muslims and the tyrannical nature of their governments.[49] By this argument, Khomeini meant to circumvent the traditional assumption by which the Shi'a clergy cleared itself from the responsibility of enforcing the religious law or struggling for political power,[50] a tendency that had remained prevalent since the Occultation of the Twelfth Imam.

Khomeini also argued that justice, in the relative – rather than ideal – sense, is an acceptable criterion for legitimising power and that the presence of the infallible imam is no longer a stipulation for securing the religious character of the state.[51]

With regard to the second barrier, jurisprudential debates mainly concern the source and extension of powers retained by the ruler. The 'ulama's involvement in politics since the Safavid era made it possible to consider the faqih as a potential vicegerent of the infallible imam. Yet, to what extent the imam's powers should be delegated to the faqih remained a controversial point. The core argument concerns the right of a fallible person to use coercive power, i.e. to take people's lives and property by inflicting physical punishments or by confiscating or limiting individual property rights.[52] To understand the irony of the argument, we have to look back to the logical formulation which the earlier Shi'a theologians developed to defend their particular doctrine of Imamate. One of the major arguments advanced in this regard was the notion of *al-lutf al-ilahi* (divine grace), according to which the designation of the imam was conceived of as an expression of such grace. 'Allama Hilli, the prominent scholar, suggests that divine grace is realised through the exemplary function of the prophets and imams. Such a function, he contends, must be of a propagating and convincing rather than an enforcing nature. The application of religious rules by force cannot be regarded as grace.[53]

Bearing this in mind, the authority of the imam to dispose of people's lives and property remained open to contrasting interpretations; some scholars implicitly denied such a generalisation,[54] others accepted it on the basis that an infallible imam would only do what was right,[55] while a third group stipulated that there should be public consent before the said powers take effect.[56] The debate concerned mainly the person of the ruler – i.e. the imam or the faqih – rather than the institution of the state. This is obviously not alien to the context within which the doctrine has evolved. Throughout the entire history of the Muslim community, the state has never been independent of the ruler; all the material means of control and sources of power have been in the ruler's hands. There were no institutionalised restrictions on his powers, nor any effective means to hold him to account. State actions were driven by his whims and desires, rather than by rational calculations relevant to the public interest. With these considerations in mind, the 'ulama were anxious that a fallible ruler empowered with the imam's authority could not be controlled; in addition to the material means that he would already possess, he would be able to have his whims sanctioned on a religious basis. As Na'ini argues, tyranny and corruption are the likely consequences of the monopoly of power by the ruler, whether he is a pious faqih or anyone else. He suggests that only institutionalised restrictions on power can block the tyrannical tendencies of rulers.[57] Na'ini's argument is not, however, unfamiliar to the Islamic culture; a Qur'anic verse explains the tendency of man to transgress all bounds as a consequence of his 'feeling of self-sufficiency' (Holy Qur'an, 96:6–7).

This argument explains why the 'ulama disagreed over the idea of power delegation. There are, however, other arguments concerning the nature of the imam's authority and its basis. Some scholars held that the divine designation of imam provided him with a supernatural character that bestowed upon him a kind of existential authority transcending the realm of man (*wilayah takwiniyah*). Thereby, the imam would exercise his authority as if the world were of his belongings.[58] The crux of this argument is that since a fallible person can by no means claim such an exceptional privilege, he is necessarily incapable of assuming the imam's authority. Another argument suggests that the imam's authority stems from his infallibility, which is realised in his knowledge and inner piety.[59] Accordingly, the two qualities – knowledge and piety – are taken as criteria that are to be met, in a relative sense, by those who seek the deputyship of imam. The former requirement has had more advocates among Iranian scholars, especially those with esoteric tendencies.[60] The majority, however, emphasise the latter.

As mentioned in Chapter One, tenth-century scholars differentiated between the office of Imamate and the person of the imam, and the state's function came to be seen as indispensable for securing the common good, which is defined in conventional terms.[61] Khomeini took the argument further and suggested a differentiation between two connotations embedded in the notion of *wilayah* (authority). Acknowledging the claimed supernatural qualities of the imams,[62] he argued that those qualities are irrelevant to the actual role meant to be undertaken by the imam in the capacity of political leader.[63] His wilayah in the political sense is of a rational and conventional nature; therefore it is linked both to his human qualities and to the particular requirements of the office. In other words, the overall authority of the imam is to be understood in two senses: it is existential (*wilayah takwiniyah*) and associated with his person,[64] and it is relative or conventional (*wilayah i'tibariyah*), concerned with society's religious and political affairs.[65] For Khomeini, the assumption of power is conceived under the latter category, where the focus is placed on the objective requirements of the office, namely to have relevant knowledge and personal piety rather than divine sanction.[66] The two qualities, in addition to public consent, were adopted by the constitution of the Islamic Republic as prerequisites for holding the office of the supreme leader (Articles 107–9).

The crux of Khomeini's argument is that the imam's authority does not belong to his person in the strict sense but to the office of ruler that he is supposed to occupy. Khomeini's account of the legal status of *kharaj* (public funds) sheds more light on his firm belief in the conventional nature of the state and religious rule. Kharaj was the main source of the treasury in the traditional Islamic state, hence Shi'a scholars tended to restrict its administration to the legitimate ruler, namely the imam. A few of them went even further, to equate kharaj with the imam's private property.[67] In contrast, Khomeini took a strong position and ridiculed the latter claim as irrational and an insult to the ethos of the Ja'afari school. His account suggests that kharaj belongs to, and is managed by, the state.[68]

Grasping the fact that, in the modern state, authority is no longer centred on the office of the ruler, Khomeini came to realise that the extensive authority presumed for the imam can take effect only if it is conferred upon the government as a whole:

> Government, which is an offshoot of the absolute authority of the Prophet, peace be upon him, is one of the prime ordinances of Islam preceding all secondary ones including prayer, fasting, and pilgrimage... The government can unilaterally suspend any legitimate contract or course of action, religious or worldly, if it is seen against the interests of the Islamic country.[69]

In another statement, he advised that the authority of the faqih is to be understood within the framework of an Islamic government. This authority comes into effect only if it secures public consent.[70] The essence of the two ideas suggests that the imam's powers are not delegated to the person of the faqih but to the state as a whole.[71] In this sense, the faqih functions as a medium through which authority is legitimately transferred from the imam to the state. Accordingly, there is no sufficient basis for arguing over the extent of powers that might be delegated. The role of the state, whether it is legitimate or illegitimate, is to manage the affairs of its citizens and their property: judges give rulings for punishing crimes, the army sends soldiers to war where they may be killed, financial departments impose taxes and other laws that limit people's rights to manage their property, and so on. Therefore, the transferability of the imam's authority should be thought of in terms of the state's functions, whereby the point is that either government is empowered with the said authority or it is not a government at all.[72]

This approach has provided a well-argued solution to the controversy over the delegation of power and the nature of the faqih's authority within a modern state. It must be said, however, that it is not yet a universally agreed solution amongst Shi'a scholars. In Chapter Four, I will introduce some contrasting opinions in this regard, many of which contest this concept of relationship between the faqih and the state, and the degree of legitimacy secured through this course.

The Primacy of the State

There are many understandable reasons for Ayatollah Khomeini's absolutist tendency: his charismatic character, being a leader of a transformative revolution, and a religious exemplar. An absolutist government has a lot of negative implications, but it has also some important positive ones. The European absolutist state of the seventeenth and eighteenth centuries served as a unifying force in the preparation for the emergence of the 'bourgeois' constitutional state.[73] Although this was usually applied to political and economic aspects, the unificatory function could be seen as an appropriate role wherever the problem of social fragmentation exists and harms national unity. I have already noted that Iranian society was characterised by a discrepancy between the conception of political order held by the state and the one held by the population. I have argued there that such a discrepancy was due to the problematic role of religion.

Ayatollah Khomeini wanted to reconcile religion with the state as the only way, at least in his view, to bring together the state and the society. He would not have succeeded in overcoming a long-established tradition of apathy by referring to the same traditions. Therefore, he had to enforce a revivalist reading of these traditions in order for them to serve his project. This was made possible by employing his personal charisma to convince the community of the validity of his proposals. Charisma is viewed by Max Weber as probably the greatest revolutionary force in periods of established tradition.[74] In such periods, Ake suggests, the hegemony of traditional institutions makes it unlikely that the population will accept, without hesitation, the state's claim to their loyalty unless it is put forward by someone whom the masses respect and trust. Therefore, 'this personal respect can be used to buttress the state until it wins its own legitimacy'.[75] The problem of political integration in new states is understood in terms of the population refraining from identifying themselves with the new system. The charismatic leader is therefore a major instrument for bridging the gap: in a sense, to make the population 'think of the state as "we" rather than "they". For Wallerstein (1961): 'political integration can only be presumed to have taken place when the citizen accepts the state as the legitimate holder of force and authority, the rightful locus of legislation and social decision.'[76]

Because of the emphasis placed on the person of the leader, and the impediments of the transitional period, charismatic rule can hardly be other than arbitrary and absolutist. In the context of Iran, this issue came to the fore in the post-revolutionary period when government policies were opposed by many religious scholars, especially with regard to the codification of laws. To handle this problem, Khomeini advanced the two correlating notions of the absolute authority of the ruling faqih and the superiority of the state over all other institutions including religious ones.[77]

The Absolute Authority of the Faqih

For Ayatollah Khomeini, the maintenance of the Islamic regime is the primary obligation of all Muslims, well ahead of most religious duties including those that are seen as essential to the faith. His argument seems logical: the state is a powerful means for creating the environment necessary to enable Islamic laws to be applied.[78]

Apparently, Ayatollah Khomeini was not fully acquainted with the compelling requirements of state affairs when he took power. In a rare testimony, he told an audience of senior judges of the lack of administrative skills among the revolutionary elite and the experimental nature of some policies adopted after the Revolution.[79] There was initially a kind of simplistic attitude towards state affairs, as Khomeini had repeatedly suggested that the available jurisprudence would be sufficient to satisfy the state requirements when a new political system was installed.[80] Shortly after the erection of the Islamic regime, its leaders found that the kind of state conceived by clerics was, to a great extent, alien to the actual reality of the situation. According to former president Hashemi Rafsanjani, the legislative business of parliament was a difficult experience due to the constant pressure from senior clerics in the Qum seminaries: 'The parliament could hardly pursue its business, for there was always a point seen by the 'ulama as incompatible with a certain religious rule.'[81]

The turning point came apparently in 1983 when Khomeini determined to free the state from the constraints of traditional jurisprudence. Until then, parliament had resorted to the notion of secondary rules (*ahkam thanaviyah*) to handle the conflict between religious rules and public interests as identified by the various branches of the state. The term 'secondary rule' denotes a reasoning methodology employed on a temporary basis as a way out in exceptional situations.[82] A common instance of such a notion is the right of the state to temporarily dictate the pricing of scarce goods, even though it violates the basic religious principles fostering private property. The repeated utilisation of this methodology came under attack from some scholars, including Ayatollah Golbaigani, the second highest ranking religious leader after Khomeini, who wrote to Khomeini and to the parliament in March 1982 protesting against the employment of secondary rules, as it represented a deliberate negligence of the established primary rules (*ahkam awaliyah*).[83] In 1983 there was another controversy over the penal code between the clerical members of the Council of Guardians and parliament for the same reason. Similar arguments arose in the following years, which brought Ayatollah Khomeini to rethink the fundamental principles regulating the interaction between state and jurisprudential institutions. In this regard, he developed the notion of *maslahat-e nezam* (the regime's interest) as a framework for conceptualising the authority of the state in dealing with the public interest. The new concept held that the application of religious rules should be dictated by their capacity to safeguard the public interest. Consequently, the role of the legislators, both the mujtahids and the members of the parliament, came to be defined in terms of identifying the common good rather than expressing the will of God or delivering religious obligations. He also redefined the faqih's authority as absolute (*al-wilayah al-mutlaqah*) and the nature of his ruling as an authoritative command (*hukm welaei*). This ruling sought to override an established notion in the old paradigm suggesting that a mujtahid is superior to the state and is not obliged to obey its rules if they do not satisfy his own judgement (especially because the majority of the officials are laypersons). The idea of the faqih's 'absolute authority' was meant to emphasise the encompassing nature of the state's authority and that all citizens are subject to its rule. The principle of maslahat-e nezam was meant to establish the state's interpretation of the public interest as a criterion for justifying its action, on a par with the established concept of religiously defined interests. Hukm welaei was meant to emphasise the coercive nature of government rulings; the government has the right to initiate compulsory orders in its own right, unlike a non-ruling mujtahid whose directive is one of instruction (fatwa).

Conclusion

Ayatollah Khomeini's project sought to adapt the established Shi'i paradigm of authority to the modern state. Given his religious orientation and the fact that he belonged to the traditional spectrum, Khomeini was not expected to disassociate himself from the tenets of the established paradigm. However, his acquaintance with philosophy and his interest in politics led him to consider the time gap that made the political aspect of the old paradigm largely irrelevant to the contemporary culture of Iran. Khomeini was probably aware that the strict limits inherent in the paradigm would not allow for the historical change that he helped to bring about. Thus, his reworking of the paradigm would concern mainly those principles that hindered his project. The extent of such a revision was conditioned by his cultural background, his intellectual capacity and the compelling requirements of the actual politics in the field.

The major adjustments he made included a new definition of the notion of justice in relative terms, whereby the personal leadership of the infallible imam was no longer a stipulation for a legitimate state. Having done so, Khomeini put an end to the idea that the Shi'as could not consider having a state of their own before the return of their absent imam, a notion that had remained intact since the late ninth century. To deal with the legal ramifications of his new definition, he entrusted the qualified faqih with the office of the imam and conferred upon him the same extensive powers claimed for the infallible imam. This is one of the notions that earned Khomeini a great deal of criticism from both religious and secular parties due to its authoritarian implications.[84] Nevertheless, a careful examination of Khomeini's writings and political behaviour would help to clarify that such a formulation was necessary for handling the theological impediments noted above. Khomeini was fairly aware of the conflict between the traditional concept of the state where the person of ruler was the most important issue, and the modern situation, where the issue of authority is concerned with the political system as a whole. What was important for him was the political system rather than the ruling faqih. This is evident by his endorsement of the constitutional amendment of 1989, which made administrative qualifications superior to religious scholarship as a criterion for candidates for the supreme leadership of the regime.

Khomeini linked the religious character of the regime with the faqih assuming its leadership, but on the other hand he stipulated the political authority of the faqih upon the existence of the political system. In other words, he did not consider the political authority of the faqih to be realisable outside of the state, since the powers presumed for the imam require a state in order for his powers to be conferred upon it. In this sense, the imam's powers are to be entrusted to the state institutions in which the faqih takes part. The faqih thus symbolises the religious aspect of the state and functions as a conduit for channelling the imam's authority through to the state system. It is this rather complex formulation that enabled a modern political system to become integrated into the broad traditional value-system and earn legitimacy on religious grounds.

In addition to his adjustment of the old Shi'i paradigm, Khomeini introduced a number of notions derived from modern political thought, among the most important of which is the notion of republicanism. His advocacy of the republic as a modern form of Islamic state earns him a unique position among Muslim scholars, not only for his acceptance of the notion in theory but also for his positive treatment of its implications and his facilitating its application in real life.

With the Revolution of 1979, the compelling requirements of state affairs brought more challenges to the old paradigm, and again Ayatollah Khomeini was the one who took up the challenge. Among his significant contributions was his endorsement of the legislative role of parliament (which had a lay majority) even in subjects with purely religious bearings, such as the codification of the Penal Law.[85] This shows, on the one hand, Khomeini's decisiveness when dealing with unforeseen theoretical challenges and, on the other hand, the secularising power of bureaucracy as stated by Max Weber.

Although the Islamic Revolution has generated a wave of radical trends throughout the Muslim world, the ideas that Khomeini introduced to Islamic thought have revitalised the debate over the relationship between religion and democracy. Following Khomeini, ideas such as the equal participation of women, universal suffrage, legislation on the basis of popular will, the separation of powers and so on seem to have had more currency among Islamist groups, in contrast to earlier periods when most of the above notions were regarded as incompatible with the teachings of Islam. Here it is noteworthy that Ayatollah Khomeini was not the first Muslim scholar to introduce these ideas; nonetheless, his assumption of power in 1979 bestowed on his reforms the authority that they would not have gained otherwise.

CHAPTER THREE

The Rise of the Reformist Paradigm

This chapter discusses the implications of the emergence of the Reformist faction. It argues that this development was influenced by the failure of the model of governance prevailing after the Islamic revolution. The Reformist model involves a serious deviation from the revolutionary one, thus I explain its rise as a paradigm shift in the sense proposed by Thomas Kuhn in his book *The Structure of Scientific Revolutions*. Obviously, Kuhn's theory meant to analyse the development of knowledge and focused mainly on the course of progress of the natural sciences. Kuhn himself was not convinced of its applicability to the field of human sciences.[1] I use it here to analyse not scientific but political progress. I believe that the theory provides a proper framework for investigating post-revolutionary transformations and especially the emergence and prevalence of the progressive force. In this respect, I would like to stress particularly the following aspects of Kuhn's theory:

1. A paradigm is a 'disciplinary matrix' for its adherents; everyone takes for granted the doctrines, presuppositions and methods of investigation offered by the paradigm as a real image of the world.[2]

2. The fault-line, i.e. the weakening factors, of a paradigm lie within its own system: that is its failure in solving puzzles that arise within the environment it has created.[3]

3. Progress is not a cumulative evolution but a paradigm shift. A paradigm breaks down through a sudden, widespread and emotional movement. Kuhn likens that shift to a 'gestalt switch' by the adherents of the old paradigm towards an alternative, characteristically incompatible one.[4] The change does not limit

itself to the solution of the particular problems that instigated the change but undermines the credibility of the whole paradigm.[5]

The course over which the Reformist model emerged and was established bears many of the features described in Kuhn's notion of a paradigm shift with some adjustment concerning his assertion that only one paradigm can prevail at a given time.[6] This adjustment was actually suggested by many of the researchers who elaborated on his theory.[7]

This chapter will begin by describing the revolutionary paradigm, how it emerged and prevailed, and the fault-line that instigated its crisis. It proceeds by describing the context within which the adherents of the paradigm started to rethink some of its major elements. And finally it shows how the new paradigm emerged, and where it succeeded or failed to deliver on its promises.

I consider this development to be the most important one since the Islamic Revolution. It involves a wholesale conversion from the classic theory of power established in Shi'ism to a new theory, more in tune with liberal democracy. Given the course of political change common in the Middle East, it is distinguished by its being led by committed Muslims, openly supported by a considerable segment of the society and implemented through democratic means. It is particularly significant, for it involves fresh approaches to such issues as the role of religion, secularism and other issues that have long been issues of contention among politicians and researchers of political development in Muslim societies.

The Revolutionary Paradigm

The fault-line of the paradigm that prevailed after the Islamic Revolution lies in its very foundations, notably the ideological justifications of post-revolutionary rule and the heterogeneity of the elite that led the country during that phase. This chapter will show that the Islamic Republic emerged without an articulate definition of rule within the newly born political system. Thus, most of the strategies adopted in that formative period were based on practical considerations. They were put in place to deal with the compelling and changing requirements of the new political arena and also to satisfy the multidirectional pressures exerted by the newly emerged political and social forces. The constant switching of major strategies indicates the absence of a solid and articulate political ideology that would otherwise have ensured consistent strategies in the middle and long terms.

My argument does not deny the post-revolutionary elite's faithfulness to their ideological orientations. Obviously, every group has a kind of ideology to guide and justify its actions. This ideology can be comprehensive, so as to provide the background for all types of political and non-political actions, or can be limited to certain aspects of political life. What I emphasise, firstly, is that the post-revolutionary elite were heterogeneous, thus, what we call a post-revolutionary political ideology was in fact a combination of sub-ideologies. Secondly, the dominant sub-ideology – that is the one held by the clergy – lacked the sophistication necessary for handling the complexities of state politics, especially for a period of extensive transformation such as that which ensued from the revolution.

The Islamic revolution 'brought together a diverse cross-section of religious and secular lay leadership, social classes and political parties as well as guerrilla movements'[8] all of which joined forces to bring down the monarchy. What lay beyond that phase was unclear to most of them, given that Ayatollah Khomeini, the leader of the revolution, had not defined the type of government he favoured.[9] Like many other Muslim scholars, he spoke of 'general principles and specific traditional Islamic institutions which provided the basis for an Islamic state'.[10] The leading role in the revolution and the revolutionary government was held by the Islamic trend, which consisted of both traditional and modern segments. According to Nikpay, an Iranian sociologist, the evolution of political religiosity during the pre-revolutionary era was substantially influenced by the challenge of modernisation, whereby the response of the religious community oscillated between the call to modernise Islam and the call to Islamise modernity. There emerged three types of religiosity:

- An instrumental type, which took Islam as merely an anti-imperialist ideology.
- An ideological type, which emphasised Islam as a basis for political and social reform.
- A jurisprudential-political type, which focused on the religious attitudes and behaviours.[11]

To locate the three trends within the social structure: the first was embraced by the nationalists or the so-called 'Pan-Iranists'; the second was embraced by both the Islamic intellectual trend and the young followers of the late 'Ali Shari'ati; and the third trend was mainly represented by the clergy. Renani, a professor at Esfahan University, places that division within the broader process of transition from traditionalism to modernity, which, according to some writers, was the major source of discontent in modern Iranian society.[12] He argues that in the course of the revolution 'two different sectors of the society revolted against two different sectors of the old regime'; for the traditional sector, the revolution was meant to stall the modernising process fostered by the Shah's regime. In contrast, the modern sector revolted against the persistence of the traditional patterns of politicisation within that regime, despite its claim to modernity.[13] The worldviews of these trends differ from each other so deeply that the plurality of opinions has served to create disharmony among the political elite instead of enriching a multidimensional, and hence unified, approach to how the new political system would be constructed.

On the other hand, on the political scene there were many political and ideological groups that, although not represented in the post-revolutionary government, were actively trying to take part in the making of the new political system. It is an inherent characteristic of revolutions that, with the collapse of the old regime, social energies are released, and a wide variety of groups and organisations emerge 'seeking to reap maximum benefits from the emerging political vacuum'.[14] Therein, a good deal of the views adopted by the ruling elite at that period and prevailing in the following years did not develop through informed debate but through the means of pressure and personal influence. In this respect, 'Ezzatollah Sehabi offers an insider's testimony on the political process during the formative period of the Islamic Republic. Sehabi was a member of various post-revolutionary institutions, including the Revolutionary Council that led the revolution, the Council of Experts, which drew up the Constitution, and the first two governments. His account includes details of the personal, ideological and cultural quarrels within the ruling elite and how the political factions outside the government substantially influenced the government's policies. In this testimony, Sehabi claims that the first draft of the Constitution was drawn up after the model of France's Fifth Republic and envisaged a liberal democratic system but was gradually changed towards social democracy and eventually towards theocracy.[15] The course of change was substantially influenced by that kind of pressure and to a lesser extent by informed debate.[16]

Despite being politically active long before the Islamic Revolution, Ayatollah Khomeini and his religious alliance did not have a political ideology that was sophisticated enough to handle the difficulties which arose in the course of its transformation from being an ideology of socialisation to an ideology of a state. Shi'ism has emerged and developed to accommodate and justify an 'out of state' type of socialisation. The anti-political character of Shi'ism did not change after its engagement in modern politics. Dabashi holds that since the early nineteenth century and 'as anti-colonial resistance began to gain momentum in Iran, Shi'ism was effectively implicated in the nationalisation of that resistance'.[17]

The historical antipathy of Shi'ism towards the state has materialised in an inherent tendency to ignore the state and politics at a scholastic level. Thus the Shi'i experience of state politics within such governments as the Sarbedaran, Safavids and Qajars is completely disregarded by the religious seminaries. These states have not only been denied legitimacy but also ignored as if they never existed. Jurisprudential textbooks and the interpretive studies of the 'ulama barely mention the many Shi'i states which emerged both in and outside Iran, even when they deal with topics related to state and authority.

Given that path of development, Shi'i jurisprudence became evidently impoverished in respect of the rules and regulations related to state and power. Books concerning political theory and current affairs published within the religious community in the pre-revolutionary era were negligible, in both number and quality. It is useful to mention here that this kind of neglect was common among both major branches of Islam, Sunni and Shi'i. The clerical contribution to the political knowledge of the Muslim community was described by Ridwan al-Sayyid as very limited.[18] The reason, according to al-Sharafi, lies in the earlier scholars' preoccupation with the ideals of the formative period of Islam as embodied by the government of the Righteous Caliphs and 'the complete neglect of the government within its historical context, as an entity subject to change in nature and dynamics'.[19] For Ayatollah Montazeri the 'ulama's unawareness of the multi-dimensional nature of the political process is to be blamed on their self-alienation from politics.[20] The same explanation is held by Hassan al-Turabi, the Sudanese scholar,[21] and to some extent al-Sayyid who argues that the antipathy between the religious and political institutions appeared long before the first encounter between the Muslim world and Western culture.[22]

The lack of a proper awareness of the imperatives and mechanisms of state politics appears to have resulted in the religious activists ignoring the complexity of the process through which the political system should be transformed. Prior to the Islamic Revolution, the prospect of political engagement had been swinging between two extremes: a traditional trend thought that state business was too complicated, tricky and even dirty to be undertaken by pious men;[23] the activist trends, on the other hand, thought that the state could be Islamised if the 'bad' holders of the key positions were replaced by good ones. Ayatollah Khomeini, for instance, tells his disciples:

> Once you have succeeded in overthrowing the tyrannical regime, you will certainly be capable of administering the state and guiding the masses.
>
> The entire system of government and administration, together with the necessary laws, lies ready for you. If the administration of the country calls for taxes, Islam has made the necessary provisions, and if the laws are needed, Islam has established them all.[24]

Ayatollah Khomeini envisaged an Islamic state with a very simple system of organisation. He deemed large institutions for legislation or judiciary unnecessary. In an Islamic government, he holds, 'a simple planning body takes the place of the legislative assembly... This body draws up programmes for the different ministries in the light of the ordinances of Islam.'[25] A large bureaucracy does not help the state to be more efficient; rather, it consumes time and money while failing to ensure the fair administration of public affairs.[26] I have already noted in the previous chapters that one of the deficiencies of the Shi'i theory of power, and hence the doctrine of wilayat al-faqih, lies in its underestimation of the part played by state institutions in comparison with the exaggerated significance given to the person of the ruler.

In addition, there has been a commonly held perception that the establishment of the rule of faith will be rewarded with the grace of God. As the Holy Qur'an says: 'If the people of the towns had but believed and feared Allah, We should indeed have opened out to them [all kinds of] blessings from heaven and earth' (Holy Qur'an, 7:96). In general, the state as an independent institution, its requirements, dynamics and its limitations related to its international relations, were largely disregarded by the religious community. According to Ibrahim Yazdi, who was a member of the Revolutionary Council and the interim government:

> Prior to the revolution, all of us thought that, as Muslims, we had the answer to every question. [We thought that] the Islamic Republic would ensure both freedom and justice; such an issue was taken for granted. No one, including the religious intellectuals and clergy, had had any doubts about that. After twenty years of

experience, we see that those questions are not as easy and basic as we have anticipated.

We thought of a state which was not against the religion, observant of the people's faith... We did not think of [such questions as] what Islamisation means exactly.[27]

The above argument certainly brings to the fore a legitimate question: how can it be said that the post-revolutionary Islamic elite lacked an adequate political ideology, whereas we acknowledge their embracing of Islam, and while the Islamic Shari'a is deemed by the elite, and indeed by many others, as a sufficient ideology in its own right, comparable with Marxism and liberalism?

To answer this question, we have to distinguish between Shari'a in the abstract sense and Shari'a in the ideological sense, as it is perceived and interpreted by the religious elite. In the former sense, Shari'a is supposed to outline a normative scheme of values and principles upon which practical rules and regulations can be grounded. For this scheme to apply to the realities of social life, there have to be efficient methods of interpretation and application. The efficiency of interpretation is contingent upon a set of factors outside Shari'a itself, including the scientific competence of the interpreter, the proper understanding of the subject matter and its location within the web of social life, as well as the implications and ramifications which would ensue from the application of certain rules to that subject. Thus my argument does not extend to question the adequacy of Shari'a *per se*, although there is room for such a question, as will be indicated in Chapter Five. My discussion is limited to the adequacy of the ideological sense of Shari'a, namely the notion of *fiqh sunnati* (traditional jurisprudence), which emerged through the process of regime consolidation as the ideological framework within which state policies would be formulated.[28]

Shari'a has been absent from real life for centuries and the traditional fiqh is said to have lost touch with the actual realities of modern life and government.[29] As Hakimi, a senior teacher at Qum seminaries, says:

One who goes through the jurisprudential textbooks will probably think that Islam is an outdated religion, a religion disconnected from the progression of human life, from politics, administration and the constructive movements in such realms as science and economy.[30]

60

The Paradigm Shapes Up

Kamrava categorises the Islamic Revolution as of the spontaneous, as distinct from the pre-planned, variety.[31] With this type, the ideology of the revolution takes shape only after 'the ultimate winners of the revolution have become clear and have established their reign over the country'.[32] What appears in the aftermath of the revolution to be the ideals and objectives of the revolutionary movements are, at best, vague promises open to differing interpretations. They are even contradictory in their eventual outcomes: 'a contradiction which is more the result of the inherent looseness of the revolutionary process itself rather than the sinister manipulation of revolutionary turn-faces'.[33] The Islamic Revolution was no exception; it emerged suddenly with no plan or preparation, says Nourbakhsh, the former director of the Iranian Central Bank:

> No one had foreseen that the revolution would succeed in such a short time. Thus we did not seriously seek to prepare a set of theories which would guide the administration of the country. Mostly, it was the personal desire of some fellows to inquire into the theories of economy, and into some aspects of Islamic economics, but nothing serious.[34]

The new system took shape through the process of trial and error.[35] To make things worse, that process took place while the country endured the effects of enormous economic and political pressures from the United States, alongside a full-scale war with Iraq. Ayatollah Khomeini was probably the one who recognised the long-term implications of that deficiency and thus rejected the proposal by some members of the Revolutionary Council for a twenty-year period of dictatorial rule in order to build the new political system before putting a constitution in place.[36] Khomeini's swift pursuit of the process of the state-building earned the Islamic regime its formal frame of identity and a crucial basis for stability. Within less than two years, there was a new constitution, a president and a parliament, all of which came about through popular ballot.

If that process had continued in the same manner, the regime would probably have accomplished the remaining mission, which is the formulation of its political ideology, thus acquiring a final identity. This was a crucial task, for it would have helped the consensus on the legal form of the new political system to evolve into a consensus on its cultural and political essence. Throughout the twenty-five-year experience of the Islamic

Republic, the major hindrance to political development has been the lack of consensus upon the identity of the Islamic regime. Despite the consensus on the religious character of the regime in the broad sense, it could not provide for a similar agreement on what is meant by each of the principles furnished by the Constitution, including the realisation of religious ideals in the public sphere, constitutional rights, the sources and limits of authority and so on. It is because of these shortcomings that factional rivalries in today's Iran are not limited to the normal differences over power distribution or the different provisions of policy making, as is the case in the democratic systems. They extend down to the very bedrock of the regime.

From 1981 the clergy-dominated alliance of 'the Line of the Imam' commenced a process aiming to consolidate its rule through suppressing or marginalising its political rivals. The Line of the Imam combined three groups: a small but powerful number of pragmatic politicians; a pro-tradition group of middle-ranking clerics and Bazaar traders and guilds; and a broad but disunited leftist collection of groups and activists. The process of regime consolidation helped the third group to claim the strongest position in the political theatre, thus its tendencies had the most influence on the political process in the formative period of the Islamic regime. The reference to some groups as leftist or pragmatic must be considered within the Iranian context, since there is a common scepticism towards the relevance of such descriptions.[37] Similarly, the inclination towards a controlled economy should not be mistaken for the advocacy of a socialist ideology, since socialism has never been accepted by the religious community.[38]

The hegemony of the left was the fruit of a combination of activist interpretations of Shi'ism with anti-imperialist sentiments which engulfed Iranian society in the 1970s. The leftist inclination became established after many of its principles were included in the Constitution.

The Constitution of 1980 represents the first and most comprehensive documentation of the political ideology of the Islamic Republic. The features of the new political system as envisaged by the ruling elite in the early post-revolutionary period were illustrated in the preamble and throughout its 175 articles (177 after the amendment of 1989). The ultimate objective of the Islamic system was defined as 'to create conditions conducive to the development of man in accordance with the noble and universal values of Islam'.[39] This objective takes effect by liberating man from all forms of tyranny and 'entrusting the destinies of the people to the people themselves in order to break completely with the system of oppression'. In political terms, people are to have full-scale participation in the political process.

The Constitution provides the basis of such participation by all members of society at all stages of the political decision-making process on which the destiny of the country depends. In this way during the course of human development towards perfection, each individual will himself be involved in, and responsible for, the growth, advancement and leadership of society. Precisely in this lies the realisation of the holy government upon earth – in accordance with the Qur'anic verse: 'And we wish to show favour to those who have been oppressed upon earth, and to make them leaders and the inheritors.' (Holy Qur'an, 28:5).

The Constitution extends the mission of the Islamic Revolution beyond Iranian territory. It asserts the 'continuation of the Revolution at home and abroad', the striving with 'other Islamic and popular movements to prepare the way for the formation of a single world community' and 'the struggle for the liberation of all deprived and oppressed peoples in the world'. Article 3 states various objectives to be pursued by the Islamic state, including:

- the elimination of all forms of despotism, autocracy, monopoly of power, as well as foreign influence;
- ensuring political and social freedoms; the participation of the entire people in determining their political, economic, social and cultural destiny;
- the elimination of discrimination and the provision of equal opportunities for all;
- a just economy compatible with the Islamic criteria, aiming to create welfare, eliminate poverty, and abolish all forms of deprivation with respect to food, housing, work, health care, and the provision of social insurance for all;
- the pursuit of self-sufficiency in scientific, technological, industrial, agricultural and military domains.[40]

The Paradigm in Action

Throughout the Constitution, as well as the speeches and communiqués by Khomeini and other leaders, there appears a scheme of five notions that make up the essence of the ideology of the revolutionary elite. These notions are: Islam, justice, public participation, independence and renovation. While in the abstract that scheme seems a meeting-point for the entire revolutionary elite, this agreement could not, unfortunately, extend to the practical level. From the early 1980s until now, the differing interpretations made each of the above principles a pivot for contention instead of functioning as an agent of ideological harmony. In the following pages I will discuss how the principle of justice was conceived and applied through two major aspects of public life, namely the management of the economy and political participation. The discussion provides an example of the way in which the revolutionary paradigm evolved and became established.

Social justice has represented a prominent theme in political and philosophical debates since ancient times. As a normative principle, it validates the processing of such major pursuits in the social life as the distribution of common resources, privileges, the organisation of public institutions and so on. There appears to be no single definition of social justice. Miller, however, suggests that it is better understood as a part of the broader concept of justice in general.[41] The early accounts of social justice are generally based on the idea that a just society is the will of God. Later accounts treated the notion in the context of natural law and the social contract. Recently, the debate on social justice came to be dominated by the contest between various socialist visions and the liberal model, most notably the contractual theory of justice, advocated mainly by John Rawls in the frame of his 'justice as fairness' model.[42] Miller holds that the conception of social justice is highly conditioned by the way in which a society is organised. He considers three social types, namely the primitive, the hierarchical and the free market-based society as distinctive frames of organisation, each with a different conception of justice:

> The social structure of a particular society generates a certain type of interpersonal relationship, which in turn gives rise to a particular way of assessing and evaluating other men, and of judging how benefits and burdens should be distributed.[43]

The market model conceives the free economic market as a just system for distributing goods and services. Rawls criticises the utilitarian character of the model as it fails to satisfy its individualistic foundation, wherein 'each person possesses an inviolability founded on justice that even the welfare of society as a whole cannot override'.[44] Rawls holds that a just society must involve two essential criteria: basic liberties are the same for each citizen, and when social or economic inequalities do exist, the distribution of social goods must benefit the least favoured:

> The basic structure of society is arranged so that it maximises the primary goods available to the least advantaged to make use of

the same basic liberties enjoyed by everyone. This defines one of the central aims of political and social justice.[45]

Similarly, the principle of justice occupies an exalted position in Islamic thought. In Shi'i belief, justice is one of the five primary principles (*usul*) of the religion.[46] According to Motahhari, justice is the essence of all religious teachings; it has an equal rank to the belief in the oneness of God, it is the basis for belief in resurrection, the reason for sending the prophets and assigning the imams and the canon of individual perfection and society's safety.[47] Along the same lines, the leader of the Islamic Republic holds that ensuring justice and fairness is the most urgent incentive for the emergence of the Islamic regime.[48] Khamenei maintains that a just system must be based on three foundations: just laws, just executives and an active role by the people. According to this view 'the only just laws are those of Islam, since Islam receives its laws from God who has absolute knowledge of the world'.[49]

Despite the aforementioned exalted position of social justice in religious traditions, its application does not match the rhetorical emphasis put upon it. That is an outcome of the absence of a sophisticated ideology which otherwise would have ensured a cumulative process towards institutionalising social justice in the Islamic system. In the following pages, I will discuss how the principle was applied within the two areas of economy and political participation.

Management of the Economy

Three factors are said to have influenced the provision of the fair distribution of income in the post-revolutionary era. First: the traditional patterns of socialisation in which society is conceived of as a collection of 'small producers, where everybody owns his own workshop and where production on a mass scale and the relations of wage-labour do not arise'.[50] Second: outrage regarding the royal regime's favouring of the upper class and major cities in the distribution of national resources. This is to be understood with reference to the fact that the major source of national income, namely oil exports, was in the hands of the state. According to Parsa, in 1974, forty-seven of the wealthiest families controlled around 85 per cent of the large firms, among which ten families owned from ten to seventy-four businesses for a total of 390 corporations. The royal family owned 137 of the 537 largest corporations and financial institutions.[51] Third: a common illusion links the lack of fairness under the former regime to its fostering of a free market economy and strong ties with the international market.[52]

It appears that the profound influence of the three factors on both the elite and ordinary people took place because of what I take as an ideological vacuum: that is, the absence of any other ideology capable of offering a better way through which the Iranian society could emerge from its difficulties. This vacuum is described by Rogani Zanjani, an economist and former cabinet member, as follows:

> In addition to the lack of administrative skills among the revolutionary forces, we had a more fundamental defect in a theoretical respect. The capitalist system evolved through systematic dialogue between theory and reality. The socialist system followed the same course. In comparison, Islamic economics as furnished by the Constitution of the Islamic Republic had never interacted with real life, neither the theories nor the people who proposed and implemented them. As a result, it was abstract and divorced from the actual executive and administrative realm of the country.[53]

For a short while, the doctrine of 'Monotheist Economy' proposed by Abulhassan Bani Sadr, the former president, gained huge popularity as a possible model for the Islamic economy but faded away in the political chaos. The doctrine, however, is more of a critique of the single crop and dependent economy than a foundation for an economic model. Bani Sadr dismisses the Western emphasis on absolute property as contradictory to the Islamic notion of the absolute ownership being the exclusive privilege of God. He holds that 'in Islam there is only the right to ownership of labour and its product and this right is relative'.[54] There were also various writings about Islamic principles in relation to the economy, none of which, however, is tantamount to a distinct model comparable to others common in the world.[55]

The lack of a coherent economic theory gave rise to the favouring of a state-controlled economy whereby the pursuit of economic equality took the form of direct redistribution of wealth from the wealthiest to the poorest segments of society. This tendency was easily accepted by the clerical circles, for it recalls a widely-cited tradition attributed to 'Ali ibn Abi Talib, the first Shi'i imam, suggesting that: 'Allah, the Glorified, has fixed the livelihood of the destitute in the wealth of the rich. No destitute person would starve if the rich did not consume the resources at their disposal excessively.'[56] It also shares some similarities with the established mechanism of social solidarity embedded in the religious duties of *zakat* and *khums*. Through these two forms of financial duties, between 2.5 and 20 per cent of added profits on an annual basis is redistributed from the wealthy to their impoverished fellows. It is not clear whether this idea was put forward in that early period. Nevertheless, in a statement by Ayatollah Khomeini, there was a criticism of some jurists who opposed a government plan to introduce a new tax code on the basis that all forms of tax other than *khums* and *zakat* were illegitimate.[57]

The move to control the market was opposed by the traditional clergy and the leading Bazaar traders, for it implicitly violates the right of property and free contract, both of which are established principles in the Islamic traditions and defined on an individual basis. In order to manage this difficulty, the ruling elite relied heavily on the *ahkam-e thanavieh*, or the secondary rules that allow the ruler recourse to his personal judgement of the public interest in a state of emergency. It is obvious that such a tendency was motivated by the elite's certainty that the established jurisprudential doctrines were not sufficient for addressing the urgent needs of the state at that time. Hence they wanted to impose their personal judgement directly on the management of the transformation of what was thought of as an unjust and dependent economy into one that was Islamic, just and self-sufficient. Ayatollah Golbaigani, the second ranking source of emulation (*marje' al-taqlid*) in the religious establishment, warned Khomeini and the MPs that the excessive use of secondary rules would probably ruin the integrity of the Shari'a.[58]

The centralist tendency came into effect through the nationalisation of the major economic sectors and land redistribution. In June 1979, the government took over the country's thirty-six banks, followed by the confiscation of nearly all the major firms in the engineering, agriculture, construction, insurance and distribution sectors.[59] Nationalised industrial firms totalled 580 by March 1983.[60] According to one report, the Organisation for National Industry acquired 564 units with around 185,000 employees in 1980.[61] *Buniad-e Mostaz'afan* (Foundation for the Disinherited), the body responsible for the administration of the properties of the ousted royal family, held 400 firms in 1982.[62] Another 177 firms were held by *Buniad Shahid* (Martyr Foundation), a revolutionary agency responsible for the welfare of the families of the revolutionary martyrs.[63] The total confiscated assets were estimated at around 31.2 per cent of the entire private investment in the country.[64]

The policy of land redistribution provides another example of the ideological confusion, as well as the political chaos, that characterised that period and resulted in many major policies being adopted without appropriate consideration of their implications. The course of land redistribution was initiated by the peasants at the peak of the revolutionary process and probably was a surprise to the political leaders. Many provinces saw peasants and workers seizing lands, factories, buildings and other properties of the figures of the ousted regime or, in general, those who were identified as wealthy or influential under the previous regime.[65] It is not clear whether the ruling elite was supportive of this type of action. Nevertheless, it brought them face to face with a drastic challenge to identify their concept of social justice: whether it rested on the respect for personal property or fostered the redistribution of private large holdings.[66]

To deal with the widespread seizure of the property of absent landlords, the government issued the 'Law for the Transfer and Revival of Land' in April 1980, promising a wide redistribution of state and privately-owned barren lands.[67] The latter category outraged the traditional clergy, voiced notably by Ayatollah Golbaigani, and resulted in Khomeini stopping any more confiscation.[68] The controversy over agrarian reform went on for years. Some of the seized lands were retained by the peasants; others were returned to their owners by the courts. The fate of agrarian reform remained unclear until 1983, when parliament approved a moderate law observing, to a fair extent, the reservations of the landlords and the religious leaders.[69] The distribution of land partially resolved the problem of landlessness on the part of the poor peasants whereby, according to official reports, around one million hectares of land were distributed among eligible families.[70] The World Bank described it as a moderate step in the right direction but not sufficient to sort out the agrarian problem.[71]

In general, the centralist policies of the post-revolutionary government, particularly its favouring of the less advantaged and rural areas, have resulted in some tangible improvements, at least in the short term. Iran's human development rating, according to UN human development reports, rose from 0.57 in 1980 to 0.61 in 1985 and 0.65 in 1990.[72] The UNHD rating index measures each country's average achievement in three basic areas of human development: a long and healthy life, education and a decent standard of living. The rating of income equality on the basis of the Gini coefficient model gives another indication of the said improvement. According to official statistics, the Gini rate has dropped from 0.512 in 1979 to 0.437 in 1989. This model supposes a five-layer pyramid of incomes where, in the ideal situation, each group should receive a share of the entire income of the society corresponding to its relative size. Since that is not the case in the real world, it calculates the rate of equality by comparing the distance between the actual share of income retained by each of the five layers with the presupposed ideal point, i.e. 20 per cent. The rating ranges from zero (equal) to one (unequal). A society with a fair income distribution would be in the range of 0.4. In the case of Iran, during the first post-revolutionary decade, the share of the 40 per cent with a low income rose from 12 to 14.05 per cent of the total income; the 40 per cent with a middle income from 30 to 37.42 per cent; while the income of the richest fifth dropped from 58 to 48.53 per cent.[73]

Public Participation in Politics

Political participation is the principal feature of democratic political systems. Nie and Verba define it as the 'legal activities by private citizens which are more or less directly aimed at influencing the selection of government personnel and/or actions they take'.[74] The degree of participation is to be assessed against the rate and scope of the government actions that articulate the expressed will of the citizens. Political participation takes different forms, the most notable of which is voting in periodic and freely contested elections.[75] In addition to its instrumental definition, 'electoral participation is conceptualised as a form of symbolic action which lends generalised support to the political system'.[76]

After the emergence of the Islamic Republic, elections were held periodically and attracted wide participation, indicating that the regime was fairly stable and popular.[77] Yet it is hardly deemed a democratic system. The reason is obvious: despite the instrumental and symbolic significance of elections, this does not suffice by itself to deliver a democratic system. First, elections have to be grounded in a conceptual basis appropriate to democracy: that is, the people being the sovereign and source of authority. Second, for elections to manifest the will of the people, rulers have to facilitate the legal and political environment so as to ensure equal opportunity for all citizens to take part in a fair and free contest.

The history of political participation in post-revolutionary Iran shows that the electoral process has evidently failed to meet these criteria. This does not mean that the elections were falsified; it means precisely that the plurality of opinions and the different segments of Iranian society were not given an equal opportunity to express themselves through the elections. Thus, the outputs of the elections might have expressed some of the various interests in Iranian society, a small or a large proportion, but definitely not all of them.

In each of the elections held throughout the twenty-five years that elapsed since the Islamic Revolution, there was political conflict over the rules of access and participation. In the legislative election of 2004, nearly all the non-conservative candidates were excluded from the contest, which was just a repetition of what happened in the 2000, 1996 and 1992 elections. The recurrent conflicts, I argue, imply an inherent misconception of the notions of 'people' and 'political participation' in the revolutionary paradigm. The theoretical ground of this misconception will be discussed in the next chapter. The following pages will illustrate the context within which the idea of participation emerged and took its current shape.

After the Constitutional Revolution of 1905–6, the Majlis became a symbol of the public yearning for a representative government[78] and, at the same time, the medium through which the secular rule is legitimised. During the Pahlavi regime, both religious and secular forces would have been ready to take part in the political process had the regime limited itself to the boundaries of the Constitution. In his *Kashf al-Asrar*, Ayatollah Khomeini indicated that the Shah could have his rule legitimised in exchange for the restoration of the Constitution, notably Article 2, which provided for a clerical body to monitor compliance of laws with religious principles.[79]

Given the exalted position of the Majlis in Iranian culture, it was taken for granted that an elected Majlis would be at the centre of the political process in the new regime. Makarem Shirazi, a conservative scholar, while maintaining that there is no reference to the electoral process in the Shi'i school of jurisprudence,[80] acknowledges its validity on a rather instrumental basis. According to this view, public participation is accepted for it serves to counter the accusation of tyranny or dictatorship. In addition, by holding elections, people's support and trust can be secured, and the temptations of the evils and enemies of the Islamic government would be beaten back.[81]

Other than the said reservation, it is obvious that the post-revolution elite were in agreement that the new political system should involve broad political participation. It appears thus that the issue was dealt with on a practical rather than a theoretical basis. In other words, the course of the revolution and its immediate outcome left no other choice.

There are three possible explanations for this. First: given that the regime was born out of a popular revolution, the role of the people was impossible to deny. The masses not only brought down the former regime but also took over the government and created an order of their choice to administrate day-to-day affairs long before the new regime stood on its feet.[82] Second: despite the old regime falling apart, the revolutionary leadership did not have all the reins of power in its hands. A sense of insecurity was heightened by the emergence of separatist movements in the provinces bordering the western frontiers, and suspicions over a possible intervention by the army or probably a plot by the United States, similar to the one that brought down the national government of Mosaddiq in 1953. In an atmosphere full of suspicion and fear, the revolutionary elite had no real force upon which to rely, other than the ordinary people who gave it faithful support.[83] Third: it was natural for a new regime to try to introduce a better form of government than the ousted one. Pahlavi rule was associated with many unpopular policies, the most notable of which was its disregard for parliament and public opinion.[84] Thus, it was natural for the new regime to take the opposite stance. Fundamentally, Kamrava maintains, the legitimacy of the new ruling elites 'depends on their ability not just to lead revolutions but to deliver on the promises they made during the revolutionary struggle'.[85]

There are of course other factors, including the wholehearted belief by some leaders in free and fair public participation regardless of all the contextual imperatives. For example, Ayatollah Taleghani, the second-in-rank leader of the revolution, was of the opinion that the *shura* (or rule on the basis of collective opinion) was the authentic method of rule in Islam.[86] However, the idea of public participation was at that time more of an acknowledgement of the state of affairs as well as a submission to the urgent need to protect the newly born regime. Ideologically based reservations might have been mitigated by virtue of the fact that the sweeping popularity of the religious leadership provided a kind of comfort, which was reflected in the feeling that, at the end of the day, people would accept the preferences of their leaders.[87]

The first form of institutionalised political participation at the grassroots level was embodied by the neighbourhood councils or *Shura-ye Mahallah* and the popular committees. Both forms denote groups of action set up in each locality and workplace to oversee common interests, as alternatives to the dilapidated state apparatus and other organisations. The group's membership was based on election, selection by respected members of the locality or self-designation.[88] After the new regime had become more securely established, many of these groups were integrated into the formal state bureaucracy. Others were put under the supervision of the locality's mosque leader, resulting in a considerable number of their members leaving because of their disenchantment with the new arrangements or being sacked for suspicions about their loyalty.[89]

The process of state consolidation, which continued until 1983, seems to have been driven by the idea that the existence of independent popular groups necessarily weakens the state and undermines its authority. Ayatollah Khaz'ali, a notable cleric, argued that 'the government would have worked better if there were no parties contesting it'.[90] Other than the local groups, which were less concerned with politics on the national level, the political parties, the interest groups and the independent media have seen the same fate. The clampdown on independent groups between 1981 and 1988 was excused by the need to consolidate the internal front during the period of war.[91] In other words, factional politics were associated with the weakening or fragmentation of society.

Generally speaking, Shi'a clergy do not view political parties as proper agencies for representing people or generating legitimacy, and when they have to do so, the party must be supervised by a mujtahid.[92] In this case, the supervising mujtahid validates the collective opinion of the party.[93] This belief appears to have originated in the scepticism of the religious seminaries about the role of modern forms of socialisation in the broader sense. Ayatollah Hairi plainly expresses his concern that the patronage of modern groups could undermine the religious establishment. Their assertion of factional loyalty serves to lure their members away from the *marje' taqlid* (religious exemplar).[94] This sentiment was not limited to groups that hold purely modernist tendencies. The former president Hashemi Rafsanjani tells us that the Islamic Republic Party was also disliked by many Friday Prayer leaders, who thought it would undermine communal unity.[95] Furthermore, Ayatollah Khomeini was widely known to have been unhappy with party politics.[96] In general, Shi'a clergy are more familiar with customary groupings and direct methods of communicating with ordinary people which take the form of prescription rather than deliberation. The lack of empathy between the clergy and modern groups might explain why most of the influential Iranian parties such as Nehzat Azadi, Mojahedin-e Khalq, Mojahedin Enghelab, Kargozaran and Mosharekat had only a few junior clerics among their members or none at all.

Since 2003, there appears to have been an increasing tendency among the conservatives to adopt modern forms of political activity, notably through political parties. This has probably been motivated by the successes of the Reformist groups in mobilising the new generations on the one hand, and the decrease in the popularity of the clergy on the other. However, this tendency goes hand in hand with the emphasis on collective action through the paramilitary organisation of *Basij*, which is regarded by the conservatives as the authentic alternative that, according to Rafsanjani, can 'fill the vacuum of real political parties in Iran'.[97] The idea of Basij (literally 'mobility') was initially proposed by Khomeini who called upon educated Iranians to help root out the poverty and deprivation of rural areas: a movement that took the form of *Jihad-e Sazandegi* (the Jihad of Reconstruction) and *Nehzat-e Sawad-Amozi* (the Movement for Literacy). The same idea was emphasised in the wake of the Iraqi attack on the western borders, when Khomeini urged Iranians to form *Basij Mostaz'fin* (the Army of Twenty Million). The organisation continued after the war under the umbrella of the Revolutionary Guard. It is currently used as a means of civil defence against a possible assault by outside powers as well as internal counterrevolutionaries. There is considerable evidence that the organisation is actually used by the conservatives against their political rivals.

The Fault-Line Emerges

For Brinton, all revolutions follow a similar course of development: moderates take over but, very soon, they give in to the radicals until, eventually, the fever of revolution settles down, commencing a Thermidorian phase,[98] a period characterised by retreat from revolutionary strategies towards more conventional patterns of politicisation. The Islamic Republic was a political system that was constructed without a pre-planned strategy. Its political ideology took shape through interaction with the imperatives of the political environment of the post-revolutionary period. Even the Constitution was a reflection of the immediate emotions and aspirations that exploded in the course of the Revolution, rather than being something that had thoroughly considered the changing requirements of society in the long term. For Renani, this is the main reason for the intrinsic contradictions within the Constitution.[99] The discrepancy between the idealistic aspirations of the revolutionary paradigm and the actual circumstances has been felt for a while but came to the fore, notably on the economic level, at the final stage of the eight-year war with Iraq. According to Zanjani, the finance minister, in 1986 there was a common feeling that the Islamic regime was no longer able to bear the burden of the war: 'I told the prime minister that we had only two options: either we stop the war or carry on the path of Imam Husayn and sacrifice the regime itself'.[100] Zanjani claims that that idea was common among the elite, but concealed during formal meetings:

In private, most of the ministers were showing a serious desire to end the war. But, in the official meetings of the cabinet, they pretended to be firm and determined to carry on with the war; they often injected Quranic verses, traditions of the infallible imams, and epic poems in their speeches.[101]

Eventually, Ayatollah Khomeini accepted a retreat from the path of Imam Husayn, not only because he was convinced that Iran could not win the war but also because 'the survival of the Islamic regime itself was perhaps at stake'.[102] That retreat was just the starting point in a chain of events labelled by Ehteshami as the Thermidorian phase of the Islamic Revolution.[103]

The final two years of the war involved many setbacks for Iranians. On the military front, the attempts to push into Iraqi territory, which apparently were intended to impose a favourable ceasefire agreement on the Iraqis, failed to make any significant impact.[104] In 1988 the Iraqis escalated their campaign to demoralise the Iranian public by directing 160 SCUD-B missiles into Tehran and other cities. The aerial bombardment of civil and economic facilities also intensified, using, in some cases, chemical weapons against both civilian and military targets on the northern front. The escalation of the 'war on the cities' went side by side with international pressures on Iran, including the increasing presence of American warships in the Persian Gulf.[105] US interference reached a climax when one of its warships shot down an Iranian passenger plane claiming the lives of 290 civilians in July 1988, prompting Iran to accept a ceasefire based on the UN 598 resolution.[106] For Khomeini, that was a deeply painful retreat: 'halting this just war is like drinking poison, death would have been easier to bear'.[107]

On the economic front, the war had a very negative impact, and the livelihood of the entire nation became gradually dependent on state expenditure, which came mainly from oil exports. Some estimates put the direct damages caused by the eight-year war at US $600 billion and the total cost at US $1 trillion.[108] The decline in the oil market, alongside the disruption of oil production by military operations, cost Iran $36 billion in oil revenues (based on the nominal levels of production and price of 1977).[109]

Iran's acceptance of the UN's Security Council resolution 598 had a variety of implications, both political and ideological. It was seen as a submission to a pattern of international relations that the Islamic Republic never recognised as legitimate. In the revolutionary paradigm, the Islamic Republic was perceived as a prelude to the universal domination of Imam Mahdi, the Lord of the Time, rather than an ordinary nation state. The revolution was meant to start from a base-country (*Umm al-Qura*) and inspire disinherited people all over the Muslim world.[110] After the war, the Iranian elite projected an image of the state as something ordinary, concerned with the national interests of its people first and foremost. Later, a prominent religious leader put this deviation from the professed ideology in plain words:

> The Islamic state is not responsible for reforming the world unless the Lord of the Time (*Imam al-Zaman*) appears. The government has to focus on construction, the urbanisation of the country and the well-being of its own people.[111]

The dismissal of Ayatollah Montazeri, the faqih-designate, in March 1989 was another major setback for the revolutionary paradigm. Montazeri was known as a man of religion, knowledge and courage and an advocate of the lower classes. He was also an outspoken critic of the government's treatment of the opposition, especially of political prisoners.[112] His dismissal came shortly after he called for a 'review' of the Islamic regime[113] indicating the changing tendencies among the elite. This event gave the public a taste of the rivalry between their leaders but fundamentally dispelled the image of the ruling elite being modest, pious and lenient. These features were officially sanctioned as the distinctive characteristics of the religious rulers who were once described by Ayatollah Beheshti, as 'the people of service and not the seekers of power'.[114]

Obviously, the elite's deviation from the revolutionary aspirations would not have taken place if the regime had been well and progressing. This deviation was regarded by some authors as a return to the pragmatic approach to local and global issues. The tendency was helped, according to Katouzian, by the collapse of the Soviet Union in 1991; and the universal decline of totalitarian beliefs and centralist policies also had some effect on the Iranian elites.[115]

This pragmatism came to be institutionalised through a major amendment of the religious-idealistic form of leadership furnished by the Constitution. Shortly after the death of Ayatollah Khomeini in June 1989, Iranians voted on a revised version of the Constitution aiming at giving state imperatives a priority over religious ones. The state leadership was separated from the religious seminaries. In the amended Constitution, the administrative and political skills were given primacy over the religious scholarship in the qualification for the office of wilayat al-faqih.

This revision also sought to establish the conventional identification of 'public interest' as the basis for determining the applicability of religious teachings. According to the previously sanctioned traditional jurisprudence, interests are identified by the mujtahid with reference to religious criteria.

The transfer of wilayat al-faqih to the then president Khamenei was relatively smooth. By putting the above changes into effect, the elite was able to exclude many contenders for the office, most of whom excelled Khamenei in respect of religious qualities.[116] The elite's choice was to ignore doctrinal considerations and focus on practical ones, whereby the regime came to enter its second decade in the hands of the pragmatist faction.

One of the major contributers to the new phase was the then Majlis speaker, 'Ali Akbar Bahramani, known as Hashemi Rafsanjani. Rafsanjani was born in 1934 to a major pistachio nut producer in Rafsanjan, Kerman, 670 miles southeast of Tehran. From the early days of the Islamic Revolution Rafsanjani showed incomparable flexibility in dealing with changing circumstances, and by so doing, he retained a role which was always crucial and decisive.[117] His published diaries, speeches and interviews reveal an image of a pragmatic and practical politician, preoccupied with action rather than ideology or aspirations. Rafsanjani portrays himself as a dutiful politician whose major concern is the continuity of the Islamic regime. Rafsanjani, who once defined the compliance with *Islam feqahati* (the jurisprudential perception of Islam) as the line of demarcation between the 'Line of the Imam' and the other Islamic factions,[118] was not reluctant to admit, in due course, that jurisprudence was not in line with what a modern state requires. In a personal testimony on the legislative process during his time as speaker of the Majlis (1980–1989), Rafsanjani says:

> Our legislative work in the Majlis was a real difficulty due to the wide gap between the jurisprudential injunctions and the 'ulama's opinions and the realities of public life. We wanted to formulate the laws necessary to promote the public interest and to ensure that the state was moving within the religious framework. Yet that endeavour was often hindered by the lack of any religious framework which was relevant to the issue in question, or because the available opinions were by no means appropriate to the obvious and actual exigencies of the society.
>
> In many cases, we were afraid of violating the religious limits and the views of some 'ulama, and that made us reluctant to proceed with some cases that we have identified as being of common interest. For instance, we debated and passed the Labour Code, then some of its parts appeared to be incompatible

with certain religious rules. The same problem occurred when the Majlis passed the Tax Code, the Criminal Code, and codes concerning cooperatives, land acquisition, private schools and so on. Whenever an important issue was dealt with by the Majlis, there was a quarrel over the compatibility of its related laws with certain injunctions or views of the 'ulama. If such contradictions and problems remained unsolved, there would be no significant progress towards the Islamisation of the laws or the management of the country.[119]

Rafsanjani's conception of reform has been a point of contention. In fact, he does not conceal his belief that economic prosperity outweighs the importance of political reforms. At times he puts this in pragmatic terms by arguing that political reforms should develop slowly to avoid possible conflicts with traditional forces. Often he puts his views in a theoretical framework and argues that democratisation must be preceded by substantial improvement in the people's livelihood to relax the lower classes' anxiety, which has previously given rise to interventionist tendencies.

Rafsanjani believes that the state is to be the dynamo and risk-taker. His major concern, according to Wright, is to 'fashion a durable state as the basis of authority and to make its survival less dependent on the credentials, personality or clout of the Supreme Leader'.[120] Concerning the economy, he believes in the role of the private sector and foreign assistance, on both the financial and technical levels.[121] Rafsanjani asserts that the concept of social justice, which was conceived by the revolutionary paradigm in the form of direct redistribution, did not prove viable. Alternatively he holds that only through a systematic and gradual process aiming to enhance economic output will the Iranian economy develop an egalitarian character and ensure a fair distribution of resources throughout the nation.[122] His desire for foreign assistance prompted him to bury the principle of exporting the revolution and to try to repair Iran's poor relationship with the outside world.[123] Iran's support for Kuwait's sovereignty against the Iraqi invasion in 1990 served to relax its relations with the Arab Gulf states and lent credibility to its self-portrayal as a stabilising power in the region.[124]

The post-war economic reforms were inevitable. The official statistics gave alarming indications. Compared with the aspiration in the early 1980s towards a strong and self-sufficient economy, the GNP in the fiscal year 1988–9 was still 6 per cent less than it was in 1978–9 (based on 1982–3 prices).[125] Alongside the decline of real *per capita* income, manufacturing output dropped sharply: in 1990, the 210 industrial units held by the

National Industries Organisation were running at 54 per cent of their nominal capacity.[126] The decline in production of the car industry was even worse: the output averages of 1988 ranged from 13 to 30 per cent of 1979 rates.[127]

With the implementation of Rafsanjani's *Siasat-e Ta'dil* (Policy of Adjustment), the economy started to show signs of revival. From 1989 to 1992, the GNP had an annual growth of 7 per cent, compared with an annual average of less than 1 per cent in the preceding decade.[128] Public services saw a similar improvement: by 1998 electricity reached 14 million homes, 40 per cent more than in 1991. Telephone lines increased from 2.45 million in 1991 to 6.69 million in 1996.[129] The rate of unemployment had dropped below 10 per cent by the end 1994. The output in agriculture and industry made a good increase and non-oil exports reached $4 billion in 1993.[130] Nevertheless, a major programme to privatise 400 firms in ten years did not go smoothly because of the pressures from both the traditional-right and left wings, as well as employees.[131]

Rafsanjani's reform policy should be viewed within the frame of limits pertaining to his own personality, immediate concerns and actual powers at his disposal. This policy was, above all, meant to address the problems of the economy. Nevertheless, it could not have been advanced without parallel improvements in state-society relations in general, due particularly to the context within which the reform programme took place, namely the conclusion of the war and the departure of Ayatollah Khomeini. The eight-year rule of Rafsanjani saw an increasing tendency to relax the rigid controls over individual and social activities. This is seen as a by-product of economic reform rather than a deliberate policy. However, it had its impact on society at large. Rafsanjani's emphasis on technocracy gave rise to modern, academic-oriented managers and professionals, most of whom had liberal propensities. Broadly, the Policy of Adjustment is seen as a project designed to redirect the Islamic Republic in both political and economic respects. As for Rafi'pour, that project has involved changing the society from a closed to an open one; relaxing traditional-religious norms; enhancing the role of professionals and replacing the old patterns of the first revolutionary decade with modern ones; and reducing state control over the market and economy.[132]

The relaxed atmosphere made a good impact on cultural life, whereby the number of periodicals rose from ninety-nine in 1986 to 662, including thirty-four dailies, in 1996. The number of books published in the same period rose from 3,812 to 14,459.[133] The economic revival and relative political openness had contradictory effects. On the one hand, the traditionalists were alarmed by the decline in people's observance of traditional-religious norms. These developments also provoked workers' fear of possible loss of their jobs in privatised firms.[134] On the other hand, the reform policies exposed the many advantages of the newly adopted model of a free market. The latter trend continued to gather momentum in the following years. By the end of Rafsanjani's mandate in 1997, the process of reform appeared irreversible. A considerable proportion of both the elite and the public came to the conclusion that the Islamic regime could no longer carry on with the revolutionary paradigm if it was to survive in the changing world. The tangible achievements of the reforms effectively proved that the free-market model, albeit with some adjustments, was the only way to secure a better livelihood for the population and prosperity for the Islamic model.

Meanwhile, the above developments have set in motion the process of paradigmatic change. The openness has effectively served to legitimise the debate over the revolutionary paradigm. Public debate of an issue elevates it from an individual or partial disenchantment to a national issue. In traditional and politically closed societies, people keep away from the controversial issues for fear of suppression, or out of the conviction that the rulers are not willing to listen. Public contribution to the course of democratisation is most likely when restrictions are limited, for it indicates that the rulers welcome the change or that they are not strong enough to suppress the movement for change.

Paradigm replacement is a unidirectional process.[135] Once the established paradigm fails to address the anomalies that have arisen within it, the process of change cannot be reversed. The timing of a paradigm shift depends on a variety of factors, including the significance of the anomalies, the flexibility of the establishment in handling discontent and, crucially, the availability of an alternative paradigm capable of invoking a wide appeal. Both internal and external factors contribute to the paradigm's appeal. On the internal level, it depends on the credibility of its advocates, as well as the numbers within society that feel alienated under the old paradigm. On the other hand, the new paradigm would be likely to have a stronger appeal if it accentuated a scheme of demands at the local level that were identical to rising trends at the international level.

The clearest indication of the emergence of the new paradigm appeared during the legislative elections of 1996, where the pragmatic-liberal candidates of the Kargozaran party enjoyed surprising success, despite the immense efforts by the conservatives to block their way to the Majlis. The conservatives wanted to trade on the explosive rates of inflation (56 per cent in 1994) and the soaring of the consumer prices (96 per cent in 1993), which had resulted from the removal of the price control system in 1993, in order to lure the electorate away from those regarded as liberals. To the surprise of all factions, the party responsible for those unpleasant policies attracted a considerable number of votes, indicating that the people were actually yearning for change and ready to bear its cost.

The left wing seems to have absorbed that lesson profoundly. After that, its language changed substantially and the language of democracy and liberalism became the hegemonic theme in its publications and public meetings. A few months ahead of the 1997 presidential elections, the anti-conservative groups united their forces to promote Muhammad Khatami and his Reformist agenda. The rise of Khatami to the presidency of the Islamic Republic is to be viewed as the turning point at which the new paradigm started to establish itself in the political theatre. At that juncture, the new paradigm was still vague, yet clearly different from the old one in various respects.

The New Paradigm

The conservatives did not underestimate the implications of the Reformist rise to power. Their resistance took various forms, from violent assaults on the persons and meetings, including assassination at the early stage, to the excessive use of the courts at later stages. After 1997, many Reformist figures were arrested and their publications closed. The hard-line Judiciary shut down thirteen publications in 2000, and forty-four in the following year.[136] A total of eighty-five papers, including forty-one dailies, had been closed by 2003,[137] including all the publications of the major Reformist parties.

The Reformist emphasis on the sovereignty of the law has effectively forced the conservatives to distance themselves from mob-like politics and particularly to denounce the actions of such minor groups as *Ansar-e Hizbollah*, which used to justify its disruptive actions on the basis of protecting religion and the revolution.[138] It has to be noted here that the supreme leader, Ayatollah Khamenei, has never shown any support for such actions, in public at least. Nevertheless, many of his close allies, some of whom hold official posts, and other notables in the religious seminaries, including Ayatollah Mesbah Yazdi, did not hesitate to support the use of violence against the Reformists and other liberal politicians. At any rate, the tendency of the conservatives to rely on the law, albeit in an extremely excessive fashion, served to expose the gap that was growing between the two paradigms. It has also worsened the split over the reform process in both the state institutions and society.

In Chapter Two it was argued that the rise of the Islamic Republic put an end to the state-society split which emanated from the antipathy between the state and religion. In the following phase, a new division arose between two versions of religion and consequently two models of rule: one that was authoritarian, grounded in traditions; and one which was democratic affiliated to modernity. Both versions have strong support from the state and society. Nevertheless, the authoritarian paradigm has the lead in the state system while the other has the lead in society. Since 1997, most of the opinion polls have shown that the Reformists enjoy a widening appeal among the public notwithstanding their recent setbacks and the overwhelming control of the mass media by the rival faction.[139] During their eight-year rule, the Reformists made enormous efforts through the parliament and the government to improve the political environment and state-society relations. They succeeded in some respects and failed in others. The viability of the paradigm should consider the framework it had set for itself. In this regard, President Khatami defined his goals in terms of comprehensive and sustainable development.[140] He explained this mission in a fashion closely similar to the concept of 'human development', which was redefined and propagated by the United Nations Development Program (UNDP). According to this concept, the aim of political development is defined as that which creates a social environment conducive to democracy, or an 'enabling environment' in order to broaden human choices.[141]

Given this sense, the main emphasis is put on the structural and institutional changes that serve to enhance the role of the people. To this extent, the Reformist paradigm could be credited with some appreciable achievements, including:

Local Councils: The first local election was held in February 1999 as a part of the Reformist principle of democracy at the grass-root level. According to Articles 100–106 of the Constitution, regional and local affairs are to be administered by locally elected councils. An executive bill was passed by the Majlis in 1982 but remained suspended because the ruling elite feared that such a huge process could not be manageable.[142] In the first election, 328,826 male and 7,276 female candidates contested 236,138 council seats. The women made a relatively remarkable gain of 300 seats.[143] Local councils are seen as a means to breaking the monopoly on power by the centrally based elite. They also provide a practical framework for helping the local and emerging elites to get acquainted with political skills and tactics, thus preparing them to pursue political careers at the national level. As for minorities, small communal and ethnic groups, the local elections provided an opportunity for partaking in the political process, although their actual strength did not help them to contest at the national level.

Political and Interest Groups: Although the Party Bill was put into effect after 1988, only a few groups took advantage by applying for formal permission. Until the mid-1990s the political scene was fairly inactive due to the sense of uncertainty regarding the ruling elite's real intentions in the post-Khomeini period. The emergence of the Reformists in 1997 unleashed a fresh spirit inciting most Iranians to believe that tangible change could be made by employing the power of public opinion. Official statistics show that until May 1997, six political parties and twenty-nine professional and interest organisations were recognised by the government. The figures rose sharply to 114 parties and 171 interest groups during the period from 1997 to 2004, among which thirty-five organisations belonged to religious minorities.[144]

The non-governmental organisations saw the same fortune under Reformist rule: according to Fakhr al-Sadat Mohtashemi, the Assistant Minister of Internal Affairs for Women, women NGOs in 2003 numbered around 600[145] out of a total of 2,500 operating in Iran. In 1997 the number of women NGOs was estimated at seventy-five.[146] These figures do not include community-based organisations (CBOs), which are far higher than these figures and fall into a different categorisation.[147] The total number of NGOs and CBOs is estimated at 20,000.[148] In respect of youth organisations, the school-based associations pose the largest organised activity in the country. The Union of the Islamic Pupils Associations consists of 8,000 groups operating in the middle and high schools. According to one report, the central committee of the Union includes 60,000 members, representing 460,000 pupils in 9,500 schools.[149] The university-based organisations are estimated by the Higher Education Minister to number 2500, representing 20 per cent of all university students.[150]

Media and Publications: The rise of a faith in the power of public opinion and the desire to take part in the political process have been reflected in the media, which has made vigorous advances under Reformist rule, as applications for new periodicals have increased, according to the Minister for Islamic Guidance, from 591 in 1997 to 2,622 in 2003. By the end of 2003, the private sector was granted 1931 permissions, representing 80 per cent of all the periodicals of the country.[151]

Khatami's government carried on the reform programme of the preceding government, but with more emphasis on its political implications and effects on the course of democratisation. In his 2004 budget speech before the Majlis, Khatami defined the function of reform as being to redirect the closed, centralised, uncompetitive and state-controlled economy towards one led by the private sector, ensuring a pivotal role for the people, and actively interacting with the international market.[152]

To advance this mission, Khatami's government had to deal with the same hurdles that brought the reform programme of the previous government nearly to a halt. It seems, however, that the overall improvement of the economy has helped with the continuation of liberalising policies, despite the constant pressures on low-income groups. The government secured renewed support from the business community by allowing it to ally with foreign contractors to execute some of the major projects in the oil sector, factory building, dams and other infrastructure projects. The previous government had taken a two-fold course: it pursued the course of privatisation but concurrently tolerated the expansion of the public sector. This process took the form of founding second and third generations of state-owned companies to execute national and infrastructure projects. According to Hashmian, the deputy minister of finance, the first generation included 176 firms, the second generation includes nearly 500 firms, and the third generation consisted of more than 1,000 firms in which the state holds more than a 50 per cent share.[153]

After 2002 at least, Khatami's government came to the conclusion that a full-scale shift towards a market economy could not be achieved without dealing decisively with the legal and cultural barriers inherent in the revolutionary paradigm, notably the constitutional favouring of the public sector and the perception that profit and foreign investments are linked to exploitation. Article 44 of the Constitution states that:

> All large-scale and mother industries, foreign trade, major minerals, banking, insurance, power generation, dams, and large-scale irrigation networks, radio and television, post, telegraph and telephone services, aviation, shipping, roads, railroads and the like; all these will be publicly owned and administered by the state.

Along the same lines, Article 81 forbids foreign investments that involve concessions granted by the government in any sector of the economy including commerce, industry, agriculture, service, and mineral extraction.

Article 82 stipulates the consent of the parliament upon the employment of foreign experts.

Efforts made by the Reformist government succeeded in breaking the legal deadlock by passing a new law to encourage and support foreign investment, despite the opposition of the Constitutional Council.[154] Other laws permitting the establishment of private banks, insurance and large industrial firms were also passed. The Fourth Five-Year Development Plan (2005–10) envisages a major transformation of the economy by expanding the programme of privatisation and allowing foreign and private firms to enter sectors that hitherto have been monopolised by the state, including telecommunications, public transport, mining, heavy industry, oil and chemicals and power stations. The plan was passed by the predominantly Reformist sixth Majlis but rejected by the Constitutional Council. The Council made 112 objections, most of which relate to Article 44. Thirty-six objections relate to Article 85, which forbids the delegation of state powers to individuals or institutions outside the system.[155] The newly elected seventh Majlis, which is dominated by the conservatives, supported the position of the Constitutional Council. It seems, however, that the plan will go on as formulated by the government since it fulfils the objectives included in the twenty-year vision which was adopted by the Expediency Council and endorsed by the supreme leader in October 2004 as the basis for the state policy until 2025.

The above reservations were already addressed by the Expediency Council, which introduced in December a new elaboration on Article 44 of the Constitution, paving the way for the privatisation of most of the public sector, including the so-called 'mother industries' and large-scale businesses. The ruling aims, according to Mohsen Reza'ie, the Council secretary general, are to shift predominance in the economy from the public to the private sector and 'to facilitate the implementation of the twenty-year plan'.[156] No other institution can revoke the rulings of the Expediency Council. Given the new consensus among the ruling elite on the course of reform, the programme of privatisation seems to have gathered momentum; according to the chief of the privatisation office, 221 companies were to be sold through the Stock Exchange by March 2005, up from fifty-two sold in the previous fiscal year (March 2003–March 2004).[157]

With the revision of Article 44 and the likely endorsement of the fourth development plan, Iran seems to have put an end to the long-running controversy over the nature of its economic system. This step has effectively drawn the final line under the ideology of social justice through state control of the market, which was adopted and experienced without success for more than twenty years.

Conclusion

This chapter has tried to analyse the rise of the Reformist trend and its implications for the political system. It takes the theory of paradigm shift proposed by the American philosopher Thomas Kuhn to explain the political development in the Islamic Republic. The discussion shows that the anomalies that instigated the breakdown of the revolutionary paradigm lie in its very foundation, notably the lack of a sophisticated ideology and the heterogeneity of the ruling elite in the early post-revolutionary period. The two factors contributed to the rise of an interventionist state. This system has proved incapable of addressing the problems of the country, particularly during the time of war and when faced with international pressures. The chapter examined the application of the revolutionary concept of justice in the economic and political spheres.

The conclusion of the war with Iraq and the death of Ayatollah Khomeini in 1989 provided the opportunity for the pragmatic segment of the elite to redirect the Islamic system towards a more realistic path. This development, which took the form of the Policy of Adjustment, although concerned with the economy first and foremost, exposed the discrepancy between the regime's ideals and the actual practice, thus setting in motion the elements of a more fundamental change encompassing the political, economic and social spheres. The effects of the change have materialised in the rise of the Reformist faction, which holds conceptions of religion and government fundamentally incompatible with revolutionary ones. While the revolutionary paradigm is grounded mainly in religious and national traditions, the Reformist one is closer to the model of liberal democracy.

The actual experience of the Reformists shows that their achievement on the political level has been limited in comparison with their significant achievements on the structural and institutional levels. Under Reformist rule, the scope of political participation was expanded through the restoration of the local government system and the enhancement of the presence of civil society, political parties and an independent media. A breakthrough was made by achieving a consensus among the ruling elite to shift predominance in the economy from the public to the private sector. This was particularly affirmed by a new elaboration on the Constitution, removing all barriers that hitherto had hindered economic liberalisation.

CHAPTER FOUR

The Conservative Vision of the State

In Chapter Two, it was shown that Ayatollah Khomeini's discourse combined modern and traditional notions. His tendency was to bring together all the factions who accepted his particular conception of Shiʿism and religious authority. This broad coalition, once named *Khatt-e Imam* (the Line of the Imam) or *Nirouhy-e Maktabi* (Devout Forces), has dominated the post-revolutionary state. After Khomeini died in 1989, each of the modernist and traditionalist trends sought to develop its initial premise into a distinct political ideology. From a cultural point of view, the conservative faction represents the traditional Islamic trend, while the modern one is represented by the Reformists. It expands on Khomeini's doctrine of wilayat al-faqih in respect of the role of clergy but distances itself from the modern notions combined in his discourse.

Being nurtured within the traditional spectrum, the conservative trend enjoys a deep-seated position in Iranian society. Hajari, a veteran revolutionary figure, takes it for the 'original' trend of Iranian society. He argues that 'every one of us bears some elements of conservatism. In Iran, religiosity and nationalism are closely associated with conservatism or bear conservative implications.'[1] The faction had the opportunity to articulate its political ideology only after the rise of the Islamic Republic. Only recently have such notions as republicanism, elections, general will, accountability and so on become common in the trend's literature, thanks to Ayatollah Khomeini, who opened the floodgates and made it possible to rethink many of the notions that hitherto were unquestionable if not completely ignored.

The core of my argument suggests that engaging Shiʿi political doctrine in the actual exercise of power will serve its evolution. In Chapter One, I discussed the course of the doctrine's evolution up to the 1979 Islamic Revolution, which resulted in the emergence of the theory of wilayat al-faqih. Since then, many unforeseen issues have arisen and challenged the professed doctrine. In the following pages, I am going to show how these issues have been addressed by the advocates of the established paradigm.

Like every discourse, the conservatives' points of view are conditioned by the particular paradigm in which they are grounded. A fair judgement about them should consider the main features of that paradigm. My comparison between the conservative and liberal views aims at a better understanding rather than a judgement. However, one might not escape the possible slip into judgement.

I will rely mainly on the works of notable conservative figures. The various works of Misbah Yazdi and M. Jawad Larijani, whose discussion of political issues is conditioned by traditional Shi'i jurisprudence, represent mainstream conservatism. The two are probably the most influential theorists within the trend.

Ayatollah Muhammad Taqi Misbah Yazdi is an outspoken cleric and a close adviser to the Supreme Leader (Ayatollah 'Ali Khamenei). Threads of ancient Greek philosophical views regarding political roles and actions are common in his and his disciples' works. Muhammad Jawad Larijani, a Western-educated intellectual, is the assistant to the Chief Justice for international relations. He is also the founder and director of the Institute for Studies in Theoretical Physics and Mathematics (IPM), a respected institution in Iran. Most of Larijani's writings are dedicated to explaining his proposal of 'the self-legitimated government': a political doctrine presented as an alternative to liberalism. Among the conservative thinkers, Larijani seems most familiar with liberal discourse. He introduces his proposals in the form of a comparison with liberalism; his critique of the latter is not, however, coherent or compelling. Both Yazdi and Larijani advocate what they deem to be a distinct course of political evolution appropriate to the religious perspective and distinct from the model of liberal democracy.

I will also cite other conservative thinkers whose works bring a fresh perspective to the trend's discourse. 'Amid Zanjani's *Fiqh-e Siasi* (Political Jurisprudence) of 1998 offers a detailed account of the normative principles underpinning the 1980 Constitution of the Islamic Republic. He provides for a better understanding of the correspondence between Islamic political values and modern constitutionalism. Sadiq Haqiqat's *Tawzi'e Qudrat dar Fiqh Shi'a* (Power Distribution in Shi'i Jurisprudence) in 2002 provides a good analysis of the idea of power distribution from a jurisprudential perspective. The book introduces the opinions of a considerable number of Shi'a scholars in this respect. 'Abbas Qaemmaqami's *Qudrat wa Mashrou'iat* (Power and Legitimacy) in 2002 represents a new approach to the nature of religious authority, its sources and the role of the faqih in relation to the elected institutions of the state.

The conservative faction is distinguished within the broader traditional Shi'ism for being politically active and by its tendency to 'change in order to conserve'. Traditional Shi'ism is historically known for being apathetic and sceptical about all kinds of change. The faction was designated conservative initially by its leftist rivals.[2] Gradually, this came to be a common designation and occasionally used by the camp itself. Nevertheless, the camp prefers to be known as *usulgara* (advocates of the principles) or *arzeshi* (value-centring) to signify its commitment to the fundamental principles of the religion in comparison with its Reformist rivals who are accused of liberalism.[3]

According to Heywood, five central themes are common to the trends of conservatism, namely tradition, human imperfection, organic society, authority and property.[4] These definitions are applicable to Iranian conservatism within certain limits, but not to the modern conservative trend (or 'the modern right' as it is commonly known), which shows certain similarities to the Reformists in some respects.

Probably the most distinctive characteristic of the Iranian conservatives is their high regard for the traditional pattern of socialisation. For them, social norms and institutions have an element of sanctity, not because they are themselves religiously sanctified but because they are seen as necessary for preserving the religious pattern of behaviour. Issues like dress code, patterns of leisure and the criticism of traditions are among their salient concerns. During the 1990s the conservative-dominated parliament ousted two ministers of culture simply because they were regarded as too lax with the growing liberalism in the local media.

The Conservative Doctrine of Power

The conservative faction upholds the established Shi'i doctrine of power as the major foundation of the Islamic regime and the source of its legitimacy. In Kadivar's account, four intellectual factors have contributed to the making of the doctrine of power in traditional Shi'ism: the doctrine of designated Imamate inherent in Shi'i theology; Plato's idea of the philosopher-king; the idea of absolute authority acquired by the perfect man in Ibn al-'Arabi's Gnostic writings; and the Persian wisdom of kingship.[5] In the following pages, I will shed some light on the above factors, for they form the background to the majority of views common in conservative discourse, after which I will discuss how these views are translated into political positions.

As shown in Chapter One, the aspiration for divine justice in Shi'ism was closely linked to the notion of a divinely designated Imamate, according to which the possibility of a legitimate government is contingent upon one of the Twelve Imams assuming power. The Shi'i doctrine of Imamate was developed to substantiate the right of 'Ali ibn Abi Talib and his descendants to succeed the Prophet as the leaders of the Muslim community. Despite the fierce disputes over the superiority of the imams in terms of their leadership qualities, the focus of the doctrine has been that the Twelve Imams are designated by God. The attachment of charisma, whether personal or divinely ordained, to the leader was, according to Montgomery Watt, a dominant idea in the Shi'i thought.[6] To this extent, the notions of justice and legitimacy came to be symbolised by the person of the infallible imam. It follows that authority is either legitimate, i.e. headed by the imam, or *ghasb* (usurped), which stands for all other authorities.[7] The major concern remained attached to the ruler, whereas the state as an independent institution has not attracted much attention among Shi'i scholarly circles until recently.

In later debates, the state came to be perceived as a conventional institution and legitimacy was linked to its performance. This new perception reflected a general tendency among tenth-century Muslim scholars to handle the puzzling situation raised by the Buyid Shi'i warlords who took over the court of the caliphate in Baghdad. In this case the *de facto* authority of the usurper was acknowledged on an ethical basis, i.e. to avert public disorder or *fitnah*.[8] This tendency has been common among Shi'a scholars and gained more currency with the rise of the Safavids in 1501. Nevertheless, the ideal type of legitimate state remained, at least theoretically, the one supervised by the imam or his deputy, i.e. the qualified mujtahid.

In Plato's *Republic*, society comprises three layers corresponding to the three levels of the individual's soul: namely, the common people, the soldiers and the guardians. Socrates gives an illustration of the statesman as a specialist who practises an art upon a community of non-specialists.[9] The possession of knowledge is regarded as the fundamental source of authority. It follows that a wise ruler might rule without being fettered by the law.[10] Plato maintains that an ideal city is to be ruled by a philosopher-king entrusted with the title of guardian.[11] The philosopher is distinguished by his acquaintance with justice, beauty, truth and the real knowledge of things.[12] According to Lambton, Shi'i circles became familiar with the notion of the philosopher-king through the works of Kulayni and Ibn Babawayh: the two influential Shi'a scholars of the tenth century. In her view, the theory of power that they proposed had bridged the gap between the political thought developed by the earlier Islamic scholars and the Greek philosophical traditions.[13]

The link between knowledge and authority has profoundly influenced Shi'a scholars. In the theoretical grounding of the exemplar's authority, the only principle agreed upon is the idea that the uninformed individual is logically obliged to refer to (and indeed obey) the advice of the informed.[14] The same argument was employed to establish the superiority of infallible imams over other rulers.[15] Garawian, a notable cleric, acknowledges the Greek origin of the notion, but argues that it seems very close to Islamic principles: 'knowledge, wisdom, and science have a self-evident authority over their antitheses'. In this sense, it is argued, authoritarianism is not unethical if supported by scientific proof:

> Under an Islamic government, there must be a bit of authoritarianism, however justified – in other words, an authoritarian government based on logic and scientific proof. I believe that wilayat al-faqih represents such a type of government.[16]

The idea of the superiority of the learned (in the social and political senses) has wide currency among Muslim thinkers, including Sunni scholars. For instance, Tabari (d. 923), a famous jurist and commentator on the Holy Qur'an, applies the Qur'anic notion of *wali al-'amr* (the guardian/ruler) to the qualified scholar, who has a greater right to be obeyed than the king.[17] Conversely, it is not strange to anticipate scholars who deny the association of leadership with knowledge in the jurisprudential sense. Esfahani, an influential Shi'a scholar (d. 1942), rejects the idea as extreme and argues that:

> The jurisprudent is qualified to theorise and interpret, whereas [the position of] rulership requires highly developed skills in public administration, organising the defence of the nation and so on. It is far from reasonable to entrust that job to the faqih *per se*.[18]

Esfahani's argument is very similar to the one advanced by Steinberger, who challenged the idea of the philosopher-king as paradoxical and logically inconsistent. In his view, the philosopher is concerned with the formulation of ideas, whereas the guardian's role is more technical and concerned with achieving previously established ends.[19]

Muhammad J. Larijani, the outspoken conservative theorist, maintains that the religious state is distinguished by the kind of objectives it seeks to achieve. For him, state objectives are defined according to the religious concept of 'the purpose of life': namely, human perfection.[20] The notion can be traced back to ancient Greek philosophy. It was embraced by many Muslim thinkers, notably Muhyiddin Ibn 'Arabi, the mystic and philosopher of the thirteenth century. Here I will use the account of Jane Clark who has made a thorough comparison between the notion of 'the perfect man' according to Aristotle (d. 322 BC) and Ibn 'Arabi (d. 1240). The Greek philosopher holds that the intellect is the highest faculty of the human spirit. The intellect develops from potentiality into actuality when it functions. For Aristotle, man has to perfect himself by acquiring virtue, i.e. preferring and cultivating the good and good qualities. Knowledge – philosophy in particular – is the means by which virtue comes about. For Ibn 'Arabi, divine revelation rather than reason is the first source for knowledge. Man can qualify for the reception of divinely ordained knowledge through purification and full submission to God. Should the self become pure, God will reveal Himself and His knowledge in the heart whereby man reaches the state of perfection. In Ibn 'Arabi's account, the heart is the point where all human faculties, including imagination, reason and sensory perception, interrelate and conjointly operate. When such a process is fully realised, man reaches his final state of perfection, whereby the purpose of creation is fulfilled.[21] The same approach was adopted by Zayn al-Din al-'Amili (known as 'the Second Martyr'), an influential scholar of the sixteenth century (d. 1557).[22] In general, the notion of 'the perfect man' was upheld by a considerable number of theologians and philosophers in Iran, including Sadr al-Din Shirazi, Haydar Amuli and Faiz Kashani.[23] As Shirazi put it: God wanted man to be His representative on earth. Thus, the pursuit of perfection is the highest level of obedience to God. Should man reach perfection, he would qualify for the exalted position of God's agency (the caliph of God).[24]

For Larijani, the Islamic state is about 'righteousness', which is realised through the addressing of the first and most crucial quest of man's life: perfection. The state is seen as worthy only if it undertakes that responsibility; otherwise it is not.[25]

According to Ridwan al-Sayyid, a Lebanese historian, the Covenant of Ardashir, a testament by Ardashir I, the founder of the Sassanian Empire (AD 212–41) was, probably, the most influential source of political theory among the Muslim scholars of the tenth century. One of its phrases, which explains the religion-state relation, was quoted forty-six times in different books written during that period. In this phrase, Ardashir suggested that 'kingship and religion are twin brothers; religion is the foundation of kingship and kingship the protector of religion. Whatever lacks a protector perishes and whatever lacks a foundation is destroyed.'[26] Arjomand shares the same view with regard to the common tendency among Shiʻa scholars.[27] His conclusion, however, does not apply as far as the contemporary Shiʻa jurists are considered.[28]

Both the notions of the philosopher-king and the religion-kingship interdependence were apparently introduced into religious Shiʻa circles through various works from the tenth century and after. However, they seem to have gained wider currency after they were elaborated in *Akhlaq-e Nasiri*, an ethical-philosophical treatise by Nasir al-Din Tusi, a highly respected Shiʻa theologian (d. 1274). In this treatise, Tusi suggests that an ideal political system would likely comprise three factors: divine law, a just king and an efficient administration of public resources.[29] The king is the essence of the political system, in both Plato's philosophy and Ardashir's testaments. The latter focuses on the king's role in respect of public order, whereas in Plato the point of focus is the king's wisdom.

The Social System

The point of discussion here is about the fundamental principles underpinning the political propositions of the conservative camp. Such issues as citizenship, public liberties, authority and so on are conceptualised by this camp or the other with reference to its particular perception of socialisation and the way it ought to be. Each political ideology is grounded on a set of normative justifications, explaining, on the one hand, the state of affairs, and on the other hand, the values to be realised through individual and collective actions. The conservative conception of socialisation is assessed here in comparison with its liberal counterpart, for this study assumes progress towards democracy as the criterion against which the evolution of political thought in Iran is examined.

Following the traditions of Thomas Hobbes, the social system is defined by the liberal theorists in terms of a social contract.[30] Before the state emerged, Hobbes suggests, individuals lived in a 'state of nature' characterised by constant and harmful conflicts incited by individuals' intrinsic desire to possess and control. The individual is illustrated by Hobbes as possessive, self-interested and self-sufficient. Prompted by their rationality, individuals willingly came to bring about the institution of the state as a mediating body assigned to protect them and solve their conflicts.[31] Thereafter, Hall suggests, the idea of 'government with consent' stood at the centre of the modern conception of the state. In liberal theory, this was conceived wholly in individualistic terms.[32] Individualism asserts the priority of the individual over society, whereby the interests of the individual are best served by allowing him maximum freedom and responsibility to act on his own behalf. Accordingly, society is conceived as a collection of self-sufficient individuals whose progress will inevitably serve the welfare of the society. Politically, individualistic liberalism embodies an opposition to all kinds of external control. Hence it tends to restrict the application of the state's powers in the public sphere, namely, the maintenance of law and order and the handling of the conflicts of individuals' interests.[33]

Liberalism presumes that all values are humanistic and all individuals are morally equal. For individualist liberals, the normative priority of the individual is conceived in two ways. First: all moral obligations and social arrangements stand in need of justification to the individual. Second: morality is conceived in a universalistic sense; morals acquire authority if they are accepted by all individuals.[34] Individualism thus came to be a central principle in liberal discourse. As asserted by Geise:

> Any secular political theory must assume that the individual, or as Kant would have it, all rational beings see their actions as potentially meaningful and evaluable, and that, as a consequence, rational self-direction, autonomy, and mutual respect constitute appropriate features of life within a good polity.[35]

Individualism, however, is a point of controversy, particularly with respect to the issue of morality, between two broad groups of liberals: those who advocate the normative priority of the individual to the extreme and the communitarians who argue for the moral requirements being justified on the basis of common welfare or the collective good of the scociety.[36] The latter trend also rejects the association of morality with individually-defined material interests. For Kant, 'the only true categorical morality transcends empirical or material interests. Only so is morality free, and beauty, too, gives free satisfaction because it pleases without engaging interest.'[37]

The conservative discourse dismisses the contractual nature of society as well as the independent identity of the individual. However, this topic has not been studied in detail by religious scholars. The available studies are few and highly biased. Misbah Yazdi's *Al-Mujtama' wa'al-Tarikh* in 1994 provides no precise conclusion on individualism or otherwise communitarianism. The bulk of the book is dedicated to illustrating his objections to both trends and promising a better Islamic alternative; but the result is that he has no coherent proposal.[38] His argument, nevertheless, seems close to the perception held by the paternalistic trend of European conservatism which deals with the issue in a rather pragmatic fashion, i.e. emphasising 'what works'.[39] It also mirrors the argument advanced by Larijani, which suggests that the state-society relation revolves around the state's competence as a problem-solver.[40]

Larijani dismisses the anthropological assumptions – namely the idea of 'the state of nature' that led to the social contract in Hobbes's theory – as well as the definition of polity in terms of a contract and offers an alternative definition: 'polity is a functional grouping tied up by a shared rationality ... The essence of socialisation is a collective action whose direction and objectives are determined by a common rationality.'[41] Larijani's definition mirrors to some extent John Locke's view of the state of nature and the pre-political society.[42]

Larijani argues that society existed before the individual, in the sense that the individual could not identify himself outside society. Individuals join society out of their need for the benefits provided through social life. They make a voluntary decision involving an informed acceptance of a common rationality and its implications.[43] This conception implies that individual rights are not natural, as suggested by Hobbes. Rather, they are determined by the particular structure of the society and conditioned by its rationality. By the same token, the state does not represent the interests of individual citizens but the collective interests of society. This argument is evidently identical to the European conservative conception of the state-society relation, where society is conceived as an organic order that emerges naturally and out of the collective need of individuals for security and familiarity rather than as a contract.[44]

Larijani faults the liberal conception of rationality, together with what he takes as an artificial association between rationality and the social contract. In his words:

> Liberalism restricts the rationality of action to its being calculable and in line with the witnessed realities ... In this precept, the actor's intention and the meaning expressed through the action are completely ignored ...
>
> Action becomes meaningful only if attached to the actor's identifying himself with the surrounding world, in the sense that he and his attitude are not detached from responsibility towards the world he lives in ... The biggest mistake of liberalism lies in its ignoring the attachment of man to his world ... What an

appalling confusion takes place that man is identified as rational
if he acquires a kind of technical competence but his essence is
ignored.[45]

Along the same lines, Misbah Yazdi faults Hobbes's idea of the self-sufficient
individual for it fails to recognise the right course of the relationship between
man and his world. He argues that there is a range of requirements for life
that lie beyond the psychological and intellectual capacity of the individual.
The individual is usually preoccupied by his immediate and calculable needs,
which are regarded as inferior to the moral and ontological ones.[46] According
to Larijani, a social contract cannot always claim rationality. Because people
are prone to error, they may agree on incorrect or irrational ends as well as
correct ones. The latter cannot be deemed rational.[47] The idea expressed here
links rationality to the action itself and not the actor.

The major objective of the social order according to liberalism is
the management of its members' conflicting interests, while in Islamic
philosophy, Larijani maintains, the major objective of socialisation is to help
the evolution of all community members towards the highest degree possible
of human perfection. This particular objective, the type of actions designed
to reach it and the set of principles supporting them are all constituents
of a collective rationality or shared belief. According to this perception,
the conservative discourse distinguishes itself from the liberal by defining
interests and actions in both moral and material terms.[48] It also asserts that
moral questions are not left to the individual, since morality is derived from
religion. Upon the basis of shared belief, the social identity is formed, good
and bad are identified, and the structure of rights and duties is formulated.[49]

The conservative perception of identity and action reflects, to some extent,
the communitarian idea of individual self, rather than the individualistic
idea. The latter conception is criticised, for the individual self is embedded
in a community and identified within shared self-understandings which
frame community life. As Sandel puts it, liberals have effectively devalued
the good by leaving its definition open to the calculations of self-interested
individuals. By comparison, there exists the prospect that all individuals
might work for a morally worthy common good.[50]

Politically, that conservative conception of the individual-society
relation is translated into the rejection of the social contract as the basis
for the state-society relation. Asifi, another conservative scholar, suggests
three implications of the social contract which contradict Islamic teachings.
Firstly, the theory denies that anyone is superior to another (in the sense

that he possesses a natural right of authority); secondly, it acknowledges the individual right to self-determination; and thirdly, it gives the individual the ultimate right to transfer the above right to whomever he likes. The three principles, he contends, are not compatible with Islam, since, in the Holy Qur'an, God is superior to all humans; He is the only one to determine the fate of His creatures and finally, authority is determined by His teachings and not by man.[51]

On the other hand, the idea of the individual's natural rights is rejected as insufficient to foster a participatory society, as Larijani argues.[52] Alternatively, he offers the idea of 'duty' as the basis for socialisation. According to this perception, a member of the political community is obliged to remain politically active throughout his life.[53] He may elect his representative or be elected. In both cases, he fulfils a social duty. On the same basis, public office is defined in terms of liability, rather than privilege. The implication of such a formulation is that the individual's political right is not the point at issue, but his duty, and thus his capacity to undertake responsibility, i.e. to serve others, at different levels.

Citizenship

The idea of citizenship signifies a set of constitutional rights enjoyed by individuals before any allegiance to their state. This modern concept was first developed during the American and French Revolutions. Its preference is for the term 'citizen' over the older term of 'subject', which signifies an inferior status of a subordinate individual prepared to obey others unquestioningly.[54] Aristotle defines the citizen as the one who can 'hold office'. This concept is fundamental to modern constitutionalism since it captures much of the idea of mutual responsibility between the state and individuals.[55]

The conservative perspective on citizenship is derived from the traditional Islamic concept of *ra'iyyah* (literally: 'flock'), which denotes a relationship between superior and inferior based on reciprocal caring and support. The oldest prescription of this kind of relation is the tradition attributed to Prophet Muhammad in which all members of society were described as guardians or shepherds (*ra'i*) responsible for those under their charge (ra'iyyah). Another basic value is the Qur'anic concept of natural equality where all human beings are seen as equal by birth (Holy Qur'an, 49: 13). The two concepts could have provided a coherent framework for the mutual rights and duties of the ruler and the ruled. Nevertheless, the historical evolution of the traditional Muslim state took a different direction whereby rights, especially in the political sense, were conferred on the rulers only, while ordinary people were commonly conceived as subjects. At certain conjunctures, some scholars have even gone further to regard the ruler as a sign of divine grace, and the people's obedience as a thankful gesture to their Creator.[56] Generally speaking, the concept of citizenship as a basis for certain political rights came to be part of religious language only recently. Thereby, its connotations are not as extensively elaborated as in Western tradition.

For Shi'ism in particular, political thought has evolved within the jurisprudential framework. Therefore, many of the normative values and concepts with political bearings have taken a jurisprudential form,[57] where the individual is perceived as a member of religious community, a believer or dutiful person (*dindar*) rather than a citizen.[58] Society is perceived by the traditional clergy as having a structure consisting of two layers: the informed elite (*khassah*) and the general, uninformed people (*'ammah*).[59] The informed elite comprises the holders of noble (i.e. religious) and ordinary knowledge.[60] One of the earliest – and widely cited – classifications of people is found in the tradition attributed to the first imam, 'Ali ibn Abi Talib, in which people are divided into three categories: 'the divinely-inspired scholar (*'alim rabbani*), the disciple pursuing the course of salvation and the ignorant mobs (*hamaj ru'a*) who follow every pretender'.[61] This tradition, according to Sadr, was meant to describe people's attitude towards acquiring knowledge,[62] but it was widely taken as a normative classification of society's members, with the religious knowledge as the criterion to determine the social, and hence, political status of individuals.[63] Generally speaking, the clerical view of the general public is rather pessimistic, for there is a large body of authoritative statements, both sacred texts and scholarly writings, attributing ignorance and selfishness to the people in general. This is one of the paradoxical tendencies within the Shi'a clergy, or at least a considerable segment of them: they depend heavily on the general public for support but do not regard them as credible and rational.

The question of constitutional rights came to be a very controversial issue in the late 1990s and early 2000s through the conservative faction's attempts to enforce its own conception of citizenship as the criterion for access to public office. In a community of believers, they argued, the axis of socialisation was the shared belief rather than mutual interest.[64] Being a citizen does not sufficiently provide for political privilege or particular rights, Misbah Yazdi asserts. The right to occupy public office, especially those with a wide influence, should be determined by the acquisition of moral competence rather than natural or constitutional rights. He argues that:

> It is commonly understood that although citizens are, in principle, equal, their rights as well as access to the positions and privileges are not as such ... We believe that these rights should be originated in God's permission. Those who live in liberal societies or democratic societies, where God's teachings are not followed, say that only the public opinion is to be observed, but we say that, in addition to public opinion, God's permission has to be sought. There has to be no view, demand, or right contradicting God's permission and God's law.[65]

This assertion is natural, since political office is a 'trust', says Lankarani. It is to be held only by those who prove both capable and trusted.[66] Although the Islamic Republic Constitution acknowledges relatively equal rights for the Iranians,[67] the traditional clerics were never happy with the idea of equal opportunity. Since the early 1980s, there have been constant attempts to redefine the constitutional criteria of political rights to match the idea of 'trust' in strictly religious terms.

The application of the above ideas has fuelled constant debates of which the most recent was the political crisis brought about by the Council of Guardians' disqualification of two-thirds of the candidates for the legislative election of 2004. During the 1980s, the traditional clerics wanted to apply the principle of 'trust' as a universal criterion whereby all the applicants for state jobs had to prove religiosity and strict loyalty to the ruling clergy. The plans were opposed by Ayatollah Khomeini, who ordered the dissolution of the committees assigned to investigate applicants.[68] In recent years, the issue has surfaced again over the right to stand for elected office. In 1995, the Council of Guardians of the Constitution was invested with the authority to investigate and determine the eligibility of the candidates for presidency, parliament and the Council of Experts. This power, known as *Nezarat-e Estesvabi* (Discretionary Supervision) came to be the focus of contention in the political fray.[69] According to the Council, the qualities to be possessed by the parliamentary candidate include among others: a practical commitment to Islam, evident loyalty to the supreme leader, a good reputation, trustworthiness and reliability. It was also stated that merely being a Muslim is not a sufficient qualification since parliament is assigned to guard the religion and provide for the promotion of ethics and virtues in society, which, in turn, requires perfect religiosity. Allegiance to the Constitution is not sufficient either, for it will allow into parliament members of illegal political groups.[70] In 2004, the majority of the Reformist candidates were barred from standing for the general elections, simply because their loyalty to wilayat al-faqih was not acknowledged as sincere. Among the names that appeared in the list of disqualifications there were 550 current and former MPs, ex-ministers and clergy members. In brief, citizenship from the conservative perspective does not provide for particular rights. The equality of citizens is acknowledged, but the constitutional rights to equal access to public office are governed by other principles, notably the office being identified in terms of trust.

Legitimacy and the Rule of Law

The question of legitimacy is concerned with two main issues: public consent and the legality of the government. In respect to the former, both the conservatives and Reformists are agreed that the ruler should not impose himself upon the people without their consent. However, the nature of the consent and its legal implications are matters of dispute.

Unlike the liberal democratic theories, political legitimacy in the traditional Shi'i paradigm is not grounded in public consent. Authority is grounded in the relationship between the Creator and the created. In this sense, legitimacy is defined in terms of *haqqaniat* (righteousness), i.e. compliance with the divine revelation.[71] Central to the conservative perception of legitimacy is the Aristotelian concept of *praxis* or 'virtuous action'. In Aristotle's philosophy, *praxis* denotes action that is an end in itself, compared with *poiesis* or production, the type of action that is done for the sake of other things.[72] Larijani employs the same formulation as the basis for legitimising political action and as an alternative to the recourse to legal framework or public consent. He suggests that 'virtuous actions are themselves legitimate whether they comply with certain laws or not'.[73]

In respect to the rule of law, the major issue that draws attention is the constitutional limits on rule. The two notions are among the notable characteristics of the modern democratic state. Power limits are closely linked to legitimacy.[74] It is realised mainly in two ways: firstly, the state's function has to be systematic, predictable and subject to predefined limits; and secondly, public office has to be defined impersonally in terms of roles, powers and functions.[75] Without the sovereignty of law, rulers cannot be held to account.

Both notions are acknowledged by the conservative camp in the broad sense. Nevertheless, like many other notions, they are conceived and dealt with on different bases and thus different scopes of applicability. Here I will focus on the applicability of the two notions to the authority of the supreme religious leader, since it is the core argument among the contesting factions in Iran.

The key principle underlying the faqih's authority suggests that his main function is to interpret the religious laws needed by society. The guidance of the faqih has a measure of sanctity since it expresses the Will of God.[76] Thus it might not be restricted to the definite boundaries of man-made laws. This is, however, acknowledged as far as the legislative role of faqih is concerned. Being a state leader, the faqih has to have the limits of his power justified on different bases.[77]

Apparently, until late 1987, the authority of the ruling faqih was commonly understood as being limited to the boundaries of the constitution. As the then President Khamenei told the congregation of Friday Prayer in January 1988, the supreme leader could not rule if the issue in question involves a possible violation of the Constitution.[78] A few days later, Ayatollah Khomeini blamed him for what he described as the failure to grasp the real significance of religious leadership. In this written statement, Khomeini asserted that the leader could unquestionably take whatever measures he sees as necessary to ensure the interests of country and religion; the leader can suspend minor religious obligations, laws and contracts, including legitimate contracts with the nation.[79]

Khomeini's statement caused a significant shift in the perception of the faqih's authority. From then on, it came to be described as 'absolute' and was added to the Constitution in the 1989 amendment (Article 57).[80] Ayatollah Mo'men, a conservative notable, maintains that the powers of the faqih are determined by religious teachings and not the legal framework.[81] The faqih is authorised to change all kinds of laws, including the Constitution, without seeking authorisation from any other institution.[82] In recent years, many of the liberalising policies of the Reformist parliament were repeatedly blocked by recourse to the above argument.[83] In 2000 the Expediency Council ruled that parliament was not authorised to check the institutions under the leader's supervision.[84]

So, how do the conservatives see the value of the constitutional emphasis on legality and power limits?

According to Article 110 of the Constitution, the supreme leader is invested with a wide range of essential and decisive powers. They include the formulation of macro-policies of the state, general mobilisation in the case of war, the supreme command of the armed forces, the nomination of high-ranking officials and so on. For the conservatives, these are just some examples – and not all – of the powers falling within the category of absolute authority invested in the ruling faqih.[85] In Larijani's account, observation of the law by the religious leader is defined in terms of competence rather than legitimacy. Laws and rules are better seen as guidelines whereby the following of predefined rules will more likely result in better outcomes.[86] The argument is based on the principle of *praxis* discussed above, whereby virtuous action is seen as self-justifying and in no need of legitimisation from an external source. As suggested by Haqiqat, rules must not restrict the action intended to achieve legitimate objectives.[87]

Republicanism and the Role of the People

The assertion of a republican regime instigated by the Islamic revolution was unprecedented in the Shi'i religious tradition. It has raised many questions concerning its implications, notably the attribution of sovereignty to the people. Since the death of Ayatollah Khomeini, many of these questions have emerged as parts of ongoing debates among the rival factions in Iranian politics.

The first hint of conservative scepticism about republicanism emerged in April 1997, when Mo'talefeh, the major right-wing party, approached the Expediency Council, the advisory body of the supreme leader, asking it to define the course by which the Islamic Republic would evolve into 'the Islamic Just State'.[88] The proposal has never been taken seriously either by the political factions or by the leader. Nevertheless, it highlighted the idea that the republic is seen as a transitional stage between the secular monarchy and what is supposed to be a full Islamic state.[89] In the view of Misbah Yazdi, the republic is a form rather than principle:

> The republic should not be thought of as a standard form of government after which we are obliged to shape our regime ...
> The vote for republicanism by the Muslim people of Iran was, in fact, more a rejection of the monarchy than an endorsement of a particular alternative.[90]

For his part Garaweian, claims that Ayatollah Khomeini accepted the idea of a republic unwillingly and was never a republican.[91]

The reservations about republicanism stem from its major ingredient, i.e. the central role of the people. The points of concern here are the grounding of authority in public consent and the legislative role of the people's representatives. According to Article 107 of the 1980 Constitution, the supreme leader is selected by the Council of Experts whose members

101

are elected by the people. The hint implied in this article is that public consent is the basis upon which the authority of the leader is granted and legitimised.[92]

The formation of the Council of Experts seems to have been a compromise to settle the traditionalist-modernist differences over the source of authority. It reflects, on the other hand, the elitist tendency inherent in Islamic traditions. In the Sunni schools, for instance, the ruler is selected by a group of higher elite. This is named as *Ahl al-hall wa al-'Aqd* (literally: 'the people who loosen and bind'), an informal body supposedly representing the various social forces. The structure of this body and the nature of its role remained open to different interpretations.[93] The idea of *Ahl al-hall wa al-'Aqd* was developed by the constitution of the Islamic Republic into a formal body assigned to select the leader and monitor his performance (Articles 107, 111).

For the conservative clergy, the process of election does not involve a conferment of authority, neither by the public upon their representatives nor by the latter upon the selected leader, since the people, says Misbah Yazdi, have never been in possession of power in order to be capable of conveying it onto the ruler.[94] The role of experts, as defined by Ayatollah Mishkini, the incumbent head of the Council, is to 'discover' the candidate favoured by God, rather than conveying on him an authority entrusted by the people.[95] Makarem Shirazi insists that the idea of election is absolutely alien to the traditions of Shi'ism: 'there is not even a small hint of the notion in the works of Shi'a scholars.'[96]

There could be different reasons lying behind the attempted relegation of the political role of the people.

Firstly, in the doctrine of Imamate, the authority emanates from above; absolute authority is transferred from God to the Prophet in the legislative sense, and through him to the imams and faqihs.[97] Therefore, as argued by Amoli, power is not the people's business. The legal status of the people is to observe the rules outlined by the legislator and not to initiate them.[98] Although he dismisses the linkage between the authority of the leader and the public will, Amoli holds that popular participation can be considered at some time in the future, provided the people have proved to have a strict adherence to religious values and the jurist's rule. He accepts the people's participation in the decisionmaking on the various affairs of the state other than that of the nomination of the supreme leader. Amoli admits, however, that such a perception is far from the one common in Western thought.[99]

Secondly, in traditional Islam, legislation is seen as an exclusive prerogative of the 'ulama' in their capacity as interpreters of the holy texts.[100] The idea that parliament is a legislative institution has been one of the most controversial issues among the Islamists. The 1906 Constitution had assigned a clerical body to ensure that parliamentary bills complied with religious principles. The solution was adopted by the 1980 Constitution. I have already noted in Chapter Two that Ayatollah Khomeini redefined parliament's role in terms of identifying the public interest. There is a considerable segment of Shi'a 'ulama who acknowledge the conventional nature of public interest and its identification on the basis of common rationality (*bina al-'oqala*).[101] Nevertheless, the idea does not seem to have been accepted by the traditional clerics in the conservative faction. This is probably due to the political bearing of the idea, namely, that parliament is to be regarded as a centre for authority, independent of the clerical leadership.

Finally, belief could be the fruit of the elitist tendency common among the Muslim clergy, according to which the general public was seen as ignorant and incapable of a rational determination of its interests. Thus the people need to have a guardian (*wali*) to guide them and protect their interests.[102] According to Mishkini, the nomination of the leader is the task of the senior 'ulama', because the people are not capable of identifying the qualified leader on their own.[103]

Although the people were denied the prerogative of being the source for authority, elections are recognised by the Constitution as the means by which political offices are filled. Apparently, the conservatives were not in a position to absolutely deny elections. Such an approach would be tantamount to the renouncement of the regime's legitimacy. Alternatively, they focused on the introduction of a different explanation for the legal nature of elections. In this regard, one finds three accounts:

1. Public consent is defined as the process by which people recognise the authority of the potentially rightful leader. It is more of a proof (*'alamat*), rather than a source or cause (*'ellah*), of his authority. The people are obliged to discover the legitimate leader and recognise his authority.[104] This implies that, at any time, there is only one potentially legitimate leader and society is obliged to identify him and help him to assume office.[105]

2. Ayatollah Hairi explains public consent in technical terms whereby all qualified mujtahids are seen as potentially legitimate rulers, yet only one can assume power at a time. Public opinion is needed therefore to make a preference among equal candidates.

This does not, however, entail any conferment of authority by the electors upon the elected person. It is more an expression of support and encouragement.[106] The crux of this account suggests that none of the candidates is *the* God-designated leader unless his authority is recognised by the majority of people. Nevertheless, the people's role in generating authority is not the point of focus in this account. It addresses mainly the possible conflict between many mujtahids competing for power.

3. Qaemmaqami suggests that legitimacy comprises religious and civil elements. The office of supreme leader (wilayat al-faqih) is distinguished from the person of its holder on the one hand, and from other state offices on the other. The office is legitimised on a religious basis, whereas the powers of its holder are entrusted and remain contingent upon Constitutional principles, namely the public's consent.[107]

The latter account assumes that state institutions, other than the office of faqih, are grounded upon the will of the nation. The role of the faqih in this regard is supervisory rather than administrative.[108] In comparison, the first two accounts hold that state action derives its legitimacy from the ruling faqih. The various branches of the state are seen as the arms of the supreme leader. The role of the people is limited to supporting the legitimate leader. This support is conceived in terms of state competence, since it helps to enhance state performance and national unity. Public preferences might thus be considered by the leader, but without him being compelled or constrained to follow their desires.[109]

The Conservatives' Frame of Reference

The contesting Iranian camps represent two distinct styles of religiosity and thinking. Each is influenced by a particular interpretation of the original sources of the religion and its basic values. In the following pages, I will discuss the ideological source of the conservative political standpoints. The Reformist one will be discussed in the next chapter.

The conservative ideology is based on a combination of three principles: religion is an all-encompassing way of life; established jurisprudence is the method for interpreting its basic teachings into practical rules; and the 'ulama are the only authoritative representatives and interpreters of religion.

Politics, like all other aspects of life, is seen as a religious affair. Conservative discourse focuses on religious life and the religious state rather than 'the role of religion', which might connote the sense of 'degree'. The values expressed through political activity and the standards observed should be defined in religious terms and sought within the religious system of values.[110] Islam is a system of beliefs concerning human existence and should be realised through day-to-day behaviour. Muslim individuals have to pay full obedience to God as He is the creator and the absolute ruler of the universe.[111]

The said obedience is realised in following His commands as conveyed through trusted experts, i.e. the religious scholars. The following of experts in each discipline is a rational obligation.[112] Their views are to be observed for they reflect the essence of the religion. In the words of Ma'refat, the historical association of the clergy with the disciplines pertaining to religion has elevated their language to the impeccable expression of Quranic themes.[113]

This notion came to be known as the *Islam-e faqahati* (the jurisprudential perception of Islam) and was seen as the major element distinguishing the conservative camp from the other factions in Iranian politics.[114]

Fiqh Sunnati

The idea that there are different interpretive readings of the religion has been understood for centuries, but it came to be an issue in Iran only in the late 1960s. There are two broad tendencies with regard to religion and religiosity. One tendency emphasises what is deemed as the ethos of the religion, such as its spirituality, ethics, knowledge and, to a lesser extent, its legal system. It is usually held by the commentators of Qur'an, philosophers, Gnostics and non-clerical intellectuals. It has remained a minor trend even though it has had a popular influence. The major tendency has been the jurisprudential one, which perceives Islam as a legal system and emphasises the idea of duty as the fundamental basis of the relationship between God and man, while paying less attention to the concerns of the former trend.

The first tendency has enjoyed a substantial rise since the mid-1970s and benefited from Ayatollah Khomeini's critique of the narrow views of the traditional jurists. However, the latter remained dominant in the religious seminaries and in the late 1980s regained territory. Khomeini's criticism was meant to encourage vitality and creativity within the traditional trend rather than to endorse its critics. The jurisprudential interpretation of Islam draws a clear-cut line between what is deemed matters of knowledge and matters of practice and asserts that what concerns individuals is the second category. Thereby it became an established attitude among the claimants to the exemplary office (*marji'yyiah*) to commence their work by publishing a *risalah 'amaliyyah* (treatise of practice). The risalah 'amaliyyah sums up the rules endorsed by the exemplar concerning the various religious duties. It also represents the link between him and his followers.

Apparently, the term of *fiqh sunnati* (traditional jurisprudence) was first employed by Ayatollah Khomeini in September 1981.[115] According to Mahamid, fiqh sunnati denotes 'the methodology of interpretation evolved and employed by the great Shi'a scholars for more than ten centuries, and documented in their major textbooks.'[116] In 1983 Khomeini expressed his favour of the methodology of Jawahiri as well as dynamic jurisprudence (*fiqh puya*):

> In respect of methodology, I believe in fiqh sunnati and Jawahiri's style of interpretation. Such a style is correct and the compliance with it is an obligation. It does not follow, however, that the Islamic jurisprudence is not dynamic (*puya*); time and place are determining factors for an efficient interpretation. Religious rules and regulations should be understood in the light of actual realities. Each system forms a particular net of social, political, and economic relations which make the subject of the ruling essentially different ... A competent jurisprudent must be aware of the changing nature of his world.[117]

The methodology of Jawahiri is attributed to Muhammad Hassan al-Najafi, (known later as Jawahiri), the Shi'a leader during the nineteenth century (d. 1847). He was famous for his frequent references to the rational and conventional definitions of public interest as the framework for the derivation and implementation of religious rules.[118] His studies are also distinguished by their concern with issues posed in the public sphere, rather than being limited to individual affairs, as was common among earlier scholars. This, according to Fakhr, is the reason for Khomeini's favouring of Jawahiri.[119] The common tendency in the religious seminaries to study topics and rules in the abstract was often criticised by Khomeini.[120]

The notion of fiqh puya was once upheld by the leftist faction of the clergy as the antithesis of fiqh sunnati, embraced by the traditional clergy.[121] With time, however, the lack of a precise definition of the notion has made it open to different conceptions, among which the most influential is the one espoused by the pragmatic faction of the conservatives which identifies the notion of dynamic fiqh with the interpretation of the religious rules in the light of the state's requirements. This conception contradicts the traditional one that calls for the state's adaptation to the jurisprudential frameworks, and the Reformist one that asserts the need for a completely new jurisprudence.

The application of jurisprudence to constitutional and political affairs has been, since 1979 at least, a controversial issue. The majority of grand ayatollahs, including Khomeini, have acknowledged the need to improve its methodology and broaden its scope. The context within which Khomeini employed the term 'fiqh sunnati' implies that he meant to disqualify the intellectual interpretation of Islam and to emphasise the clerical one. He strongly rejected the calls for a 'completely new jurisprudence' proposed by some modernist clerics and intellectuals and described such a tendency as a 'starting point for the destruction of the religious seminaries'.[122] In the speeches where he emphasised the notion, Khomeini criticised the intellectuals' tendency to disregard the leading role of the clergy or to claim for themselves a role in the leadership of the religious community in opposition to the role of the clergy. This is a major theme in Khomeini's thought and political practice. In brief, the notion of fiqh sunnati denotes the established Shi'i jurisprudential methodology. Nonetheless, for Ayatollah Khomeini, jurisprudence can appropriately address the challenges of modern life and the state only if the 'ulama familiarise themselves with actual conditions of the world surrounding them and develop their methodology to suit the new conceptions and realities.

The major implications of the jurisprudential version of Islam include:

1. Political philosophy, as well as political theory, has to be adapted to the jurisprudential framework; jurisprudence has the capacity to foster both.[123]

2. The implementation of religious teachings is the major objective of the state. Given the sufficiency of religion to address all types of problems posed in social life, the state is obliged to formulate its policies and programmes in accordance with religious criteria. Power relations and the public interest are defined in religious terms and in accordance with religious standards.[124]

3. Public demands are legitimised, hence undertaken by the state, on the basis of their being identified by the religious ruler as 'common interests' rather than an expression of the public will. The idea is justified on the basis that the Islamic government is bound to undertake right actions only. Taking action in itself constitutes its value and thus its justification. Some actions are

in themselves good; others are bad. Being desired or detested by the public does not change their nature. The ruler is eligible to select the acceptable demands of the people because he holds the best knowledge of good and evil.[125] The idea that interests are defined in religious terms has been a matter of wide debate. Some conservative figures came to make a distinction between 'discerning' and 'determining' of interests. In this view, society was said to have the capacity to undertake the former whereas the latter was to be reserved for the faqih.[126] The suggestion is based on the argument that religious rules might constitute interests that were not disclosed for the ordinary believer (*masaleh khafiya*), thus they should be taken for granted as they came from God.[127]

Conclusion

The conservative faction emerged within the traditional spectrum of Iranian society and expressed its concerns. Its political manifestation was prompted by the challenges of the administration of the state and modern ideas unleashed by the rival factions during the post-revolutionary epoch. The conservative ideology expands on the established Shi'i paradigm of authority which is made up of four components: the doctrine of designated imamate; Plato's notion of the philosopher-king; the association of absolute authority with the perfect man, from Ibn al-'Arabi's Gnosticism; and the Persian wisdom of kingship.

Unlike the liberal notion of individualism, the conservatives place more emphasis on the community. The individual-society relation is not based on a 'social contract' but perceived as natural and stemming from the individual need for social life. Society is defined as a functional grouping bound together by a shared belief that conditions the identity of its members and their roles. In such a system, the focus is placed on duty rather than right. The objective for which the system functions is to maximise the collective interest of the members. The interests are defined in both material and moral terms with the latter given superiority.

The conservative discourse acknowledges the equality of all human beings by nature. However, political rights, particularly access to public office, rest on moral competence and strict adherence to the clerical leadership. Political legitimacy and the rule of law are recognised by the faction in the broad sense. Their applicability, however, is conditioned by other principles. Aristotle's notion of *praxis*, or idea of the action that is an end in itself, is adopted as the synonym of legitimate action. According to this precept, action is legitimised if it is seen as right, i.e. there is no need for public consent for it to be carried out. The righteousness of an action is secured upon its compliance with the religious rules as identified by the religious leader. By the same token, the performance of a right action is not restricted by law. Thus the authority of the religious leader is seen as absolute and not bound by constitutional limits.

The faction's scepticism about republicanism stems from the latter's major implication, namely, the central role of the people in governance. In the conservative discourse, authority is not based on public consent; neither does the state represent the nation's will. The highest authority is held by the religious leader who is nominated by the senior clerics. The role of the people is to acknowledge and support his rule.

The conservative ideology is based on a particular interpretive reading of religion called *fiqh sunnati*. According to this perception, religion is taken as an all-inclusive ideology encompassing all the aspects of life. The state is seen as responsible for implementing the religious rules and ensuring the citizens' observance of religious teachings. The 'ulama retain a central role, for they are the authoritative spokesmen for the religion.

The evolution of the conservatives' political ideology during the post-revolutionary period was more of a reaction to the challenges posed by the secularising function of the state and the modern notions unleashed in society. Being a reactive movement, the conservative faction has dealt with theoretical challenges from the platform of defending the continuity of religious tradition, rather than initiating a new vision. This position has constrained the faction's argumentation within the framework developed by its rivals. In other words, the course of the argument over state, religion, modernisation, etc. is led by the Reformist factions. In the short and medium terms, this particular course of debate will help to articulate the faction's views. But, over the long term, it will exhaust its theoretical resources, since it will have helped to establish its rivals' principles as the centre of debate on the national level. In my opinion, this possibility represents a key point in the analysis of the future developments of the conservative-reformist debate.

CHAPTER FIVE

The Reformist View of the State

This chapter discusses the principal elements of political discourse of the Iranian Reformist camp and the religious principles upon which they are grounded. It offers a brief introduction to the influential theorists of the trend. Then it explains the rise of the discourse and its relation to the pre-revolutionary discourse on the religious reformation. Through discussion of its conception of republicanism, legitimacy and democracy, I try to locate the discourse within modern political thought. The discussion of its conception of the role of religion in politics reveals the boundaries differentiating the trend from the established religious paradigm.

The emergence of the Reformist trend signified the rise of liberal tendencies in Iranian society during the 1990s.[1] Two factors can be seen behind this development: socio-economic changes during the first post-revolutionary decade and the revival of intellectual activity, together with the emergence of a new self-awareness, notably among the young generation.

The Socio-economic Background

As a demonstration that the Islamic revolution belongs to the less advantaged class (*mostaz'afin*), the post-revolutionary government has made huge efforts to improve the country's infrastructure, focusing mainly on the countryside. A wide variety of development programmes was carried out by both the government and the voluntary organisation of *Jihad-e Sazandagi* (the Jihad of Reconstruction) and *Nehzat-e Sawad-Amozi* (the Movement for Literacy). In addition to the ideological motives, the government's focus on the countryside aimed to enhance food production in order to counter the shortage in foreign income during the war with Iraq and the economic embargo by the United States. The development programmes have included the building of a huge infrastructure of roads, communication systems, electricity supply and primary schools. These programmes have had a direct effect on the society's culture and served to connect the rural population to the main path of the political and economic processes of the country after decades of isolation. 'Abdi specifies three manifestations of the said development in the realm of politics. The first is the elevation of the level of education of the population in general. This is seen in the growth of the percentage of students at the middle and higher levels of education, as well as in the overall expansion of literacy. The second manifestation is the decline of clerical influence over the population to the benefit of the independent media and other modern means of communication. And third is the change of lifestyle of rural communities, which gradually became open to trends familiar in urban areas.[2]

Between 1976 and 1996, the literacy rate among Iranians aged six years and over rose from 47.5 per cent to 80 per cent, including 70 per cent of the rural inhabitants. In 1976 roughly 18 per cent of the women in rural areas and 64 per cent in the urban areas were literate. In 1992, the figures had risen to 62 per cent in the rural areas while in 1996, urban female literacy was estimated at 82 per cent. Similarly, the number of students at all levels of education rose from 7.25 million in 1979 to 19.32 million in 1996, of which 1.2 million were at university.[3] Reza'ie focuses on the change of status among employees. During the same period, the number of self-employed workers rose from 182,300 to 528,000. The other indicator is the elevation of women's employment status. Despite a decrease of 2 per cent of working women (from 16 per cent down to 14 per cent), the percentage of women occupying executive and professional posts rose to 38 per cent.[4] The flourishing of education on the national level is seen by almost all development theorists as a major stimulus for social change, in the sense of attitudes, worldviews and political orientations. It helps to bring about a new self-awareness reflected directly in the willingness to participate in public affairs. The electoral behaviour in the 1997 presidential election provides strong support for this assumption. The voting of the peripheral regions and countryside was similar to that of the major cities, which are usually regarded as more politicised. Piran, a professor of sociology at Tehran University, holds that the significant role of the youth in that election indicates the emergence of students as a major reference group in Iranian society. Bearing in mind the increased tendency on the part of the rural population to follow the urban lifestyle, the two factors have led to the modernist discourse expanding rapidly and its representatives winning the widest appeal at the expense of the pro-tradition camp.[5]

111

The Role of the Intellectuals

Boroujerdi ascribes the rise of the Reformist discourse to the arrival of a new generation of Islamist thinkers on the Iranian intellectual scene.[6] The term 'intellectual' denotes 'someone for whom ideas, science, art and culture are so important as to determine not only the aim of everyday life but also the roots of political thought and action'.[7] When it comes to the politics of development, Shils broadens the definition to include all those whose education or profession belongs to the modern world. In this view, the social position of the intellectual is emphasised as being contrary to the pro-tradition segment of society; thus he assigns the attribute to 'all persons with an advanced modern education'.[8] The term 'religious intellectuals' (*roshanfikr deeni*) denotes the group of thinkers whose worldview is conditioned by the basic principles of religion. Based upon historical experience, 'Alavitabar places the group between the traditional clergy and the secularist thinkers. He identifies the religious intellectual trend with three distinctive preoccupations:[9] developing a rational interpretation of religion and religious principles; criticising the current social system, its institutions, relations and attitudes; and emphasising the values of liberty, equality and progress as prerequisites for the social organisation.

Vahdat explains the advancement of intellectual discourse in Iran within the frame of an identity revival. The process involves a bifurcation of the ambivalent self-identity that characterised the Islamic discourse of the 1960s and 1970s. It is argued that the philosophical approaches of the three main architects of the revolutionary discourse, 'Ali Shari'ati, Ayatollah Khomeini and Murtaza Mutahari, have shared a characteristic ambivalence towards subjectivity, resulting in their political views promoting unclear conceptions of citizenship. While none of the three denies human subjectivity, they do not regard it as independent either, but contingent upon God's subjectivity, as it is expressed in the monotheistic society (*jame'ah tavhidi*). The construction of such a society is viewed by the three scholars as the main objective of the Islamic Revolution. With the course of bifurcation, the conservatives have leaned towards the traditional position in which a religious-based subjectivity embodies the negation of citizenship and its related political rights. By contrast, the Reformist discourse has developed in line with the modern notion of individual subjectivity and its political embodiment as universal citizenship.[10]

For Bashiriyeh, the above development demonstrates the transformation of Iranian political culture, which eventually helped individuality to emerge as the basis for independent self-awareness. Since the revolution, he argues, the dominant group has made intensive efforts to restructure the national identity of the Iranians. The ideal citizen has been described as one ready to give up or degrade his sense of belonging to all social institutions other than the one offered by the official ideology.[11] The identity of the Islamic Republic has been introduced as absolute, solid and perfect, while other identities including those that are national, ethnic and culturally based have been regarded as inferior or contradictory to Islam.[12] In addition to satisfying ideological objectives, this course has been designed to unify the sources of power in the hands of the state. Thus, the first post-revolutionary decade saw the political theatre purified of any institution that might symbolise or mobilise different identities. The political parties, professional associations, as well as the independent press, were weakened or even dismantled; and the public sphere was freed for the officially sanctioned identity to flourish.

From the early 1990s there was a reverse cycle aided by both internal and international developments. It was characterised by a decline in the ideological components of individual self-awareness and a reciprocal growth of individualism in the liberal sense.[13] Thus, the inclination towards individualism and the general tendency to embrace notions pertaining to liberal democracy are not phenomena limited to the intellectual elite. This was rather a common tendency shared among all groups of society that, at a certain point of time, felt alienated.[14] Furthermore, it could be said that it is the change in the hearts and minds of the people that made the environment conducive to intellectuals voicing their claims. This argument can be supported by the fact that the landslide victory of Khatami in 1997 was no less a surprise for his supporters than for their rivals.[15] The idea indicated by this event is that the people were more ready for change than the Reformist elite.

Prior to the Islamic Revolution, intellectual discourse within the religious sphere was pioneered by the founders of *Nehzat-e Azadi-e Iran* (the Movement for the Liberation of Iran), notably Ayatollah Mahmoud Talegani, Mahdi Bazargan and Yadullah Sahabi, all of whom were active supporters of the former Prime Minister Muhammad Mosaddiq and his National Front during the 1950s. Since its earliest stage, the major objective of this trend has been to reconcile Islam with modernity. Apparently the immediate aim was to defend religion against the rising secular trends unleashed by the modernising policies of the Pahlavi regime. The trend thus had to distinguish itself from the traditional clergy, in both its discursive language and its anticipated audience.[16] It reached a climax with 'Ali Shari'ati who dedicated himself to reinterpreting Shi'i history, traditions and thought in a fashion directly contradicting the established paradigm espoused by the clergy. This has inevitably led to his discourse taking an anti-clerical character.[17]

During the 1960s and 1970s intellectual discourse was influential mainly among the urban middle class in general and university students in particular. It has been noted in Chapter Two that the majority of pre-revolutionary supporters of Ayatollah Khomeini consisted of educated laymen and young clerics with modernist, mainly leftist, tendencies. The trend developed its Reformist character after it was alienated from the state in the late 1980s. After an interval of passivity, it returned to the political fray through the means of independent media. The common theme among the four Reformist periodicals published between May 1990 and October 1991 was criticism of the official ideology of hegemony, notably traditional fiqh. The four publications were shut down after a while by the hard-line dominated judiciary.[18] Their relatively short life, however, made public the variety of contesting opinions in the community, in contrast to the image displayed by the ruling elite illustrating a uniform society, fully adhering to the official discourse. The daily *Salam* and the monthly journal *Kiyan* pioneered the new discourse. The former served as the political voice of the emerging Reformist trend while the latter voiced its intellectual principles and concerns. *Kiyan* was published in October 1991 by a group of young thinkers who, a few months earlier, were forced out of the state-owned *Kayhan Farhangi*. In addition to its journalistic role, *Kiyan* served as a centre for communication and debate among non-conservative intellectuals. Through the *Kiyan* Circle, a weekly gathering of writers and supporters, it brought together a relatively large number (sometimes up to 107) of academic researchers, professional writers and political activists from different walks of life. The Circle has provided the Reformist publications and groups that appeared in the 1990s with a considerable number of their writers, new ideas and informed activists.[19] This explains why *Kiyan* has been regarded by some analysts as a milestone in the history of Iran's cultural press.[20] In addition to *Kiyan*, Jalaipour mentions two other circles through which the Reformist discourse has taken shape, namely the Centre for Strategic Research based in the office of President Rafsanjani, and the 2,500-member group of postgraduates sent to Western universities through Rafsanjani's initiative to renovate the academia and state administration in the early 1990s.[21]

Main Figures and Themes in the Reformist Movement

The Reformist trend has among its activists a relatively large number of intellectuals and professional writers. The trend benefits also from its acquaintance with the broader intellectual and academic community of the country. Many of the names appearing in Reformist publications belong to political figures and scholars of different tendencies, including the modern right wing, the secular nationalists and the liberals. Among the many theorists and analysts advocating the Reformist manifesto, there are a few who have a special appeal to the members and supporters of the trend. Here I will introduce three of them, each representing a distinct tendency within the Reformist camp: Abdol-Karim Soroush, an academic figure; Muhammad Khatami, a cleric; and Sa'eed Hajjarian, a political activist. Later in the chapter, I will introduce Mujtahid Shabestari, the outspoken critic of the established school of jurisprudence. The three thinkers share the same principles held by the Reformist movement, but they differ in regard to their areas of interest and the audience that they appeal to. Soroush, for example, focuses on the value of justice, which he deems as having the highest value and as the essence of human ethics. He has dedicated his *Akhlagh-e Khodayan* (Morals of the Gods) to show how basic moral values and virtues are linked to justice.[22] Khatami is more concerned with the practical means to curb authoritarianism. Thus he focuses on accountability, the rule of law and the constitutional framework of political action. In comparison, Hajjarian emphasises the modernisation of the political system, including such ideas as rationalisation, the representation of various interests, the division of labour and so forth. Soroush tries to establish his arguments outside the particular limits of the political system, supporting the idea that the current system is transitional, whereas both Khatami and Hajjarian hold that the Islamic Republic is potentially capable of developing a democratic character, and thus they focus on the dynamics of development from within the system and its institutions. To sum up, Soroush seeks to establish a democratic discourse outside the prevailing system while the other two are more concerned with the process of democratisation within the Islamic system itself.

Abdol-Karim Soroush, the pen name of Hussayn Haj Faraj Dabbagh, was born in 1945. He studied chemistry in Tehran and London, where, in the late 1970s, he switched to philosophy. After the revolution, he taught philosophy in Tehran University and served on the Council for Cultural Revolution before moving to full-time research and lecturing in 1995. Since his early career as an author, Soroush has attracted much attention; nevertheless, the peak of controversy over his opinions occurred after he published a series of articles on the relative nature of religious teachings. The articles entitled *Qabz va Bast Theoric Shari'at* (The Theoretical Contraction and Expansion of Shari'a) have marked the shift of Soroush's focus from criticising Marxism and religious traditions in general, to the criticism of the traditional fiqh and clerical culture in particular.[23] The thesis focuses on the evolutionary nature of religious knowledge and the contextual limitations of the sacred texts aiming to draw a clear line between religion and religious knowledge. It argues that the latter is acquired through scientific means, thus it is subject to the same rules that are applied to other disciplines. It is profane, subjective and changeable, with no supremacy over any other disciplines, let alone having sanctity or immunity from criticism. According to this account, the perception of religion, the formulation of its practical rules and the way man exercises what he believes in are all based on subjective and contextual understandings of religion. Thus what is introduced by religious scholars as the Will of God is nothing but their own perception of Divine Will.[24] Soroush's methodology and his discourse in general are deeply influenced by Karl Popper's philosophy of knowledge.[25] He often uses Popper's notions of science being probabilistic and of falsifiability as the criteria to distinguish science from pseudo-science. The main target of Soroush's critiques, however, has been the claim of authority based on absolute knowledge, holiness and human perfection, as they inevitably lead to authoritarianism.[26] In addition to *Qabz va Bast*, Soroush has published numerous books and articles, most of which have been provocative.[27]

Sa'eed Hajjarian is regarded as the chief strategist of the Reformist camp.[28] While Soroush's main focus has been the religious character of the polity, Hajjarian has focused on the process of socio-political change after the Islamic Revolution: its dynamics and the way it reflects on the culture, behaviour, roles and institutions in both the state and society. Following Max Weber's traditions, Hajjarian views the rise of the Islamic state as the first step toward secularising the institutions that were hitherto regarded as religious or based on religious principles. Hajjarian was born in 1953 and served as an intelligence officer and deputy at the Ministry of Intelligence. He was among the few analysts who predicted the transformation of electoral behaviour in the early 1990s as a reflection of the structural changes during the post-revolutionary period as well as the conclusion of the war with Iraq and the absence of Ayatollah Khomeini. Thereby, he played a central role in regrouping and transforming the ex-leftist groups into the driving force of political reform.[29] Hajjarian's opinions are expressed mainly through detailed and well-written articles. In fact all of his books are made up of previously published articles. His beautiful yet provocative writing has earned him a large audience. His *Sobh-e Emrooz* was one of the top daily

116

newspapers in terms of circulation before it was shut down in April 2000 by the conservatives.[30] His most controversial book has been *Az Shahed-e Qudsi ta Shahed-e Bazaari* (From the Sacred Witness to the Profane Witness). It describes the process of secularisation of religious institutions as a reflection of their involvement in the political process. His *Jumhouriat: Afsoun-zedaei az Qudrat* (Republicanism: Demystification of Power) deals with the notion of republicanism as a grounding principle of the people's sovereignty and its manifestation through the state institutions and the state-society relationship.

Muhammad Khatami, the outgoing president of the Islamic Republic, is more famous for his personal charisma and moderate behaviour. A cleric and son of a local religious leader, Khatami was born in 1943. He served as an MP, chief editor of *Kayhan* newspaper, minister of information and the director of the National Library. His interest in literature, epistemology and the sociology of religion has earned him a prominent position among the intellectual elite.[31] Probably the harassment he has experienced at the hands of the conservatives throughout his political career has prompted him to develop a keen interest in the religion-power relation. His *Ayen va Andisheh dar Dam-e Khod-kamegi* (Religion and Intellect Trapped in Tyranny) offers a detailed account of the way political thought in Islam has evolved under the influence of autocratic rulers. Its main goal is to address such questions as why Islamic traditions lack the normative structure to foster a democratic discourse.

Other than the above three, there are numerous thinkers whose opinions have enriched the Reformist discourse, including Mohsen Kadivar,[32] 'Alireza 'Alavitabar, Akbar Ganji and finally Hossein Bashiriyeh, whose sociological analyses are acquiring influence among the Reformists, notwithstanding his secular orientation.

The Reformists favour a model of government similar to the one common in Western liberal literature, where the state is conceived as a contractual institution representing the various interests of its citizens. In this regard, the Reformists are fairly aware that such a conception cannot be grounded in the established religious paradigm. According to Shabestari:

> The Constitution of the Islamic Republic introduced to religious thought a number of novel notions, including: the rights of the nation, the sovereignty of the nation, [...] freedoms, the separation of powers and so on. The religious scholars' endorsement of these notions is also unprecedented in the religious community. The concept of 'nation' is also new and has no reference in the religious

traditions [...] The truth is that since there is no definite form of government in the Qur'an and the traditions of the Prophet, the door is open for the Muslims to integrate such concepts into their political and social culture.[33]

The Reformists argue that the religious framework is not the right place to conceptualise the issue of state authority.[34] State and politics are better thought of within the framework of political philosophy whereby, Ganji argues, principles and institutions are determined on the basis of rational ends and common sense.[35] I will discuss the Reformist conception of religion and its role later in the chapter. The following pages will discuss their major political views, including republicanism, legitimacy and democracy.

Republicanism: the Question of Sovereignty

As far as the nature of authority is concerned, a republican government is distinguished by its concern with the interest of the public. Thus Coker holds that 'it is not necessarily connected with any particular form, but it most naturally associates with the representative form'.[36] Elson quotes an American writer from the nineteenth century defining the republic as the type of government in which 'the supreme power is entrusted by the people to councils, composed of members chosen for a limited time'.[37] In Plato's philosophy, the ideal republic combines three groups corresponding to the three components of human soul: the appetite, the spirit and knowledge. The appetite is associated with the sphere of private interests, thus it is represented by the commercial class. The spirit mirrors the public sphere and is represented by the executives and soldiers, and finally knowledge is associated with authority and is represented by the lawmakers or the philosopher-kings. In comparison, Aristotle has focused on power distribution; for him, power can be held by one or few persons or be distributed among many. Historically, the distinction between a republic and a monarchy rests on the basis of whether political obligation is a matter of consent or of obedience.[38] James Madison, the American politician and theorist, emphasises the methods by which the various interests are fairly represented in the state. Thus he asserts the public's control over the rulers, the general election of people's representatives and the separation of authorities in order to enable them to be reciprocally checked and controlled.[39]

Republicanism represents a key element in the Reformist discourse. It is also a controversial issue in Iranian politics. The quarrel over the republican character of the Islamic regime revolves mainly around the question of sovereignty. Those who presume that sovereignty is exclusively God's are more in favour of the rule by the few, namely the religious elite who possess the knowledge of God's teachings, whereas the advocates of the people's sovereignty prefer an open and participatory political system. As noted in Chapter Four, the conservatives have been reluctant to accept republicanism due to its main connotation, i.e. the sovereignty of the people. This reluctance resembles a common tendency among the Islamists outside Iran, where the sovereignty of people is seen as contradictory to the sovereignty of God.[40] Just recently some scholars came to differentiate between two distinct connotations of sovereignty. Political authority (in the strict sense of powers relating to the executive branch of the state, as distinct from both the legislative and judiciary) has been acknowledged as residing with the people, while legislation is to be restricted to the framework laid out by the religious scholars. Accordingly, elections are accepted as a proper method to choose state officials as well as legislators. Nevertheless, the elected officials have no right to legislate or execute any decision beyond the limits of Shari'a. As held by Zanjani, 'in a monotheistic legal system, the Will of God is the ultimate source of rules and laws. It is also the basis upon which citizens give obedience and observe the law.'[41]

Compared with the conservative view, the Reformists emphasise the idea of representation as the essence of authority. Therefore, a republic is defined as a particular type of power relation with distinct criteria and principles including:

- It is a social contract comprising reciprocal rights and duties whereby the rulers are responsible before the people.
- State functions are limited to the public sphere where interests are shared by all society members; the will of the nation is the source for authority, and the common good is the objective to be pursued by the state.
- The polity members are equal and citizenship is the basis underpinning the state-society relation. All citizens have the right to share in the making of decisions concerning their future, the way they are governed and the system through which their common interests are handled. The sum of individual rights makes up the national sovereignty.[42]

The Reformists assert that the political system set up by the Islamic Revolution is a legitimate contract sanctioned on the basis of religious principles and formulated in the 1980 Constitution. Legitimate contracts involve a mutual, plainly expressed consent, as well as equal rights for the contracting parties.[43] Hajjarian relies heavily on Article 56 of the Constitution, which implies that the supposed sovereignty of God is effectively invested in the people:

> Absolute sovereignty over the world and man belongs to God, and it is He Who has made man master of his own social destiny. No one can deprive man of this divine right, nor subordinate it to the vested interests of a particular individual or group. The people are to exercise this divine right in the manner specified in the following articles.

The same idea is held by Ayatollah Montazeri, who chaired the Council of Experts, the board assigned to draw up the Constitution[44] and it mirrors, to some extent, the division of state authority into civil and religious categories, as illustrated by Qaemmaqami, the conservative author, and noted in Chapter Four. It contradicts, however, the mainstream conservative assertion that the public interest and the powers of the supreme leader are pre-defined by the religion.

Political Legitimacy

Although the Constitution of the Islamic Republic regards the popular will as a major source for legitimacy, and indeed, the Constitution itself was endorsed through a referendum, the post-revolutionary leadership has been, to a large extent, of a charismatic nature, at least until the death of Ayatollah Khomeini in 1989.[45] Charisma can secure the legitimacy of the political system, although not without limitations. By its very nature, charisma is inextricably linked to the persons whose achievements are regarded as exceptional at a certain historical juncture. Thus, its legitimising function is rather limited to the lifetime of the charismatic leader and the particular circumstances that signified his achievement. With the passage of time, charisma endures a process of becoming routine, thereby ceasing to function as a legitimising agent.[46] Ibrahim Yazdi, the leader of Nehzat-e Azadi Iran, uses this argument to conclude that the Islamic Republic is faced with a legitimacy crisis brought about by the poor performance of Khomeini's successors and their lack of charisma. He cites the 1997 presidential election as an example, when the establishment's candidate endured a humiliating defeat. He argues that the voting there was more 'against' than 'for'.[47]

Some moderate figures in the conservative camp admit the existence of a legitimacy crisis. For instance, Hassan Rohani, the secretary general of the National Security Council, describes it as the major challenge facing the Islamic regime nowadays.[48]

Generally speaking, the Reformist camp is in agreement that the traditional principles underpinning the political system of the Islamic Republic are hindering its evolution. If it is to cope with the challenges of a changing world, it has to be legitimised on a legal-rational basis, namely the observation of the law and respecting the will of the people.[49] This argument is consistent with the camp's conception of sovereignty, according to which political legitimacy, and hence the religious character of the state, are linked to popular consent.

In this regard, two trends can be traced among the Reformists. The first trend is represented mainly by the senior clerics, notably Ayatollah Montazeri and Sane'i, which emphasises the religious character of the state, but regards society as the bearer of religious truth. Thus Montazeri asserts that the absolute authority of God is invested in the people, who pass it through to the rulers by the means of their expressed consent.[50] The Prophet and Infallible Imams are no exception. Their political authority too was sanctioned through contracts (*bai'a*) with the people.[51] Montazeri suggests that the state can be identified as Islamic insofar as its policies conform to the religious norms.[52] Ayatollah Yousef Sane'i, another figure within this trend, is concerned particularly with the excessive use of religion to claim permanent authority. He argues for the political role of the clergy to be restricted to the monitoring of the state's compliance with religious rules and the defending of the people against any state arbitrariness. Sane'i ridicules the idea of people being irrational or in need of a guardian. For him, the religious character of the state does not necessarily confer authority upon the clergy. There is a clear line distinguishing the legitimacy of an action from the authority of the actor. This principle is applied even for actions that are unequivocally legitimate, such as the congregational prayer. In his words:

> A cleric cannot even lead the religious congregation in prayer against the will of the congregation, let alone assuming political leadership [...] the role of jurisprudence and its students is to offer the rules. The identification of how these rules are to be applied, in other words the identification of the interests of the people, rests with the people [...] The people have proved capable of identifying and solving drastic issues, defending the country, and preserving the dignity of the religion [...] Those who deem the

people or their majority as ignorant are mistaken. The people are rational and [their will is] a proper reference for the legitimacy of ruling [...] We [the clergy] should act to protect and guide the people not to be their guardians. Guidance means to show the right way, not to repress and impose or excessively interfere in people's affairs. The idea that the people do not know what is good and bad for them is absolutely against both reason and religious traditions.[53]

The second trend is represented by the Islamist intellectuals and some junior clerics who dismiss any divine character of power and hold that Islam has no political system of its own.[54] Although Islam sanctions a set of norms to be realised by the polity, the Islamic state is just like any other state: conventional, led by fallible people and evolving through the normal process of accountability, responsibility and the experience of wrong and right.[55] For this view, 'legitimacy is originated in justice. Being religious or not is not a criterion for the legitimacy of the government.'[56]

The first trend is not new to the Shi'i seminaries; it can be traced back at least to the early twentieth century. During the Constitutional Revolution (1905–6), a number of eminent scholars challenged the tendency to link the legitimacy of the state to the perfect ruler. As 'Allama Na'ini wrote in 1908:

A perfect man satisfying the requirements illustrated in the Shi'i traditions, is impossible to find [...] Even if one is found, the so-called internal perfection is not a sure means of restraining him or his state from developing into a tyranny.[57]

Alternatively, Na'ini holds that justice is achievable only by integrating society into political matters. Thus he illustrates a political system involving representation, a written constitution, definite limits on power and civil liberties to ensure accountability.[58] For Na'ini and his colleagues, people are rational enough to determine their own good. He compares the political system to a jointly owned firm and regards it as the kingdom of the people.[59] This trend remained minor and isolated in the Shi'i seminaries. Nevertheless, it seems to be gaining more currency nowadays among the religious seminaries both inside and outside Iran.[60]

In addition, the Reformists assert legality as the second pillar of legitimacy. The sovereignty of law has been one of the central themes in the writings and speeches of the Reformist figures. In a challenging speech before the Council of Experts dominated by traditional clerics, Khatami declared:

> I have repeatedly said, and I particularly told the supreme leader that the Constitution is the highest institution of our regime. Wilayat al-faqih is significant for it has been signified by the Constitution. Outside the Constitution, wilayat al-faqih is just a theory like the many other theories of jurisprudence.[61]

The Reformist emphasis on the observation of the Constitution concerns mainly the constitutional limits on power. Contrary to the conservative position, Montazeri renounces the idea that the ruling faqih possesses absolute authority and maintains that society has the indisputable right to impose stipulations upon which the faqih is entrusted with the state's power. It might be embedded in the Constitution or in the form of a political agenda specifying the terms of rule and political commitments.[62] Apparently, the latter idea concerned the temporary and time-limited mandate and the direct election of the leader, which arose after the death of Ayatollah Khomeini.

Democracy

With the Islamic Revolution, the Iranians had the opportunity to have a say in how their country would be run. As suggested by Beetham, revolutions usually lead to the expansion of popular involvement in the new political order.[63] Ten years after the Revolution, popular influence on the Islamic regime seemed to have decreased by and large.[64] Certainly the transition from a revolutionary situation into a consolidated state changes the balance of power and the sources of influence to the advantage of the professionals and elites. The extent of potential influence retained by the people depends, however, upon the new political system developing an institutionalised exchange of input-output between the state and society. The extent of the state's observation of public opinion and demands depends on the system being modelled after either a democracy or an autocracy.[65] On the other hand, the political system's development of democratic features is certainly helped, or otherwise hindered, by whether the nature of the society's political culture is participatory or parochial. There has to be a general conviction that the country's problems can be solved through the participation of the people in decisionmaking and political matters in the broader sense. This requires, according to Lerner, 'an expansive and adaptive self-system, ready to incorporate new roles and to identify personal values with public issues'.[66]

Despite the familiarity of the Iranians with the notion of political participation since, at least, the Constitutional Revolution, many scholars are reluctant to deem the Iranian political culture as participatory.[67] Zibakalam, a university professor, ascribes the lack of a democratic ethos in Iran to the country's long history of despotism.[68] Katouzian links the said phenomenon, until the oil era at least, to the ecological limitations of the country, which dictated a type of political economy that was not conducive to equitable power distribution. He challenges the Marxist-inspired theory of the Asiatic Mode of Production, or Oriental Despotism, as irrelevant to the context of Iran. He argues that, historically, the state has been able to remain independent from society. Iran is a vast and mainly arid desert. Production used to be dispersed among scattered villages, none of which was able to produce a surplus large enough to generate political power.[69] Thus, he argues 'the distinctive characteristic of the Iranian state is that it monopolised not just power, but arbitrary power, not the absolute power in laying down the law, but the absolute power of exercising lawlessness'.[70] Lerner makes a similar argument to explain the lack of a participatory political culture in Iranian society. His account, however, focuses on the extremism associated with life under the said ecological limitations and emphasises that it is a hindrance to the emergence of a mutual understanding or 'empathy'.[71] He defines the latter notion as the capacity to see oneself in the other fellow's situation as well as the readiness to incorporate new roles and take part within collective actions.[72]

With the emergence of oil as the major source of national income in the 1940s, the Iranian state acquired a rentier character. Accordingly, the state has not only remained independent from the society, but society has also come gradually to be dependent on the state's expenditure for its livelihood.[73] Given the religiously justified passivity as discussed in Chapter One, and the excessive use of security apparatus by the state during most of the twentieth century, despotism became by and large the ordinary fashion of politics in Iran. The course of democratisation therefore requires much more than drawing up a good constitution or establishing a parliament, although these are undoubtedly essential for any democratic system. This shows how arduous the course of democratisation in Iran is.

The Reformists have to deal with a wide range of issues: constitutional, institutional, cultural and political, none of which is easy. Given the particular state of affairs in today's Iran, the cultural issue seems to be the most urgent. The question put by Binder in the introduction to his *Islamic Liberalism* is certainly voiced by many people: 'Is the discourse of Islamic liberals a form of false consciousness, an abject submission to the hegemonic discourse of the dominant secular Western capitalist, or is it practical, rational, and emancipatory?'[74] For post-revolutionary Iran, the Western and secular orientation of democracy has been even more troublesome, due to the religious character of the regime and its anti-Western orientation.

Generally speaking, for most of the fifteen years following the 1979 revolution, the term 'democracy', indeed most of the Western-oriented terms with political connotations, were rarely current in the Iranian mass media or in the language of the leaders and propagators. As Esposito and Voll rightly noted: 'for Khomeini, as for some other Islamists, the term "democracy" is often associated with the West and thus Western penetration, as well as with a society governed by human rather than divine law.'[75] When Khatami launched his electoral campaign in 1997, he used the term *mardomsalari-e deeni* (religious people's sovereignty), a Farsi equivalent to the term 'religion-based democracy'. Khatami's conciliatory term did not gain a smooth reception in traditional circles until recently[76] when it came to be employed occasionally by some conservative figures as identical to their own conception of religious regime, i.e. the representative system supervised by wilayat al-faqih.[77] Thus the use of the terms 'democracy' and 'religious democracy' remained, at least until 2002, distinctive characters of the Reformists' political language.[78]

The argument over democratisation in Iran demonstrates three distinct areas of interest. The first concerns the functional sense of democracy, namely its being a method of public representation and peaceful transfer of power through general elections, the separation of powers, universal suffrage and so on. The second concerns its philosophical foundations, namely the sovereignty of the people, equality, natural rights, etc. The third concerns the ideological orientations of democracy, namely its origination within Western culture. The second area has attracted a good deal of the conservative argument, as was shown in the previous chapter. Nevertheless, the third area has been the centre of contention. In this regard, democracy is seen as a reflection of the historical experience of Western communities, so that it embodies their response to the particular challenges they have endured.[79] As it is nonsense to import problems, it is by the same token illogical to import their solutions.

The major argument put forward by the Reformists to affirm the relevance of democracy to the Iranian context is the idea that state tyranny has been the major defect in the modern history of Iran.[80] The state manipulation of power and resources served to humiliate the people and hinder the course of progress. Democracy provides a viable model for changing the balance of power so that society masters its government.[81] Shabestari takes the argument further and argues that democracy is as necessary for religion as for society. He emphasises the two components of democracy, namely civil liberties and equality, and contends that only 'through the model of liberal democracy can the two major objectives of the religion, namely justice and emancipation, be realised'.[82]

The Reformists acknowledge the ideological orientations of democracy but do not see them as inextricably part of the model. Being of foreign origin does not affect its value. For Khatami, democracy is best seen as one of the pillars of modernity.[83] In addition to its political components, modernity enjoys a considerable interest among Iranians as it symbolises a common desire to restore the historical status of Iran as a great nation. Khatami condemns both the childish imitation of other models as well as the stubborn rejection of ideas merely for being foreign.[84] In contrast, he urges Iranian intellectuals to study critically what he takes as the pillars of modern civilisation, which include liberalism, individuality, priority of rights and rationality. In this view modernity represents a phase in the long history of humanity; it has to be read, criticised and dealt with as one of the solutions reached by man in his constant struggle for progress and integrity. It is a human achievement bearing advantages and disadvantages and not a locked system to be either taken up or rejected.[85] Khatami therefore argues that for democracy to be established, its principles have to be re-grounded in the local cultural web. The localisation of democracy aims to maintain its major theme, namely the sovereignty of people, and concurrently to enable the people to choose the appropriate methods to put it into action.[86] For him, the localised version of democracy is relevant to Iranian concerns, especially the religious character of the nation.

The Idea of 'Religious Democracy'

The idea of religious democracy was initially proposed by 'Abdol-Karim Soroush, the Reformist thinker, apparently as a counterargument to the conservative notion of ideal polity.[87] The idea began to attract national attention after Khatami made it the slogan of his campaign for the 1997 presidential election. Soroush's focus had been the philosophical basis of democracy and its relevance to religion, whereas Khatami's was the political application of the doctrine. The association of democracy with religion has

126

triggered a good deal of argument. Many of Khatami's opponents and friends alike saw his proposal as rather ambiguous and intrinsically inconsistent.[88] The Reformists acknowledge these reservations but argue that with an analytical approach to both religion and democracy, the two would show a good capacity for mutual accommodation.[89]

Apart from its religious character, the Reformist conception of democracy bears little difference from the universal model, especially in respect of its functional and philosophical dimensions. 'We are arguing over an established model, well-defined and widely exercised, rather than a utopia,' says Ayatollah Shabestari.[90] This model proposes a set of principles and institutions that aims to minimise the faults of political administration through the maximum possible engagement of the population in policymaking and reducing the personal influence of leaders.[91] A democratic state is distinguished by an observation of public opinion and an absolute respect for human rights.[92] For democracy to mature, democratic values should run through every part of public life, including the economy, education, media, justice and so on. On the political level, however, the democratic system has three features at least:[93] a comprehensive, meaningful and periodical contest for power; universal participation in the election of leaders and the determination of political choices; and social and political freedoms, notably the freedom of expression and organisation.

The notion of civil society occupies a pivotal place in Reformist discourse. Reformists promote the notion based on both a theoretical and a practical basis. On the one hand, the robust activity of civil society organisations is regarded as a crucial catalyst for the process of democratisation. On the other, the notion is put forward as an antithesis to that of *huzur dar sahneh* (presence onstage) or public mobility, which is taken by the conservatives as the real embodiment of public participation but regarded by the Reformists as an example of populism, rather than democratic participation.[94] A good part of Reformist literature is dedicated to condemning populism and its manifestations in local politics.[95] According to Khatami, populism unfolds through the ruling elite considering itself the source of right, or the faultless group and so on. People are praised by the rulers, their active role in politics is welcomed, but they can neither hold their rulers to account nor do they have the final say in respect of the polity's major concerns.[96] He maintains that for collective rationality to function in a systematic and informed fashion, the political system should be designed appropriately to feature such standards as a high level of public participation in decisionmaking, a fair distribution of power and resources, transparency, accountability, guaranteed liberties and equal rights for all citizens.[97] For Jalaipour, the principal factor that distinguishes democracy from populism and crowd politics is the institutional differentiation and distribution of power between the state and the society. This is realised by the state acknowledging the role of civil society and providing it with legal protection so that it can efficiently channel public demands through to state institutions.[98]

Religion and Democracy

The Reformists' conception of the religion-democracy relationship derives from their basic differentiation between the function of religion and that of the state. For them, the state is about representing the various interests in the social theatre and handling its conflicts. Thus it needs a model of administration capable of solving conflicts in a peaceful manner, and that is the model of democracy.[99] Religion, for its part, is mainly about man's existence, ethics and attachment to God. The realm of the state is characterised by pragmatism, compromise and finally violence. In contrast, religion is a realm of surrender, selflessness and voluntary action. Soroush specifies the difference between religion and state in that the former is a realm of mystery (*raz*) whereas the state is a realm of reason and material realities.[100] In brief, religion and state seek different objectives as well as different ways of functioning. Democracy, therefore, is a method appropriate for the state and not for religion. It is possible to seek a reading of religion appropriate to democracy, Hajjarian argues, but strictly regarding the function of the state, not the religion itself. Put differently, religion can foster a democratic state just as much as it might be used to legitimise an authoritarian one. In either case, the central question is about the state, and not religion or democracy.[101]

In this regard, it is argued that Islam has no particular model of government, whereas democracy has nothing to do with religion.[102] In other words, democracy is a model of government and not an ideology; thus it is not contradictory to religion but to the other ruling models, namely autocracy and oligarchy. Within a democratic system, both religion and the ruling model have a distinct role. Religion provides the values, the objectives and norms to be realised by the political system. On the other hand, democracy as a model of government defines the methods by which those purposes are fulfilled. Thus it determines the institutions, the process of decisionmaking and the standards of administration.[103]

The religious character of the state is understood to be in two forms:[104]

1. The Islamic state is accepted as such by Muslim society. The state is deemed Islamic in reference to the basis that the society is the audience addressed by Divine revelation; hence, it is the agency that assigns religious value to institutions and actions in the public sphere.

2. The state is observant of the religious criteria of ruling. Religious criteria are defined in accordance with the particular method of interpretation of the religion held by the reformist trend. In this regard, it is argued that most of the principles concerning rule, including justice, freedom, equality and so on, are religiously sanctioned but not of religious origin.

Standing by his theory of the contextual nature of religious knowledge, Soroush argues that the observation of religious teachings on the part of the government cannot be other than subjective and contextual.[105] Basically, the policies and institutions that enact the principles are man-made. Statesmen consider how to apply the principles and design the methods to deliver what they think is right. Their perception and the methods of enacting the theoretical assumptions have an inevitable influence on the final outcome. In this case, human reason determines the objectives – and priorities – which are supposed to have been meant by the sacred text, the way to have them delivered and the criteria against which the purpose is determined to have been satisfied. This process can be carried out in accordance with the judgements made by a few people from the higher ranks of the state, or it can be carried out through a systematic recourse to the collective rationality of the whole society. In either case, the result is a human conception of God's will and not the will of God itself. To this extent, the preference for the latter method over the former cannot be questioned. That process is deemed by the traditional clerics as religious, for it delivers religious rules, while the Reformists perceive it in terms of an exploration of the common good, whether it is fostered by religious teachings or initiated by society members. Thus it is more of a rational technique than a religious process.

The Reformists' Frame of Reference

The Constitutional Revolution has opened a prolonged debate on the religion-state relation and Islam's capacity to foster a modern way of life. The emergence of the Islamic Revolution unleashed more questions, many of which are still attracting the attention of intellectuals both inside and outside Iran. Some of these questions have been already addressed through the discourse of the religious reformative trend that paved the way for a new phase in religious thought.[106]

Naturally, the intellectual debates in the post-revolutionary period have been highly influenced by the political arrangements that ensued from the revolution. The change of the social structure, roles, positions and the political rivalry among the post-revolutionary elite have collectively shaped the contemporary course of intellectual debate. Reformist thinkers bear some of the universal characteristics of intellectuals: they are critical of the state of affairs, and their general tendency is anti-traditionalist and anti-clerical. Obviously the harassment they have experienced at the hands of their conservative rivals since Ayatollah Khamenei's rise to supreme leadership has driven them to be preoccupied with such ideas as hegemony, traditions, authoritarianism and the excessive use of right.[107] Thus their discourse has focused on such ideas as plurality, modernity, democracy and power limitation. These ideas are being applied to both religious and political spheres, simply because the centre of controversy has been the issue of authority. In the Islamic Republic religious and political authorities are inextricably linked together on the constitutional as well as the political and social levels.

One of the consequences of such debates has been the rethinking of the role of ideology as a hindrance to rational thought, as well as to individual emancipation. The term 'ideology' explains how values, expectations and prescriptions for the organisation of society are structured to produce a harmonised system of meanings and explanations about the self and the world. McClosky defines ideology as systems of belief that are elaborate, integrated and coherent, that justify the exercise of power, explain and judge historical events, identify political right and wrong, and set forth the interconnections (casual and moral) between politics and other spheres of activity.[108]

The concept owes its place in modern intellectual debates to Marxist tradition. From this perspective, ideology is linked to class interests, and thus it is commonly seen as a means employed by the dominant classes to justify and affirm their hegemony.[109] Despite the focus on domination and hegemony, the function of ideology is more justified. It is employed literally by every group, including those opposing the sociopolitical order and the alienated, since, as suggested by Shils, ideology involves an aggressive alienation from the existing society.[110] It is not strange, thus, to see it commonly associated with groups of the extreme left or right.

The Reformists' criticism of ideology aims apparently to undermine the universality of the particular paradigm of religiosity espoused by the clerical elite. The paradigm is called *Islam-e faqahati* (the jurisprudential interpretation of Islam) and is officially presented as the pure Islam of Prophet Muhammad (*Islam-nab-e Muhammadi*), as distinguished from the one held by the intellectuals, which is deemed by the conservatives to be tainted with liberal or socialist views.[111] For Soroush, indeed most of the Reformist thinkers, the glory of Islam and its deep influence on man's soul is contingent upon its being equally available to every human being.[112] In this account, religion is a direct path linking man to his God, with no medium or guide other than his own soul. Contrastingly, a religion in power could develop into an ideology of domination. Soroush insists that a religion-based ideology is not immune from the common symptoms of other ideologies: it conceals reality, degrades reason and hinders the free exchange of information and opinions.[113] Being a state ideology, religion will have its function altered from inspiring the high morals into justifying class domination.[114]

Soroush's critical position with regard to religious ideology is not limited to the ruling clergy. Earlier, he criticised Shari'ati's perception of religion, which was modelled after the socialist notion of class struggle.[115] Shari'ati argues for Islam, Shi'ism in particular, as an ideology for activism. In the absence of an ideology of resistance, Shari'ati argues, Islam would continue to be a utility at the disposal of the higher classes, from both the state and the religious establishment.[116] Retaining his assumption that religious knowledge is subjective, relative and temporary in nature, Soroush blames Shari'ati for treating his interpretation as the only rightful perception of Islam. In his final analysis, Shari'ati's ideology was useful in a certain epoch but is outdated now, thus it is better dealt with as a landmark in the history of the nation and not as a continuously valid trend of thought.[117]

A good deal of Soroush's works are dedicated to defending the role of intellectuals in advancing religious thought and social life alike. He argues that: 'No revolution can be sustained if it fails to regenerate its theory, and that is the job of intellectuals.'[118] Intellectuals play a historical role for 'they always motivated the clergy to regenerate; they are needed today more than before because the clergy has engaged with power and become more ready for degeneration'.[119] The major defect of clerical knowledge is seen in its adherence to the past, which has made it ignorant of the modern realities of society and culture:

We see no significant contribution by the clergy to the debate on such questions as rights, freedom, justice, happiness and the other theoretical issues related to modernisation [...] In comparison, the intellectuals simultaneously recognise the significance of the traditions and modern knowledge, they analyse the traditions in the framework of modern notions and practical requirements, and by so doing they bridge the present and the past.[120]

The Reformists' reading of religion is grounded in the principle of the plurality of interpretation. Indeed pluralism, in respect to religion and culture as well as politics, represents one of the axes of Reformist political ideology. Soroush has entitled one of his controversial books *Siratha-ye Mustaqim (Right Paths)* as a direct challenge to the doctrine of the single right path commonly held among Muslims. The Reformists' reading seeks, therefore, to undermine the clerical claims to having the sole authoritative interpretation of the religious fundamentals. The relevance of the latter to current realities is dismissed on three bases:[121] it serves to marginalise the political role of the people; it serves as a pretext to suppress those who hold different opinions; and it lacks scientific authenticity.

The most rigorous argument over the scientific authenticity of traditional jurisprudence was advanced by Muhammad Mujtahid Shabestari, a cleric and doctor of philosophy. Shabestari was born in 1936. He trained in the Qum seminaries and held the title of Ayatollah, signifying his attainment of the degree of *Ijtihad*. Between 1970 and 1979 he worked as the director of the Islamic Centre in Hamburg, Germany, where he became familiar with modern Christian theology. Shabestari is preoccupied with the reconciliation of religion and modernity. Like Soroush, he calls for the differentiation of religious knowledge from religion.[122] However, he focuses on the methodology of interpretation of the sacred texts and the methods of application of religious rules. His discourse is deeply influenced by the philosophical hermeneutics developed by Protestant theologians. Hermeneutics initially aimed to discover the values and message embedded in the sacred texts. In the twentieth century, however, it was expanded, notably by Martin Heidegger (1889–1976) and Hans-Georg Gadamer (1900–2002) to emphasise the broader realm of art and literature and to take human existence as its main question. In his *Hermeneutics, Ketab va Sunnat (Hermeneutics, the Scripture and Tradition)* and *Naqdi bar Qara'at-e Rasmi az Din (A Critique of the Official Reading of Religion)*, Shabestari offers many reflections on Heidegger, Gadamer and Karl Barth (1886–1968).

Heidegger signifies pre-understanding as the agency to determine what we understand, hence he holds that there can be 'no understanding without pre-understanding'.[123] Gadamer terms this as the 'horizon' or the totality of our being as determined by the totality of past and present experiences.[124] Thus, hermeneutic consciousness has an open horizon, a horizon in motion and constant change. According to Gadamer:

> The projecting of the historical horizon, then, is only a phase in the process of understanding, and does not become solidified into the self-alienation of a past consciousness, but is overtaken by our present horizon of understanding. In the process of understanding there takes place a real fusing of horizons, which means that as the historical horizon is projected, it is simultaneously removed.[125]

Shabestari employs the idea of 'horizon' to undermine the method of literal interpretation common in the Shi'i seminaries. This method is based on the idea that the grammatical construction and the historical context of the text convey the plain meaning that is taken as a correspondent to the intention of the legislator. Following philosophical hermeneutics, Shabestari contends that the linguistic form of Divine words corresponds to the horizon of the recipient community. This is understandable, for the Divine message has to capture the hearts and minds of its primary recipients in order to be embraced and passed through to other communities.[126] The Divine message is about the values transmitted through forms and not the forms themselves.[127] He argues that the literal interpretation has lost its rational bedrock, for it has sanctioned forms that are contextual and temporary. This explains the gulf between religious teachings and the imperatives of contemporary life.[128]

Shabestari takes the basic values of religion as the only institution possessing sanctity and universality. Values can embody different forms at different times. Almost all religious rules concerning aspects of life other than mere worship do not have a universal or sacred character.[129] This includes both the rules developed by scholars and those stated in the sacred texts. For Shabestari, each generation can formulate, on the basis of collective rationality, the institutions and regulations fulfilling the particular imperatives of their time. Nevertheless, forms should serve rational ends without violating the basic values of religion. One of the examples he notes is the model of government. He argues that Islam does not specify a certain model as its favourite. What concerns the legislator is the essence of government, i.e. justice, and not its form.[130]

Shabestari's hermeneutical approach, together with Soroush's theory on religious knowledge, offers a distinct interpretational approach to religion.

The approach features a number of key notions, summed up by Kadivar in seven principles:[131]

- Man is self-sufficient by virtue of the fact that he bears the spirit of God and reason, which is deemed as the internal messenger of God.
- The role of religion is more one of guidance. It might interfere wherever man proves incapable, but for most of the aspects of life, apprehension, explanation and regulations are to be sought in science and collective rationality, rather than religion.
- Science is a distinct realm of human activity. It interacts with religion, yet each of the two retains its own sphere and objectives. This assumption is applicable to the natural, empirical, as well as human sciences.
- As a public affair, politics is a realm of reason and collective rationality where good and bad are discovered through methods of trial and error. In this realm, no value or rule is Divinely-sanctioned (*ta'abbodi*) or beyond human appraisal and verification. In the public sphere, religion offers basic values and general criteria according to which Islamic politics can take shape. The observance of such values and criteria is generally of a negative sense, i.e. it shows the final limits not to be breached rather than defining a plan to follow.
- Islam does not specify a definite model for state administration.
- Other than the fixed rules concerning mainly the worship of God, most religious rules are changeable in accordance with common sense and rational ends.
- Religion aims mainly to enrich man's consciousness of his existence and his understanding, thus ensuring his harmony with the surrounding world.

Secularism

As noted above, the secular character of democracy has been the chief point of contention among the conservatives. For the Reformists, however, secularism is not seen as an inextricable part of democracy. Compared with the mainstream Islamists who indiscriminately reject secularism as contradictory to religion, the Iranian Reformists seem largely tolerant of it. This position is clear in their handling of such issues as the religion-state relation, culture, social behaviour and so on. They tend, however, to be careful not to stand with the outspoken advocates of secularism. They insist on the claim that what they offer is an intellectual reading of Islam, distinct from both secularism and religious traditionalism.[132] To counter the conservative accusation that the Reformists' perception of religion is secular-oriented and Western-inspired,[133] Reformist thinkers insist on the differentiation between secularism as an ideology and secularisation as a process. The most rigorous account in this regard was made by Saʿeed Hajjarian in his controversial book *Az Shahed-e Qudsi ta Shahed-e Bazari*. Hajjarian denounces secularism but argues that the process of secularisation is inescapable.[134] Following the traditions of Max Weber, he asserts that the state is the most powerful means for secularisation. Thus he emphasises the rise of the Islamic Republic as the first step on a road leading eventually to the rise of a completely new type of religiosity.[135]

In 1996, Hajjarian provoked a fierce argument by claiming that Khomeini's theory of *wilayat-e mutlaqah* (the jurist's absolute authority) serves effectively to secularise religious law or, in his words, reconcile fiqh with mores by reproducing the former within the limits of the latter.[136] Until the rise of Ayatollah Khomeini, Hajjarian argues, Shiʿi jurisprudence has been resistant to the new trends unleashed by the changes of its own social environment and the world. Khomeini's charismatic personality helped to impose his ideas at the expense of many of the principles established by the religious community.[137]

Hajjarian argues that Ayatollah Khomeini was aware of the cost to be paid for the adaptation of jurisprudential rules to the legal system of the state. He emphasises Khomeini's development – and indeed enforcement – of the rational-oriented notion of *maslahat-e nezam* (the regime's interest) as a major instance of the way in which the state affects the function of religion. According to this notion, the expediency of the political system is a criterion to determine whether parliamentary legislations can be blocked on the basis of being incompatible with religious principles. As he puts it:

> The integration of the institution of jurisprudence into the institution of the state, and particularly the hegemony of the idea [propagated by Khomeini] that equates religion with politics,[138] led to the political institution imposing its requirements and features upon the religious institution. The State, particularly in modern times, is the strongest machine of secularisation. Statesmen act on the basis of conventional rationality and when the institution of jurisprudence is amalgamated with the state, the former will inescapably adapt to that type of function.[139]

135

To debate about secularism from a neutral platform is not an easy task in any Muslim society, let alone a religious system, as is the case in Iran. The issue, however, is too controversial and challenging to be brushed aside. It sits at the very heart of the debate on development, modernity and democratisation. The failure of the Muslim elites to properly address the issue has effectively hindered the emergence of a robust discourse fostering democracy and liberalisation in Iran as well as other Muslim societies. The problematic nature of secularism, especially its applicability to modernisation and democratisation, forms a major part of the Reformist discourse. There seems a general acquiescence that a degree of secularism is inevitable, yet new approaches have to be advanced in order to formulate a kind of localised conception of secularism: a conception that is able, on the one hand, to explain the functional correspondence between the religious and non-religious factors of worldly affairs, and on the other hand, to allow for an active role for both religion and reason, each in its own right.

To put it differently, unlike the conservatives, who think of a religious world, the Reformist thinkers are convinced that there are, in the real world, two distinguishable realms, religious and non-religious. The application of reason in general, and to its own realm in particular, does not necessarily entail a contradiction with religion.[140] This realm is universally called secular. The notion was developed within the Western frame of knowledge and, due to this particular course of evolution, it took an antireligious flavour. Yet this contextual condition does not change the actual situations, nor does it constrain other societies to develop a similar conception of the differentiation between the religious and nonreligious. On this basis many of the Reformist thinkers, notably Hajjarian and Soroush, made substantial efforts to formulate the term '*urf* as a synonym for secularism and '*urfi-shodan* for secularisation. The two terms have the same meanings as the English terms, but with a less aggressive connotation. '*Urf*, an Arabic term common in Farsi, means 'convention' or the ideas and modes of behaviour that are considered acceptable to most members of a society, hence it closely relates to common sense or public consent.

Hajjarian puts forth the same idea with regard to the integration of religious values within social institutions. He also employs the notion of a civil religion to emphasise the difference between religious values in the abstract and social actions based upon them.[141] He argues that the process of enactment of religious beliefs by the community involves a compromise between religious ideals, society's perception of them and the limitations pertaining to social institutions. Hajjarian holds that the conversion of religious values and ideals into localised conventions is an unstoppable process and represents a permanent associate of socialisation. The exchange between religious ideals and conventions takes two forms: conventions are created or modified to satisfy certain principles, or the principle is applied in a certain manner to satisfy an established convention. Thus he contends that many of the so-called religious traditions, especially those concerning social behaviour, are, in fact, social mores acknowledged by religious leaders, thereafter invested with religious values.[142]

Soroush specifies three connotations of secularism: action being based upon a non-religious platform; interpretation of the world and man outside of the religious framework; and such notions as science and politics being understood to be independent from religion. He favours the third connotation and asserts that like politics, science, art and philosophy are all independent institutions. Thus he equates the course of secularisation with the exploration of this independence:

> We had better replace the term 'the separation of religion and politics' with the term 'the independence of politics from religion'. Yet we have to bear in mind that not only politics is evidently independent from religion, but that philosophy, art, sciences and many human affairs and social institutions are the same. Thus the separation must be taken in the sense of [obtaining] independence and people become secular by their recognition of that sense.[143]

He argues that secularism does not necessarily exclude religion from public life; yet he warns that the implementation of the religious legal system necessarily requires the spiritual character of religious teachings to be excluded, for they derive a good deal of their supernatural features from being mystical (raz), whereas society's administration and the management of worldly affairs require rules and values to be capable of delivering tangible and calculable ends.[144]

The difference between secularism and secularisation is generally understood in terms of the former being more of a philosophical position about the way things should be, while the latter denotes the process through which that philosophy takes effect.[145] Hajjarian views the process of secularisation as a result of the transfer from a primitive community into a modern polity.[146] The process is caused by the division of labour, the codification of law and the separation between public and private spheres.[147]

Given the religious orientation of the trend, it obviously advocates a robust role for religion in the state and society but without a similar role for the formal religious authorities. To put it differently, Reformists acknowledge the role of religion but want the religious establishment to be independent from the state.[148] Thereby the debate can be seen as revolving around the definition of the line separating the jurisdiction of religion from the jurisdiction of man. The debate is rooted in the primary disagreement over the role of religion and its ramifications. I have already noted that the conservatives define religion as perfect and all-inclusive and religious scholars as the only legitimate source of religious standards. It follows that both the state and society are realms in which the rulings offered by the religious authorities are to be enacted. This idea is termed as *din hadd-e akthari* (the maximal application of religious rules).[149] In contrast, the Reformists are for *din hadd-e aqalli* (minimal application of religious rules).[150] In practice, the former notion means that every action should conform to religious advice, whereas the latter notion expresses a negative sense: every action can be carried out unless it breaches an agreed religious principle.

In the final analysis, the Reformists' argument over secularisation serves to affirm their primary position concerning the conventional character of the state. As with Soroush, they believe that the state's claim to a religious character will inevitably lead to religion converting into a conventional order, just like the state law. It will thus lose its essential character, which is to be a force of spiritual inspiration to human life.[151] Spirituality is not a state business; it cannot be taught or enforced by the means of law but through the constant dialogue between man and God. Piety is a level of morality at which man sets his reason and senses free from the narrow borders of material reality. Thus he challenges its limits and pursues the territories hidden behind it.[152] Shabestari argues that state interference in religious affairs will inevitably lead to religious tyranny. During the post-revolutionary period, such interference was responsible for the violation of civil rights and the alienation of the youth and women, as well as the intellectual elite.[153] On top of that, it relegated the role of religion to the limited scope of law, rather than facilitating its most important function, namely the generation of morals and meaning for the social life.[154]

Conclusion

The rise of the Reformist discourse signifies the expansion of liberal tendencies unleashed by structural changes during the 1980s and the revival of the intellectual discourse of religious reform. It advocates modernity from a religious platform distinct, however, from both the clerical and secularist trends. The common theme in this discourse is the criticism of the official ideology of hegemony, notably traditional fiqh and the advocacy of such notions as modernity, republicanism, democracy, plurality and power limitation. Their conception of democracy shows little difference from the universal model. The Reformists reject secularism but take secularisation as an inescapable outcome of the integration of religion into the state system.

For the Reformists, Islam is capable of developing a democratic discourse. It depends, however, on the method through which its fundamentals are interpreted. Thus they advocate a particular reading that rests on humanism and collective rationality. Their principal argument suggests that Islam does not advocate a particular model of government. The religious character of the state is understood either through Muslim society acknowledging the government as such or by the state being observant of basic religious values.

The Reformist discourse has a good potential for reconciling Islam with modernity, especially with regard to political affairs. It involves a robust exchange with modern thought on the one hand and religious principles on the other. Regardless of the controversy over the authenticity of its reference to either modernity or religion, which is, like every account, subjective and open to question, the discourse has had a strong appeal to the modern spectrum of Iranian society. The appeal of the Reformist approach has expanded beyond the Iranian borders from 2003–07, especially to the Arab world where the works of Reformist thinkers draws increasing attention amongst Arab intellectuals.

CHAPTER SIX

The Composition of Political Factions

In the previous chapters, I have discussed the political ideologies of the two major camps contesting for power in Iran. The aim was to explore the principal points of contention and their ideological foundations. Needless to say, ideology makes no difference unless it is translated into political action by powerful forces. For the political system to develop a democratic character, democracy has to evolve from an idea dreamed up by a few pioneering individuals into a popular demand. And here lies the role of political groups that transform general ideas into issues of interest, in political or social terms, for a large segment of society. In other words, democracy has to be integrated into society's culture, intertwining with the various aspects of its daily life, and thus evolving into a symbol of the people's aspirations for a better future. The study of factional structures in certain societies helps to understand properly whether the democratic forces are capable of delivering tangible change or not.

This chapter discusses party politics in Iran and the way it reflects on the political system. I will start with a brief introduction to the role of political parties and the forms of identity expressed by them. The chapter proceeds with a brief account of the Islamic Republic Party, which is regarded as the forerunner of the active factions in today's Iran. The discussion here is limited to the major factions in both the conservative and Reformist camps, among which three parties are assessed in more detail: the Coalition of Abadgaran, for it represents a prototype of the new generation of conservatives which, in my opinion, will lead the camp in the future; Kargozaran, a pragmatic-liberal group representing the bureaucratic and professional elite; and finally, Mosharekat, which represents the modernist middle class with liberal and quasi-secular tendencies.

My argument is that, although the Iranian social and political system is suffering from the symptoms of backwardness common to pre-industrial societies, it has, nevertheless, some good opportunities to develop politically. The current process of reform, although slow and shaky, shows that political groups could play a decisive role in turning public opinion into a determining agent for opening up the political system and reshaping its structure.

The body of literature dedicated to factional politics in Iran is relatively small. This is quite understandable for, at least until the late 1990s, the country's factional structure has not taken a definite shape. As this chapter will show, most of the currently active political parties were established or took distinctive shape in or after the mid-1990s. Generally speaking, most of the analyses and information about the Iranian political factions were offered through more general writings on political reforms. Inside Iran, the structure of party politics has attracted wider attention in recent years.

Two points are worth noting here. First: analysis of the factional structure of Iran was advanced mainly by Reformist writers. The conservatives seem less interested in sociological analyses, or probably they are convinced that political rivalry does not necessarily indicate a fundamental difference among religious forces. As for Nateq Nuri, the former parliament speaker, political rivalry consists more in 'different tastes' than different ideologies.[1] Some recent accounts offered by the conservatives are of a defensive nature, aiming to stress the 'otherness' of the Reformist parties on the assumption that, by advocating liberal democracy, those parties are no longer identified as religious forces.[2] Second: all the concerned writers take for granted the allotting of the political factions in Iran into categories of the left and the right. The current attribution of groups to the conservative or Reformist camps has not completely replaced the former categorisation. It is understood that political rivalry was caused by differences over the economic policy of the government,[3] which makes it natural for groups to be identified as left or right. The persistence of such categorisation, despite the fact that the economic factor is no longer an issue of rivalry, remains, however, a point of question. Relating to this point, it must be mentioned that the left was primarily regarded by many researchers – outside Iran in particular – as radical or fundamentalist (see, for example, Menasheri 2001, Baktiari 1996, Tachau 1994), and the conservatives as moderate. From the mid-1990s onwards, these designations were swapped between the two factions. Such a categorisation seems to be based on the political behaviour of the parties in question. In my opinion, it is not relevant to categorise the political factions as radical or moderate, since every faction can bear both characteristics, each in its own right. In addition, the criterion to which this designation corresponds is by and large subjective and variable.

The Role of Political Groups

The flourishing of party politics signifies the shift in society from an attitude of passivity to one of activity. Communal groupings emerge when certain segments of society develop a collective identity revolving around a particular range of demands or interests. Political parties are formed to handle the type of problems that require a change of state or of its major policies. They also deter the inclination of the state apparatus to overstep the boundaries of law and represent a counterbalancing force to the arbitrariness of bureaucracy.[4]

The relevance of party politics to the course of democratisation in developing societies is almost self-evident. Through organised and collective action, the aspiration to participate in public affairs evolves from mere individual or sporadic desires into a tangible and persistent movement capable of delivering an influential discourse competing for hegemony. Political groups help the course of democratisation by forming public opinion and integrating the general people into the political process.[5] The proponents of the elite theory view them, says Lester, as 'the principal agencies for accomplishing the selection and representation of political elites'.[6] The ability of parties to fulfil these functions is, however, contingent upon the actual state of affairs within the context in which they operate.

The question of 'how the political groups identify with their social bases' has drawn wide attention from Iranian researchers. Apparently, the debate stems from a previous disagreement over the principal determinants of social alignment, i.e., the way one identifies with a certain reference group. One trend views the social system as being divided on the basis of class; another emphasises the cultural elements of identity as the distinctive factor of one's preferences; and the third trend proposes state interventionism as the centre of political rivalry.

The first approach elaborates on the economic theory of political behaviour. Society is perceived as a collective system of upper, middle and lower classes, each of which acquires a distinctive identity and preferences. This approach sees party politics as the political expression of the conflicts of interest among the social classes. Political parties are formed to promote and defend the particular interests identified with a certain class.[7] Hence the political groups are identified according to the class they represent. Many researchers deny the existence of such clear-cut class divisions in Iran and dispute the relevance of this approach.[8] Beeran views the traditional landowners and traders of the Bazaar as the only group potentially capable of developing a definable social class with a political function.[9] Such a development, however, was hindered by the lack of security of private property, which prompted that group to take refuge in the shadow of the state instead of developing a class-based association of its own.[10]

The second approach assumes that one's identity develops through interaction with the other members of one's community. One's political preferences thereby embody the norms and values common to this reference group.[11] Elaborating on the theories of political culture, Hossein Bashiriyeh, a prominent Iranian sociologist, holds that social and political rivalry in Iranian society emanates from a cultural split between traditionalism and modernism. Each embodies a distinctive range of interests, concerns and relations. In this view, the political rivalry extends the conflict between the tendency to maintain the inherited social system and the one that seeks to change it.[12]

The third approach presumes that party politics revolves around the extent of state intervention in private affairs, which are technically varied from the state's basic purpose. For this approach, the political factions are categorised along a right-left divide. The former is associated with minimal state intervention while the left is associated with interventionism.

It is almost agreed that none of the active factions in today's Iran can be identified exclusively with one of the above categories, but neither is it fair to deny their applicability altogether. The relevance of each of the above categories is better understood in a relative sense.[13] Nowadays the Iranian political groups are commonly categorised as for or against the political reforms President Muhammad Khatami proposed in 1997. In the conservative camp Mo'talefeh and Rohaniat Mobarez represent the traditional upper class. They advocate minimal state intervention in the economy but maximum supervisory intervention in other areas. The Coalition for the Development of Islamic Iran (Abadgaran) represents the middle class. It holds similar political and cultural views but in a more moderate fashion. It also seeks more egalitarian economic relations, which inevitably entails state intervention in the economy. The three conservative factions are commonly categorised alongside the right wing.

In the Reformist camp the party of Kargozaran-e Sazandagi (Executives for Reconstruction) represents the modern upper class. It advocates minimal state intervention in all areas but emphasises a leading role for the state in modernising the economy. Mojahedin Enghelab, as well as Rohanion Mobarez, is commonly identified as leftist. They call for an egalitarian economy promoting the interests of the lower class. In respect of political and cultural issues they advocate moderate intervention by the state. Their middle-class ally, Mosharekat, is more of the centre left. It advocates full-scale democracy, a free-market economy and cultural liberalism.

The Structure of Party Politics in Contemporary Iran

The Iranian political scene was described by Menasheri as fluid and constantly changing in its positions and alliances.[14] During recent years, especially since 2000, positions and alliances seem more stable, with most groups having defined themselves in line with or against the model of democracy. Post-revolution party politics can be divided into three phases: the period of uncontrolled proliferation in the first three years; the period of the regime consolidation, which lasted until 1991; and the period after 1991.

According to Tajik, more than eighty groups appeared during or soon after the revolution, representing all walks of life.[15] This relatively large number reflects the variety of interests that had the opportunity to be expressed through the revolution.[16] It is understandable, however, that the majority of these groups by and large lacked coherence in terms of ideology, organisation and political agenda. Such defects make it difficult to formulate a proper categorisation of the many groups of that period. With recent developments, a range of groups that are well defined and coherent can be seen, each of which represents a particular range of interests and social segment. As I am concerned with the theoretical development of the religious-based Shi'i doctrine of power, my discussion will be limited to the political groups that fall within the religious spectrum.

The first major Islamist grouping to emerge was the so-called 'Line of the Imam' (Khatt-e Imam), a broad alliance of supporters of the religious agenda proposed by Ayatollah Khomeini. Apart from some independent figures, the Line of the Imam was dominated by three broad organisations, namely the Islamic Republic Party (IRP), Sazman-e Mojahedin Enghelab Islami (SMEI) and Jame'ah Rohaniat-e Mobarez (JRM). Each of the three groups was composed of left- and right-wing factions. The leading role in the first party was played by the pragmatic trend led by Ayatollah Muhammad H. Beheshti, 'Ali Khamanei and 'Ali Akbar Hashemi Rafsanjani. The leading force in the Mojahedin was the left wing led by Behzad Nabavi, while Jame'ah Rohaniat was dominated mainly by right-wing senior clerics, notably Ayatollah Mahdavi Kani. Although party politics of today are far different from those of the early 1980s, many of today's active elements have trained in the above groups.

The Islamic Republic Party (IRP)

According to former president Hashemi Rafsanjani, the Islamic Republic Party was planned shortly before the Islamic Revolution but was endorsed by Ayatollah Khomeini only after the revolution succeeded. The purpose of the party was to organise the religious forces against their rivals, including the liberals, Mojahedin-e Khalq, the communists and so on.[17] Muhammad H. Beheshti, the cofounder and first leader of the party, suggested that the party had been meant to be the political wing of the 'ulama.[18] Kamarava takes the formation of the IRP as an instance of the clerical tendency to 'redirect the popular enthusiasm generated during the revolution into an organised, institutional support base'.[19] The party's manifesto states its chief objective, however, as the promotion of a 'comprehensive Islamisation of the society in which Islamic values, commands and laws govern all social relations'.[20] The party dominated political life from its formation in 1979 until its disbanding in 1987. The IRP was more of a loose and ill-managed grouping of the various movements that accepted Ayatollah Khomeini as the absolute national leader. In a sense, the party was a bit like an archetype, exemplifying the religious trend with all of its intellectual variety and political concerns. According to Beheshti, the crucial deficits of IRP were poor organisation and lack of cohesion, the absence of a precise ideology and an inefficient induction process. The party expanded without a pre-planned strategy, whereby its organisations, even at the higher ranks, were infiltrated by its rivals. In June 1981 the party received a devastating blow when a bomb claimed the lives of seventy-two of its top leaders. A few weeks later, another bomb killed the president and the prime minister (who was also the recently elected party leader). These events devastated the IRP but made its government determined to suppress all its opponents without mercy. In fact, all other groups were suppressed during the period from 1981 to 1983.[21] The absence of rival groups has had a negative impact on the party. With no serious rivals, says Rafsanjani, the party had no objectives to pursue and its members lost their enthusiasm to carry on.[22] Eventually, it was disbanded in 1987 on the advice of Ayatollah Khomeini. It was said that Khomeini was not happy with the fact that the dominance of the IRP caused discomfort to many of the religious notables who chose to remain independent. Khomeini saw this situation as a likely threat to the unity of the religious trend.[23]

As indicated earlier, the party had within its organisation three distinct trends – a traditional right wing, a religious left wing and a pragmatic wing – all of which were fairly represented in successive governments; nevertheless, their relationship was never friendly. As early as October 1981 parliament voted against the right-wing candidate for prime minister in favour of the leftist Mir Hussayn Mosavi against the wishes of Khamenei, the newly elected president.[24] In August 1983, two right-wing figures resigned their ministerial posts in protest over the state's handling of the economy. Interestingly, the president, parliament, the prime minister and the resigned ministers were all of high rank in the Islamic Republic Party.

With the conclusion of the eight-year war with Iraq in August 1988, the Iranian government began to ease the rigid policies concerning political and social activities. A major step was the restoration of the Party Bill, which had remained suspended since its formulation in 1981.[25] However, the political atmosphere remained uneventful until the death of Ayatollah Khomeini in June 1989. The absence of the regime's founder effectively removed the major barrier hindering party politics, namely the idea that independent activities might harm the unity of religious forces. One month after the death of Khomeini, four groups were granted official recognition under the 1981 Bill. From among those recognised, three were deemed Islamist left-wing, including the Islamic Republic Women's Association led by Zahra Mustafavi, the daughter of Khomeini, Majma' Rohanion Mobarez and Fedaiyyan Islam.[26] After his election in July 1989, President Rafsanjani undertook what he called the Policy of Adjustment (*siasat-e ta'dil*) whereby the state acknowledged the plurality of ideas and promised less restrictions on independent activities. In the following years, the political scene saw the emergence of various groups, five of which would claim a major influence during the following decade. The political groups in Iran used to be identified as either right- or left-wing. From 1997, they would be categorised as reformist or conservative.

The Conservative Camp

The conservative camp emerged within the traditional religious community in order to promote its aspiration for a pure religious state based on established Shi'ism.[27] The essence of the trend consists of an alliance between the religious seminaries and the notables of the traditional Bazaar.[28] The two groups made up the major opposition of the pre-revolutionary governments. Despite the close links binding the religious exemplars and their local representatives to the Bazaar traders, the alliance remained undefined with no particular organisation representing its political concerns, at least until the Islamic Revolution. Anjoman Hojjatiyeh was probably the first inclusive organisation embracing the concerns of the religious trend, notwithstanding the group's intentional limiting of itself to purely religious causes. Hojjatiyeh was established in 1957, aiming to counter the proliferation of the Bahai faith.[29] It upheld the Shi'i traditions as its official ideology, including the assumption that Shi'as had to stay away from politics until the return of the Twelfth Imam.[30] Throughout the decade preceding the revolution, the group's relationship with Ayatollah Khomeini and his young supporters was far from friendly. This position earned it the tolerance of the Shah's government on the one hand, but the hostility of the revolutionaries on the other. The revolution was a devastating blow to Hojjatiyeh, which saw the majority of its members deserting their professed doctrine to join the revolution. In 1979 an attempt by the group's leader, Mahmoud Halabi, to reconcile with Ayatollah Khomeini failed, due to the latter's scepticism and conviction that the group retained affiliations with the remnants of the ousted regime.[31] Eventually the group decided to disband in July 1983, apparently after Khomeini publicly criticised their political leanings.[32] Most of the group's members then joined the other right-wing groups and the government.[33] It is widely believed that the group retains underground activity at the present time.[34] Ayatollah Khaz'ali, an advocate of the group, implicitly admits the continuity of its underground existence, however within a smaller scope.[35] The association of the conservative camp with Hojjatiyeh attracted wide attention during the early 1980s when the conservative faction of the first post-revolutionary parliament was ascribed to Hojjatiyeh.[36] Such a strong relation is no longer emphasised.

Hojjatiyeh is not significant, however, for any direct action but for the way its ideology has shaped the political thought of the religious trend, especially its particular conception of pure Shi'ism. The group's principles have deeply influenced the conservative camp. The reflection of its principles on political and social action could be understood only by comparing it with the type of values upheld by revolutionary figures prior to and after the revolution. These include:

- The strict commitment to traditional Shi'ism, which is reflected in the form of sectarian fanaticism as well as hostility to all reformist trends.
- Being preoccupied with the threat of the surrounding world. For this camp, conspiracy theories constitute the main framework within which to conceive the position of the foreign countries towards Iran. This tendency explains as well the camp's exaggerated emphasis on protective policies.
- The tendency to exercise self-designated authority over all

other people in order to ensure their compliance with virtuous behaviour, while, in comparison, individual and public rights and freedoms are left neglected. This tendency is directly reflected in the strict rules concerning dress, personal appearance and leisure activities.

In my opinion, many of the rigid policies held by the state, the cultural policies in general and the policies concerning minorities and women in particular cannot be understood without examining their roots in the model advocated by Hojjatiyeh. The group's ideals are still alive through its many veterans, who found their way into the leading posts of the conservative camp as well as into society and the state system.

The conservative camp consists of around fifteen groups,[37] most prominent among which are Jame'ah Rohaniat, Mo'talefeh Party and the newly formed Coalition of Abadgaran. We will look at each of the these in detail below.

Jame'ah Rohaniat Mobarez (JRM)

Rohaniat-e Mobarez (the Association of Combatant Clergy) was established a year before the 1979 Islamic Revolution, aiming to bring together the politically active clerics under the umbrella of Ayatollah Khomeini. Starting with a few members, the group developed into a central force in pursuing revolutionary causes.[38] After the revolution, it expanded its membership, although the determining role remained in the hands of a few leading members holding its top positions. Despite its leading role, JRM does not identify itself as a political party. It has not applied for official recognition nor has it had an official organ.[39] JRM had among its membership figures representing both the right and left wings. In 1984, the right wing became more distinct when four of its figures launched *Resalat*, a daily newspaper that became the leading tribunal of the traditional conservatives. By 1988 the left wing walked out to establish its own clerical association, making JRM a purely conservative group. JRM is organically linked with the Association of Professors of Qum Seminaries (*Jame'ah Mudarressin Hawzah 'Elmiyyah Qum* [JMHI]). The two associations share ideals and objectives as well as some leading members. Since JMHI is the state-recognised commanding body of the clerical community, the close link between the two suggests that JRM is the political proxy of the former body. According to Rafsanjani, the former president and a leading member of Rohaniat, most of the political positions, as well as nominations for elections on the part of the group, were decided in consultation with the Qum professors' association.[40] The group advocates a market economy but is strict on social and cultural affairs. As Taqavi, the group's spokesman, says:

> The cultural trend in the country has lost its balance ... They [the liberals] propagate maximum freedom unobservant of any rule or principle, notwithstanding the likelihood of endangering others' rights and freedoms. The culture of society shows increasing signs of vulnerability, incited by the cultural encroachment of the enemy, as well as the presence of the sell-outs (*khod-foroukhteh*) and western-struck (*gharbzadeh*) intellectuals in the country's cultural domain.[41]

Between 1992 and 1997 Rohaniat and its allies were the dominant force in parliament and the state institutions. They were overpowered by the leftist camp in the presidential, local and legislative elections of 1997, 1999 and 2000. Since then the group seems to have lost its energy. In the presidential election of 2002 it refrained from nominating or supporting any of the candidates. In the local elections of 2003 and legislative elections of 2004 the group was not accounted for, and the commanding role was taken by the young pragmatists loyal to the person of the Supreme Leader.

Mo'talefeh Party

Hezb-e Mo'talefeh Islami (Islamic Coalition Party) has been considered by some political figures as the dynamo of the traditional conservatives.[42] It was formed in the wake of the Khordad Revolt, a civil insurrection that erupted on the arrest of Ayatollah Khomeini in 1963.[43] At the outbreak of the Islamic Revolution the group resumed its activity among the traders of the Tehran and Esfahan Bazaars, where it recruited the majority of its members.[44] The group joined the Islamic Republic Party until its dissolution in 1987. From then on it was established as an independent party. Between 1981 and 1997 five of its leading members had ministerial posts; others had parliamentary seats, the headship of the Open University, the Chamber of Commerce and Buniad Mostaz'afan, the largest state-owned holding corporation.[45] Being dominated by wealthy traders, the group was sensitive to the state's handling of the economy. In 1983 two of the group's members gave up their ministerial posts in protest over the cabinet's endorsement of the first development plan, which had a strong leftist flavour. In general, Mo'talefeh was the strongest opponent of the economic strategies adopted by the government after the revolution.[46] This tendency is seen in line with that of the Reformists, which is to amend the Constitution's articles that affirm the state's interference in the market. On the political front, the party advocates wilayat al-faqih as the only religious basis for political legitimacy, hence it only recognises groups whose adherence to the doctrine is unequivocal. These are designated by the party as *khodi* (insiders) compared with *ghair-e khodi* (outsiders), i.e. the groups which are not wholeheartedly loyal to the doctrine. The idea of political pluralism is applicable to the insiders only; outsiders should be barred.[47] Religious pluralism is seen by the party as nonsense; in the words of 'Abbaspour, a member of the party's central committee:

> Religious pluralism, whether within or without Islam, is inconsistent with the principles of the authentic (*nab-e Muhammadi*) Islam. Those who advocate such notions have to seek the advice of the real experts of Islam. Otherwise people would view them as heretics. What conception of the religion do they have to boldly tell us that neither Shi'as nor Sunnis possess the absolute right?[48]

For a while Mo'talefeh was felt to have lost its appeal.[49] In the general elections of 1996 three of the group's top leaders lost their seats, despite the overwhelming victory of the conservative camp. The same misfortune occurred in 2000. In the 2004 elections the conservative alliance refused to support the nomination of the group's leader and his deputy on its list, indicating a significant fall-off in the group's popularity.[50] During its 2004 congress, the group's leaders were urged to surrender their roles to the younger generation.[51] Mo'talefeh's influence is largely dependent on its close links with the religious establishment and clergy members in general. Historically speaking, the clergy has been dependent on the market traders for financial support. Although a large segment of the clergy joined the Islamic government, the majority remained independent. This includes the most influential figures of the religious establishment, i.e. the great exemplars, their local representatives and senior disciples. This is one of the interesting points about the behaviour of the Shi'a clergy, whose endorsement of the government entails no submission to, or financial dependence upon, it. Mo'talefeh secures its influence by supporting the cultural and charitable activities promoted by the clergy. It has, for example, the upper hand in Komiteh Emdad, the largest charity in the country. It also provides a good deal of the budgets of the religious schools, mosques, educational programmes based on voluntary basis and so on. However, Mo'talefeh could not translate these impressive works into reciprocal support for its political agenda and figures.

The group's dependence on the clergy has so far helped it to secure a relatively strong position, particularly in the institutions supervised by the Supreme Leader. Due to the group lacking the capacity to act politically on its own, its future seems uncertain. Its major clerical affiliate, Rohaniat Mobarez, has lost its political primacy, whereas its middle-class affiliate, the Islamic Society of Engineers, is moving away from its traditional affiliations towards the newly formed Coalition of Abadgaran.

E'telaf-e Abadgaran Iran Islami

Despite its low profile, Abadgaran-e Iran Islami (the Coalition for the Development of Islamic Iran) was widely expected to win the highest stake in the legislative election of 2004, thanks mainly to the Council for the Guardianship of the Constitution, which arbitrarily removed the majority of the Reformist candidates from the contest. Abadgaran first appeared on the eve of the local elections of 2003, where it achieved a surprise victory and removed the Reformists from the council of Tehran. Statistically, the Reformists won the majority of the seats contested in that election, notably in the peripheral areas[52] but failed in the capital and major cities. The failure was taken as an indication of the political mood of the society, the urban middle class in particular. Among the thirty members of Abadgaran who secured the council of Tehran, only two members were relatively known: 'Abbas Shibani and Mehdi Chamran. The others were completely new to the political arena, including Ahmadi-Nejad, the new Mayor[53] (who, in June 2005, won the presidential election).

The emergence of Abadgaran was explained in different ways, with the most common explanation linking it to the structural changes within the conservative camp. After 1997 there was increasing discontent within the camp over its performance, policies and particularly the hegemony of the traditional and elderly figures. The sentiment reached a climax in mid-1999 with the clash between university students and the police.[54] The events were a great shock to the regime. The mood of the universities used to be seen as the barometer of the general mood of the nation. The student protests and ensuing clashes with the police and Basij, the revolutionary reserve forces, indicated the erosion of traditional support for the religious leadership among students. The events frustrated younger conservatives, resulting in a widespread demand for a meaningful change to the structure and language of their camp. The defeat of the conservatives in the local and legislative elections of 1999 and 2000 respectively made the call for change more credible.

It is believed that, since then, the commanding body of the conservative camp, known as 'The Alliance of the Line of of Imam and Leader', has broken up, notably after the retirement of Ayatollah Mahdavi Kani, the ailing leader of Rohaniat Mobarez. Another board was formed wherein the commanding role of the traditional clergy and Mo'talefeh was entrusted to younger groups comprising mainly pragmatic bureaucrats and academic figures. The new E'telaf-e Nirohaye Enghelab (The Alliance of the Revolutionary Forces) was closely managed by the office of the Supreme Leader through his special adviser, Nateq Nuri, and chaired by Muhammad Reza Bahonar, the leader of the Islamic Society of Engineers.

Nuri, a middle-rank cleric, was born in 1943 and studied in the Qum seminaries. He served in Jihad-e Sazandegi (Jihad of Reconstruction), as interior minister (1981–5), parliamentary speaker (1992–2000) and finally as a member of the Expediency Council. Bahonar was born in 1953. Despite his long record of service in the parliament and Expediency Council, he remained in the shadow of his superiors. With the elections of 2004, he was promoted to the position of deputy speaker of the Majlis. During recent years Nuri has been a strong advocate of change within his camp. In February 2004 most of his speech before the congress of Mo'talefeh was dedicated to urging the group to adapt to modern methods of party organisation, to focus on the young generation and for its leadership to be invested in the young members.[55] The idea of regeneration was also asserted by M. Jawad Larijani, the conservative theorist, and explained within the framework of the regime's renovation.[56] The idea is seen as significant, for it reflects a common cry among the young members and supporters of the camp who feel alienated by their leaders. This feeling was voiced by many activists. Hussayn Harandi, the deputy chief editor of *Kayhan* newspaper and an activist in the radical group *Ansar Hizbullah,* explains the emergence of Abadgaran as a solution to the long-running conflict between the upper and lower echelons of the camp:

> Our forces have made a remarkable success this year. Trusting their own intellect, they broke out of the moral hegemony of a score of notables whom we highly regard and respect. However, we have stopped paying them blind obedience. In the past, our activities were restricted to the frameworks they defined and we had to disregard our own viewpoints and sacrifice valuable time in order to secure their satisfaction. Today, however,

> *Hizbullah* forces have reached the conviction that only the
> supreme leader would receive full obedience. Pure obedience as
> a religious principle is realised in the strict following of a single
> leader. Unfortunately, until recently we have been caught in the
> outdated ideas of our elders. Now we are free, we have realised
> that we could free ourselves. We will retain respect for our elders,
> nevertheless we have to tell them that the direction is no longer
> dictated by them.[57]

The Abadgaran Coalition was formed within the Alliance of the
Revolutionary Forces, headed by Nuri and Bahonar, to express the new
tendencies of the conservative camp. The group is dominated by the Islamic
Society of Engineers and *Jam'iyat-e Esargaran Enghelab Islami* (The Society
of Devotees of the Islamic Revolution). Esargaran was formed in 1996 to
promote the interests of the veterans of the revolution and the war with
Iraq.[58] The society remained relatively unknown until the election of
Ahmadi-Nejad, one of its activists, as Mayor of Tehran in 2003. The group
is seen as a minor player in Iranian politics in terms of size and daily activity.
It is based mainly in the southern suburbs of Tehran,[59] an area dominated
by lower-class migrants. The group operates within the conservative camp
and shares its ideals; nevertheless, 'Ali Darabi, the deputy leader, asserts its
modernist orientation as the principal feature distinguishing it from the
traditional groups such as Rohanion, Mo'talefeh and the association of Qum
professors.[60]

Esargaran explains the country's current difficulties as an 'administrative
deficiency' and puts the blame on 'incompetent politicians and executives'.
The group's second congress put forward a fifteen-article agenda to solve the
country's crises, nine of which focused on the state administration.[61] For
Ahmadi-Nejad, the solution rests on the faithful forces of Hizbullah taking
over the state:

> We have already witnessed the trend of failure and destruction
> rising wherever the venues of service and work are deserted by the
> revolutionary and Hizbullahi forces.[62]

> For the group, the Islamic regime does not face a crisis in respect
> of legitimacy or political ideology, hence the call to follow the
> liberal model is nonsense.
>   The doctrine of wilayat al-faqih represents a new trend in
> the political philosophy and the foundational principles of
> sovereignty [...] With the collapse of socialism, the world is bound

to choose between liberal democracy and an Islamic Revolution. The liberal discourse is falling apart due to its lack of capacity to open up new perspectives for humanity as well as its impotency to renovate its philosophical and intellectual foundations. Thus it is not an exaggeration to claim that the discourse of the Islamic Revolution penetrates the heart and mind of today's man, even without his realising it.[63]

The group dismisses both the programmes of 'economic development' pursued by Hashemi Rafsanjani and 'political reforms' proposed by Khatami. Hussayn Fada'ie, the group's leader, is suspicious of notions of political reform and civil society, which he regards as a mask disguising chaos and indiscipline. He is also worried about the return of the counter revolutionary forces under the umbrella of the Reformists.[64] Esargaran seeks to cooperate with the religious trend of the Reformists, notably Rohanion Mobarez, but rejects any dealing with Moshrekat, for it is regarded by the group as a secular and counter-revolutionary force.[65] In a sense, the group's leaders look hopeful about a project joining the 'good' ideas of the Reformists with the 'good' people of the conservatives to form the real force of future Iran.[66]

It is still early to judge the policies of the new conservative generation as expressed through Abadgaran. Their proclamations, however, indicate a distinctive moderation. Abadgaran asserts that it is a 'working team' rather than a party or an advocate of a certain political ideology.[67] It has already declared its respect for the political openness called for by the Reformists; nevertheless, it expresses concern at the rise of non-religious attitudes. 'We are not going to turn the clock back on reforms', says Haddad 'Adel, the parliament speaker. 'We will only adjust the clock's hands.'[68] In respect of the economy, Abadgaran pledges to carry on with the Reformists' policy of liberalisation but with some adjustments aiming to strengthen the middle class, as suggested by Tavakkuli, the chief economist of the group.[69]

To apprehend the general flavour of the new group's tendencies, I would like to borrow Quchani's comparison between the orientation of Abadgaran and that of the traditional segment of the conservative camp. It is argued that the established alliance between Mo'talefeh and Rohaniat Mobarez represents a model of power relations grounded in the unified interests of the proprietors and clergy.[70] The alliance derives its power from outside the state but employs the state to secure its interests.[71] By contrast, Abadgaran comprises mainly petit-bourgeois elements that have made their careers within the state bureaucracy, whereby property does not represent a pivot of interest or a source of political power. On the other hand, the clergy is not seen by this group as a distinct class or political elite but as a professional group.[72] In fact, their discontent with the excessive involvement of the clergy in state matters is no less than the Reformists', although they express these sentiments in a rather muted fashion. It is not surprising, therefore, that the Majlis, dominated by Abadgaran, has been the first since the revolution to be chaired by a non-clerical speaker, a step that has disappointed the Association of Professors of Qum Seminaries.[73]

Both Abadgaran and the traditional conservatives emphasise the religious orientation of state legitimacy. For the latter, however, the state secures legitimacy if it is supervised by the clergy, who act as the interpreters of religious principles, while for the former, legitimacy rests on the state's pursuit of social justice, notably realised in the equal distribution of material goods.[74] Abadgaran therefore seems more interested in economic issues, as they are the main subject of social justice, while its elders are preoccupied with cultural issues. For Haddad 'Adel, 'issues such as *hijab* (dress code) and the like are neither a priority for society nor for the Majlis'.[75] Instead, Bahonar, the deputy speaker, argues that the most urgent concerns include unemployment, low income and inequality, as well as corruption. He goes further to acknowledge the Reformist principles of economic development:

> We share with the religious reformists [i.e. Rohanion] the idea that reforms should concern principally a comprehensive endeavour to boost the rate of national production, ensure a fair distribution of income, equality, and the sovereignty of law.[76]

Given the emphasis on social justice on the one hand and the lack of interest in political reforms on the other, Abadgaran can be justifiably categorised as pragmatic and an advocate of statism. For some analysts, the group's rise is explained in terms of 'state reconsolidation' after a period of duality of power under the previous parliament.[77] Despite his conservative inclination, the Supreme Leader is more identified with the pragmatic trend as much as his immediate advisor, Hashemi Rafsanjani.

The Reformist Camp

The core of the Islamist left consists of Sazman-e Mojahedin Enghelab Islami (SMEI), the clerical Majma' Rohanion Mobarez (MRM) and Anjoman-e Islami Daneshjouyan (The Islamic Society of Students), later known as Daftar-e Tahkim-e Vahdat. The trend appeared in the early 1970s with the flourishing of leftist tendencies in Iran.[78] At the time, political opposition was dominated by the Tudeh Communist party, while the Islamist trends were seen to be generally impotent, as in the case of the formal religious establishment, or highly influenced by socialism, as was the case with the militant group Mojahedin-e Khalq. The Islamist left had overwhelming popularity during the first post-revolutionary decade, enabling it to secure a majority in parliament until 1992. After the rise of Ayatollah Khamenei to supreme leadership in 1989, the faction came under intense pressure to force it out of the political arena.[79] According to Mosavi Lari, the minister of internal affairs and a member of Rohanion, the conservative campaign took the form of slander and intimidation.[80] The faction's decline was worsened by the sweeping victory of the right wing in the general elections of 1992, which caused the left wing to lose almost all its positions in the government.

The transformation of the leftist faction into a democratic movement was incited by the change of the political atmosphere in the early 1990s, on both internal and international levels. The conclusion of the war with Iraq in 1988 and the death of Ayatollah Khomeini in 1989 resulted in a wide decline of revolutionary and leftist tendencies among the population. The international development, notably the collapse of the Soviet Union in 1991, also has an impact in this respect. As noted in Chapter Five, proposals for religious reform had been already in the public domain since early 1988. Nevertheless, they were viewed as an elitist concern. The earliest political expression of the Reformist trend emerged in February 1991. Ayatollah Mosavi Khoainiha, a radical leftist cleric, published his daily paper *Salam*. Its early issues focused on the critique of the economic policies of Rafsanjani's government but gradually developed a general theme of political reform, criticising the autocratic rule and calling for openness and plurality. In October *Kiyan* appeared as a monthly journal dedicated to new thinking on religion and the state. Coming at the right time, both publications gave a great boost to the Reformist tendency and drew attention to the split within the religious trend on both theoretical and political levels. In fact, they paved the way for the Reformist trend to be recognised as an insider force, although distinguished from the mainstream within the political system.

Kargozaran Sazandegi

Kargozaran Sazandegi (The Executives for Reconstruction) was formed in January 1996 by sixteen of President Rafsanjani's assistants and cabinet members. The party's immediate aim was to defend the reforming agenda of Rafsanjani, which is known as *Siasat-e Ta'dil* or the Policy of Adjustment. The most significant point in the party's experiment has been breaking the clerical control of the nomination for the Majlis. After the 1984 legislative elections, there was a common feeling that only the candidates supported by Rohaniat Mobarez had the chance of winning the elections. This was particularly asserted in respect of the major cities. President Rafsanjani's technocratic group used to fight elections on the conservative lists. On the eve of the 1996 legislative elections Rohaniat Mobarez decided to exclude the group from the camp's lists due to their liberal leanings. The decision was apparently influenced by Mo'talefeh, which, according to Shadlo, had warned that it would block its financial contributions, which made up the bulk of the camp's budget for the electoral campaign.[81] As a reaction, the party was formed and allied with the leftist camp to fight the elections against the conservative lists. The result was impressive; the party and its allies won forty-one seats,[82] although the majority (around 170 seats) remained with the traditional right.[83] The unexpected success of the new group was surprising to both factions. The general impression, however, was that the political atmosphere was about to change decisively. The influence of the clergy showed a relative decline compared with the rise of lay professionals. Kargozaran's successful alliance with the left wing was the first indication of the emergence of the Reformist camp. On the other hand, that success has drawn the attention of the left to the increasing appeal of such ideas as political reform, democracy, freedom and so on.

The emergence of Kargozaran highlights the conflict between the revolution and the state as different institutions with distinct objectives, requirements and mechanisms for action. Such a difference was obvious since the first days of the revolution. The post-revolutionary interim government made an abortive attempt to bring the revolutionary forces under state control. The decision came at the wrong time and thus failed to make any difference. That was, according to Barzin, a result of the hostility of the then powerful revolutionary forces to state bureaucracy. It is argued that the left wing deemed the state bureaucracy to be inherently conservative and lacking in sensitivity to popular concerns, while the religious-traditional trend was suspicious of its inherent tendency to expand its control over social and cultural activities.[84]

After a decade, most of the state institutions, as well as the state-owned industries, came under the dominance of the revolutionaries who would gradually adapt to the distinctive preoccupations of bureaucracy. The rise of the professional and pragmatic forces in the wake of the eight-year war with Iraq effectively blurred the lines between the state and the revolutionary institutions. This was just another example of how the bureaucracy relaxes the fever of revolution and accommodates its forces. Through their presence in the state's upper and middle ranks, the new bureaucrats came to recognise the difference between paying lip-service to political objectives and having the means to put them into effect. The advance of this trend aided the rise of a rational and pragmatic type of culture at the expense of idealism and passionate types of action familiar to the revolutionaries. In a sense, the rise of Kargozaran reflected the decline of revolutionary momentum and the emergence of a new reference group, characteristically pragmatic and professional.[85]

Since its formation, Kargozaran has remained an elitist circle limited, in terms of membership, to high- and middle-ranking professionals and executives.[86] The bureaucratic background of the party has earned it some of its distinctive features, such as the advocacy of statism, pragmatism and technocracy.[87] Its advocacy of economic development and its moderate attitude in respect of political and cultural issues have earned it the support of the urban middle class. Nevertheless, this support has not been translated into organisational power, simply because the party itself shows no interest in expansion. According to H. Mar'ashi, the deputy leader, 'the party is more concerned with the quality than the quantity of its membership, thus it focuses on attracting the elite.'[88] Such a tendency emanates from a conviction that the elite collectively represents the real power for change in the country. In the words of Gholam Hossein Karbaschi, the party leader:

> The political party is an effective means for bringing about a consensus among the national elite [...] Such a consensus is the most agreeable basis for development and the most viable means of countering threats to national security [...] If we fail to bring together the national elite and introduce a consensual long-term strategy, the socio-political system will gradually wear out and erosion will be a serious possibility.[89]

Economic progress is the major preoccupation of Kargozaran. Indeed, it deems itself the pioneer of the idea in the Islamic Republic.[90] The party is of the idea that political, cultural and economic development are so intertwined that any reasonable progress in the political arena cannot be achieved without a considerable improvement in the living standards of citizens. To achieve such an objective, the country has to push towards a level of urbanisation and economic efficiency that meets international standards. The predominance of the economy among the party's concerns is the principal source of contention between it and other supporters of

President Khatami, since the latter's overemphasis on political development, says Muhammad Hashemi, a leading figure in the party, 'will get nowhere'.[91]

During his first term in office (1988–92), President Rafsanjani's plans to liberalise the economy won stable support from the traditional conservatives, in spite of being modelled on the advice of the International Monetary Fund. The support has by and large declined during his second term due to his tendency to elevate the industrial sector to the status of mainstay of the Iranian economy at the expense of traditional trade, which hitherto made up an essential part of the conservatives' strength.[92] The inclination of the party towards a modern industrial economy caused some analysts to identify it as the representative of the modern upper class.[93]

The party advocates a strong and effective government. Its model of government lies between the rule of an experienced oligarchy and a representative government. The best rule is embodied by the professionals who enjoy the trust and support of the public.[94] In fact, the party prefers the rule by technocrats to the rule by politicians. Hussayn Mar'ashi, the deputy leader, describes the party members as Muslim technocrats: 'technocracy is part of our essence'.[95] According to Centeno, the most common perspective on technocracy is a variant of elite theory 'that asks whether or not an oligarchy of technicians controls the administrative, economic, and political arms of a given state'.[96] The idea had long been established in the traditions of the Greek philosophers as well as the nineteenth-century works of Auguste Comte (1798–1857) and Saint-Simon (1760–1825), where the idea of the separation between ownership and the effective control of power was applied to decisions taken by those who control the means of production, namely, the learned technicians.[97] In the 1930s the idea attracted more attention aided by the flourishing of the assumption that progress is indebted to the advancement of technology. On the other hand, technocratic rule was criticised on the basis that the technician's view of his fellow human being is likely to be utilitarian, i.e. people are to be treated as a means of production.[98] The core distinction between technocratic and democratic rule lies in the philosophy of government, being an administration of things or a representative of its citizens' interests.[99]

Kargozaran's focus on the technical skills of state officials discomforts the conservatives who see them as inferior to an ethical commitment.[100] Its economic policy is another point of contention and seen, as Bahonar argues, to be inconsistent with the revolution's values: 'they [Kargozaran] put rationality and rational administration before a religious one, while the others [the conservatives] emphasise simultaneously economic development, justice, values and the maintenance of the regime.'[101] In response, Muhajerani, a senior member of the party, argues that it is logical that each working unit is administered by the most learned. Technocracy is not a value-free model of rule; the party's focus on skill does not contradict its religious commitment.[102]

The party views the religious establishment as an essential ally of the government. However, it prefers the former to be subordinate to the latter, rather than vice versa, as argued by the clergy.[103] At the same time, the party is less interested in the theoretical issues related to religion and religious reformation. It takes a pragmatic approach to the application of religious rules and emphasises the calculable interests borne out by the rule rather than its metaphysical authority. Rafsanjani's experience as chairman of the Expediency Council offers a good example of the way he likes to organise the interaction between religion and government. In this respect, the relevance of religious rules is judged upon their capacity to deliver the interests identified by the government or parliament. The party's standpoint towards wilayat al-faqih is another example of its pragmatism. As Karbaschi says:

> We accept wilayat al-faqih within the frame of the people's sovereignty [...] The faqih is the leader elected by the majority and not the appointee of God. The authority of the faqih is grounded in the Constitution. In fact our acceptance of wilayat al-faqih is originated in our adherence to the Constitution.[104]

The party holds a liberal propensity for social and cultural issues, forwarding an agenda entitled *tasahul va tasamuh* (Leniency and Tolerance). Karbaschi, the former mayor of Tehran, and Muhajerani, the former minister of information, shared responsibility for putting the agenda into action. Consequently, the two have been singled out for criticism by the conservatives. In 1998 the mayor was sentenced to five years in prison and banned from political activity for ten years.[105] Muhajerani, who dedicated two of his books to defending his liberal agenda,[106] was forced out of the cabinet in 2000. In 2004 he was subjected to a smear campaign to force him out of the political arena amid rumours about his possible nomination for president in the 2005 elections.[107]

The party operates within the Reformist Second Khordad Front. After pioneering political reforms in the early 1990s, the party was overtaken by other Reformist groups, due to the advance of the Reformist discourse, as suggested by Muhajerani.[108]

It is commonly felt that Kargozaran's sole purpose is to win elections. After its formation, its activity was limited only to election times. The lack of any broad organisation and membership puts some constraints upon the party's movements. Its efficiency in political contests is widely dependent upon its alliance with other factions. For this reason, the party has to be very moderate and intrinsically pragmatic in dealing with political and social issues, keeping a reasonable distance from all active factions.[109] This tendency can be interpreted as a strength, as all other factions can see the party as a possible ally. The other side of the coin, however, suggests that the party is no more than a halfway ally. It could be allied with on a tactical basis but with no security in the long run.[110]

The relationship between the party and the former president Rafsanjani is quite complex. The party leaders do not deny the 'special' link with Rafsanjani. In the list of the party founders, there are four Rafsanjanis, including his younger brother and daughter.[111] The central committee comprises mainly Rafsanjani's former assistants. Muhajerani admits that the party observes the views of the former president regarding major issues but denies that he is the party's 'Godfather'.[112] Rafsanjani is one of the top three men of the regime; nevertheless, he could neither protect the party leaders from conservative hostility, nor did he help them to have access to the state institutions dominated by the conservatives, such as the judiciary, the armed forces and so on.

Mojahedin Enghelab

Sazman-e Mojahedin Enghelab Islami (Organisation of the Fighters of the Islamic Revolution) was established in 1980 as a merger of seven smaller groups. Apparently, it was meant to counter Mojahedin-e Khalq, the quasi-Marxist Islamist group.[113] Its presence in the state was noticeable after the revolution. Many of its members have occupied senior positions in the armed forces, intelligence units, cabinet, academia and parliamenta. The group is seen as the dynamo of the left wing and generally treated by both the pragmatist and right-wing factions in a manner that is far from friendly.[114]

Since 1982, Mojahedin Enghelab has been in decline. First, Ayatollah Khomeini outlawed the membership of military personnel in political groups, resulting in scores of the group's cadres walking out. A year later, thirty-seven leading figures left the group in the middle of internal differences over its leftist tendencies. Finally the group was disbanded in 1986 on the advice of Rasti Kashani, a senior right-wing cleric designated by Ayatollah Khomeini to oversee the group's operations.[115]

In 1991 the group was restored by the left wing. In 1994 the group started publishing *'Asre-ma,* a fortnightly paper which deeply influenced the political scene in this period.[116] It was known for its thorough analysis on issues previously left untouched, including the structure of the political scene, the composition of influential factions, state-religion and state-society relations and so on.[117] It also paved the way for the next wave of writings on such issues as democracy, civil liberties and the role of modern elites. Before it was shut down by the judiciary in March 2002, *'Asre-ma* was among the most influential publications of the country. It played a prominent role in advancing the reformist discourse among the supporters of the left.

The Mojahedin Enghelab of today is far removed from its professed principles of the early 1980s. Its leftist tendency has been extensively modified; it came to advocate public consent, rather than wilayat al-faqih, which it upheld in the past as the basis for the legitimacy of the regime. Its rigid interpretation of religion was also replaced by a more liberal one.[118] The group has been harshly treated by the conservatives and slandered as being secular, a conspirator and so on. In 2002 the Association of the Professors of Qum Seminaries (JMHI) issued a communiqué declaring the group religiously illegitimate and appealing for its exclusion.[119] This came shortly after Hashim Aghajari, a leading member of the group, was arrested and later sentenced to death for blasphemy and insulting religious beliefs.[120]

The group made a crucial contribution to the rise of the Reformist camp, and after 2000 it became a major partner in the government. It is this determining role that caused the group's rivals to regard it as the hidden power behind the Reformist camp,[121] not least because the dominant partner of the camp, the Mosharekat party, is led mainly by former members of Mojahedin.

Mojahedin Enghelab has never had clergy members within its organisation,[122] probably because of an anticlerical tendency common among those who have been influenced by 'Ali Shari'ati. It resembles Kargozaran in its elitist composition. The group remained relatively small and dominated by professional politicians and intellectuals.[123] It also emphasised an industrial-based economy against the dominance of traditional trade.[124] In respect of the state-society relation, most of the group's views resemble those held by the Mosharekat party. Mojahedin was banned from participation in the legislative election of 2004. Since then it has tried to shift from its tradition of elitism and secrecy to being a popular and broad-based organisation. The new policy of expansion was declared in the group's seventh general congress, the first held in public, in April 2004.[125]

Majma' Rohanion Mobarez (MRM)

Rohanion (Assembly of Combatant Clergy), the faction of the clerical left, has been the closest group to Ayatollah Khomeini. Its differences with the mainstream traditional and pragmatic right came to the fore after the death of Muhammad Hussayn Beheshti, the leader of the Islamic Republic Party in June 1981. Beheshti was able to keep the revolutionary groups together despite their contradictions.[126] The leftist group was operating within the clerical association of Rohaniat Mobarez (JRM) until 1988 when an internal dispute reached deadlock, days ahead of the legislative election.[127] The conservative trend was generally supported by the senior clerics, the religious establishment and the pragmatic wing of the Islamic Republican Party. The leftist faction had the support of Ayatollah Khomeini, Mojahedin Enghelab the younger clerics and the student organisations. According to Rafsanjani, Khomeini's support of the faction was due to its being informally led by Ahmad, Khomeini's son and his personal assistant.[128] Apparently, the group was the only political party whose formation was publicly endorsed by Khomeini, not surprising when ten out of twenty-seven of its founders had been working at Khomeini's office and six others were among his representatives. Like Kargozaran, Rohanion lacks the basic features of a political party. It has no organisation of its own, no distinctive ideology and even no definite position with regard to many of the issues posed in the political fray. The final communiqué of its first congress (November 2003) expressed a deep concern over the hegemonic attitudes of the conservatives and emphasised the group's commitment to reform. Nevertheless, the position taken in respect of many controversial issues is mostly vague.[129] The viewpoints expressed by the group's members diverge widely, implying the lack of a coherent ideology that otherwise would have fostered collective and united positions towards the major issues posed in the political arena.[130] The group had a good link with the students' associations, brokered notably by Mosavi Khoainiha, which was a great help to Rohanion in political contests. Since 2002, however, this relationship seems to have weakened due to disillusionment and the rise of secular tendencies among students. In the legislative elections of 2004, many of the group's candidates were disqualified. The others have failed to retain their seats, including Mahdi Karroubi and Majid Ansari, two leading figures with pragmatic tendencies. The failure was blamed on the Reformist allies' retreat from the fray. In fact, the group was not capable of winning battles on its own. The withdrawal of its younger allies has left Rohanion with no means to fight.[131]

163

Jebhe Mosharekat Iran Islami (JMII)

Despite its short history, Jebhe Mosharekat Iran Islami (Islamic Iran Participation Front) has proved remarkably competent in mobilising the people behind its programmes. Only six months after it was established, the party secured the majority of the local councils elected in February 1999.[132] This was followed by a similar victory in the legislative elections held in February 2000, securing the upper hand in both the Majlis and cabinet.[133] The party is categorised as liberal-democratic. Some Iranian analysts view it as a social democratic party in line with the modern left, apparently because of the leftist orientation of its founders.[134]

The seeds of the party were planted in the 'Ayen Circle', a group of intellectuals who during the period 1994–5 were busy preparing to publish a new liberal-oriented journal. With the nomination of Khatami, the group's leader, for the presidential elections in early 1997, the circle shifted to the headquarters of his campaign. With Khatami elected as president, the circle's focus moved towards establishing a political party advocating the proposals that won him the presidency.[135] The party was established by a group of 110 politicians, professionals and journalists. At this early stage, Sa'eed Hajjarian was said to have been the brains behind the party;[136] traces of his opinions are easily found throughout its publications. For many Reformists, Hajjarian is the principal theorist of the political reforms in today's Iran.[137] Like many of the party leaders, Hajjarian has been a member of Mojahedin Enghelab. The two groups are so interlinked that their rivals deem Mosharekat to be the public proxy of Mojahedin.[138]

Mosharekat is thought to be the largest political group in respect of membership and regional presence.[139] Before it was shut down by the conservative-dominated judiciary in July 2002, the party's newspaper, *Nourooz*, was one of the top Iranian dailies in terms of circulation.[140]

According to 'Alavitabar, an Iranian analyst, three trends could be identified within the Mosharekat party:

1. The traditional left with religious orientation originated in the Line of the Imam, which developed into a moderate advocate of broader public participation and controlled political contest.
2. The centre left, oriented in the intellectual, religious Reformist trend which supports a quasi-secular democracy.
3. The professional politicians who hold pragmatic, liberal views and moderate religious attitudes.

'Alavitabar suggests the latter trend is more likely to determine the future direction of the party. If it happens, the party will develop into a professional political party, whose activity revolves around the contest for power.[141]

The party's proposals have so far proved to have a significant appeal for the new generation. Its main slogan 'Iran for all the Iranians' had a great influence on those segments of society that felt alienated, notably the youth and women. Thus it is widely believed that the party has attracted to the political fray a segment of the population that had hitherto been indifferent. An opinion poll carried out in January 2004 showed that, despite the public dissatisfaction with the performance of the outgoing parliament, which was dominated by Mosharekat, the party was still the favourite among the electorate.[142]

Political reform represents the major preoccupation of Mosharekat. It holds the idea that the new socio-political situation of the country and the world requires an extensive rethinking of political culture, structure and the standards by which the Islamic state functions.[143] It advocates liberal democracy as the only model of government capable of meeting the challenges of modern times. Thus it emphasises such notions as civil constitutional rights, the establishment of the public will as the essence of the regime's legitimacy, the sovereignty of law, transparency and accountability as the major objectives of the Reformist movement.[144] For the party, the rise of the Reformist trend embodies the shift of the revolutionary movement brought by the Islamic Revolution towards rational, practical, peaceful and locally developed forms of action. Muhammad Reza Khatami, the party's leader, argues that the course of democratisation has been hindered by idealist tendencies, populism and autocracy on the part of the conservative rulers and, on the other hand, by the yearning on the part of the secular opposition for an intervention by foreign forces.[145]

The fifth general conference of the party (2003) dedicated a good deal of its time to considering what the party members, indeed most of the democratic forces, take as a dead end reached by the Reform movement. Nevertheless, in the final communiqué, the party reaffirmed its primary principle of peaceful struggle within the limits of the Constitution and the country's laws. This assertion was meant to highlight the line distinguishing the party from the groups seeking a wholesale change of the Islamic regime as well as the friends of the party who see no way out under the current system.[146]

The party views the extensive powers retained by the supreme leader in the absence of a systematic means of accountability as a major source for political irregularities.[147] Its four-year parliamentary experiment is characterised by serious endeavours to adjust the legal system and power relations to enhance public rights. The controversy between the Mosharekat-dominated Majlis and the conservative-dominated Council for the Guardianship of the Constitution shows that the former was principally aiming to enhance the people's influence on the political process.[148] For Mosharekat, the Constitution of the Islamic Republic has fundamental defects, yet this cannot be entirely blamed for the hesitant progress of reforms; as Reza Khatami says:

> The existing Constitution has serious shortcomings in such respects as the definition of the power relations and power distribution within the political system [...] Given that, we do not believe that the advance of reforms is contingent upon the change of the Constitution [...] We believe that the fundamental defect in the country is the lack of an absolute and impartial sovereignty of law [...] Even if our Constitution and other laws are perfectly democratic, given the current situation, there is absolutely no guarantee of having them implemented. Therefore the ultimate assignment of the reformist movement must be to establish the sovereignty of law.[149]

The party is of the opinion that the course of democratisation can only advance properly with structural changes leading to the balance of power becoming in favour of the society and its democratic forces. The seventh general conference saw a strong emphasis on the role of political parties and other civil society groups as the principal means of translating public opinion into political power.[150]

The party identifies itself as the intellectual trend of religious reformation. It advocates a wide role for religion in both public and private life.[151] However, it rejects the extension of the sanctity of religion to the state. It deals with the religious branch of the state, including wilayat al-faqih, the Council for the Guardianship of the Constitution and so on, on a legal or a political rather than a religious basis. In the same line, the party does not see religion as a part of the state's business and calls for the separation between the religious establishment and state institutions.[152]

Although President Khatami is a member of the clerical assembly of Rohanion Mobarez (MRM) rather than Mosharekat, his campaign promises and intellectual publications make up the essence of the party's teachings.[153] Therefore, it is widely believed that he is actually the founding father of the party: a similar relationship to that of Kargozaran with Rafsanjani.[154] Two points, however, might be considered in this regard. First: as a large and country-wide organisation, the making of Mosharekat's common views and positions is primarily a function of the organisation rather than the persons of the leadership. This function was very clear in the seventh congress held in July 2004.[155] Second: the presence of a considerable number of intellectuals, professionals and politicians within the party's organisations enhances the value of collective opinion and reduces the influence of individual charisma in the process of decisionmaking. Amongst all of the political groups in the country, Mosharekat seems to have the largest number of thinkers and professionals. On the other hand, many intellectuals who have been alienated during the last two decades were able to voice their ideas through the party-inspired publications.[156]

Prior to the legislative elections of 2004, all of the party's candidates were disqualified by the Council for the Guardianship of the Constitution, forcing the party out of the contest. Previously, it was thought that the party was not going to win the same majority as it enjoyed in the sixth Majlis (2000–4). In the second local election of 2003 the party endured a sweeping defeat in the major cities at the hands of the new conservative Coalition of Abadgaran. This setback was blamed on the party's failure to deliver on its promises at the local level, in addition to its engagement in fierce rivalries that frustrated its electorate.[157]

Conclusion

Despite the emergence of political parties after the Islamic Revolution, their effectiveness became tangible only after the changing of the political environment in the 1990s. The Iranian parties, notwithstanding their many defects, have helped at least to hinder the evolution of totalitarianism, which seems to have been pursued by both the left wing in the 1980s and the conservatives in the 1990s. This shows that political groups are, even in difficult circumstances, crucial for maintaining pluralism, and, when the situation improves, they can be helpful in accelerating the course of democratisation.

This chapter shows that among the factions discussed, only two have the shape and machinery of a modern party, namely Mo'talefeh and Mosharekat. Three other groups, namely Rohaniat, Rohanion and Kargozaran, are more like elitist clubs with no coherent organisation. The first two appear to be increasingly losing their power and political influence, probably due to the general decline in the hitherto exemplary status of the clergy.

Some analysts assumed that Iranian politics were characteristically fluid. I contend that such an assumption has to be taken very reservedly. As we have seen throughout the chapter, the composition of each of the two broad camps remained by and large stable. The change of positions and alliances resulted mostly from the sharpening of the lines that differentiate the factions from each other. In my opinion, these changes resemble the overall evolution of the political system of the Islamic Republic. Since the rise of the Reformists in 1997, however, the line separating the modernists from their traditionalist rivals has become clearly demarcated as it never was before. This was aided by the accentuation of the different ideologies behind the two trends.

Most of the assumptions about fluidity relate to the changing alliances during the running for general elections. It is a matter of fact that the majority of party politics in Iran revolves around elections. As Baktiari rightly noticed, the Majlis has been at the centre of elite factionalism and power rivalry: 'who controls the Majlis, and in what numbers, has become an important indicator of factional victory in revolutionary Iran'.[158] This chapter shows that four of the eight parties studied have been formed shortly before elections. The others have weakened after they lost elections. It is understood that power represents the pivot of party politics, and a party is defined as 'a team seeking to control the governing apparatus by gaining office in a duly constituted election'.[159] The problem with the Iranian parties, however, is seen in their exaggerated attachment to elections, and hence power, in the sense that if there is no election, there is no activity, while for the course of democracy to mature, an effective opposition is as necessary as an effective government. This requires the political groups to remain active at all times and not only at the time of elections. This idea seems to have been finally understood as we see three groups, Mo'talefeh, Mojahedin and Mosharekat, declaring plans to expand their organisations and focus on civil society, a typical propensity of 'outside-government' party politics.

The rise of the coalition of Abadgaran has attracted little analytical attention outside Iran as it was generally perceived to involve more of change of personnel rather than of ideology.[160] In this chapter I have tried to locate this development within the structural transformations of the society, which inevitably affect the conservative camp, as well as the other parties. For the conservatives, however, it signifies that domination within the camp has shifted from the traditional clergy and market traders to the middle-class technocrats. The change will probably ease the camp's rigidity; nevertheless, its implications in the course of political reform are still open to question.

168

CHAPTER SEVEN

Ahmadi-Nejad in Power

The 2005 presidential election results came as big a surprise to the mainstream conservatives as to their Reformist rivals, exactly as did Muhammad Khatami's election in 1997. Defying all the pre-poll surveys, Mahmoud Ahmadi-Nejad rose from being the weakest contender to become winner. More astonishing was the fact that two of the Reformist candidates – Mustafa Moein and Mahdi Karroubi – and the conservatives' main candidates – Ali Larijani and Muhammad Baqer Qalibaf – could not even clear the first round.

Once again, Iranian politics proved to be capricious and unpredictable. However, such a description does not explain the real story. This chapter discusses the questions raised by many observers about Ahmadi-Nejad and the shift towards radicalism in Iran as exemplified by his rise. I will start by focusing on his personal career and attitude. This chapter will also analyse his electoral victory and its implications. The political ideology of the new conservative generation represented by Ahmadi-Nejad will also be discussed in this chapter. The conclusion will show some of the outcomes that ensued from the shift towards radicalism in the country and the possible developments in the short term.

The President

Mahmoud Ahmadi-Nejad was born in 1956 in Aradan, a small village near the city of Garmsar, one hundred kilometres southeast of Tehran. The following year, his family moved to the capital, looking for a better life. He was awarded his first university degree in civil engineering and obtained a PhD in planning and transport engineering from Tehran's University of Science and Technology in 1997.

During the war against Iraq, he served in the engineering corps of the volunteer forces (Basij) where he met many of his present associates. After the war, he assumed several positions, the highest of which was the governor of Ardabil, in north Iran, from 1993 to 1997. About this time he joined a group of war veterans to form *Jam'iyat-e Esargaran Enghelab Islami* (Society of Devotees of the Islamic Revolution) with a declared purpose of promoting the interests of the ex-soldiers, war victims and their families. He entered the political fray on the national level after he was appointed mayor of Tehran in 2003, a position that made him a well-known figure and paved his path to the office of president in June 2005.

Once he entered the political arena, Ahmadi-Nejad was viewed as a radical and populist figure. His attitude and lifestyle portrayed him as a statesman of a different class. The house he lives in, the car he drives and the clothes he wears are all similar to those of the average Iranian, far below the usual lifestyle of the elite. In my opinion, he does not pretend to be a down-to-earth man; this is what he is, at least up to the day he became a president. His attitude as a civil servant exemplified the same character. As a Tehran mayor, he was a man of action, a boss who spent time with his staff in their various fields rather than staying in his office, issuing orders and reading reports. When difficulties arose he would not hesitate to break with the bureaucratic strictures. This way of life and working touched deeply the hearts of the common people. Iranian culture venerates rulers who serve without being affected by the display of power. This does not mean, however, that Ahmadi-Nejad has overlooked his political aspirations. His attitude is rather used as a tool for his campaign. Apparently he viewed the popular appeal of such behaviours as proof of his being a different leader: a real alternative to all those who preceded him in power. During his electoral campaign for presidency, Ahmadi-Nejad portrayed himself as the saviour of the nation and the only contender with a pure understanding of what religion is all about, what inspired the revolution and what the people feel and need.

The radical attitude of Ahmadi-Nejad is explained by some analysts as a personal propensity sprung from a particular social and professional background. Hooshang Amirahmadi, an Iranian Professor at Rutgers University, describes him as a 'very egoistic and name-seeking individual who likes to become popular, controversial and a centre of attention'.[1] Many clues to this attitude could be traced in his speeches. For example, I quote a part of his speech to some senior clerics about his UN visit:

My arrival into New York and then the United Nations were

extremely exceptional. In the streets, in the buildings, the Iranian delegate was the centre of everyone's attention as if no other one was in there. Last day when I gave my speech, all the heads of states were present. One of the audiences told me later: 'once you started, a beam of light has suddenly appeared and took around you'. I have personally felt that thing, [I felt] the atmosphere suddenly changed and everyone there was completely silent and surprised. This is not an exaggeration, I have seen it. Everyone there was looking to know what the Islamic Republic had to say.[2]

A Victory with Many Questions

At five o'clock in the morning of 18 June 2005, Mahdi Karroubi, former parliament speaker and presidential candidate, retired to bed after having received promising reports of his advancement in the previous day's poll. He was not the only one to know about it. The official website of the Internal Affairs Ministry broadcast live non-official figures from every ballot box counted.

> At eight o'clock that morning, I got up to find a completely different picture. A candidate whose votes were far behind the others had just jumped to first position. For me, this proved what my assistants previously had said about the wide interference by certain organisations in the process of elections, the use of public resources and the partiality of some state organisations, including the Council for Constitution Maintenance, in the favour of a particular candidate.[3]

Two other candidates, Mustafa Moein and Hashemi Rafsanjani, also accused the so-called 'hidden forces' of manipulating the elections as a part of a wider plot to make up the rules of the game. The organisations indicated here include mainly the Revolutionary Guard and its sub-organisations of Basij, the state radio and television, as well as the organisations for Friday Prayer. The partiality of these institutions, as well as other publicly funded organisations, was evident during the election campaign and also on the polling day inside and around the polling stations.[4]

Despite these accusations, one cannot credit the victory of Ahmadi-Nejad merely to this alleged intervention. Other evidence, statistical and non-statistical, indicates that his campaign had a stronger appeal amongst the major cities' lower classes. Ahmadi-Nejad's campaign traded very efficiently on the weak points in Reformist rule, particularly the bad effects of their economic reforms. In comparison, the Reformists had failed to capitalise on their strong points. They entered the elections disunited and lost the crucial support of the university students. The latter boycotted the elections due to ideological disputes and their disappointment with the performance of the Reformist government. Since the 1990s, the students have been viewed as the strike-force of the leftist and then the Reformist faction.

Ahmadi-Nejad's victory can be analysed in relation to three aspects: his electoral campaign; his rise as a sign of regeneration within the conservative camp; and the accumulation of all state powers by the supreme leader. We will discuss these three aspects in detail here.

Two notions have made up the major theme of Ahmadi-Nejad's electoral campaign: egalitarian distribution of the national resources and the nation's capacity to deal with its problems on its own. The two notions were formulated in very simple yet sensational pledges, targeting a principal concern for the majority. Regarding the first notion, he repeatedly told his audiences that Iran's problem has never been a lack of resources but poor management. The huge resources are poorly handled or even taken away by the powerful urban elite who control the market and influence the government. Every town in Iran, he claimed, could be more prosperous than Dubai or Kuwait, the prosperous cities on the other coast of the Persian Gulf, if trustworthy and capable hands were put in charge.

Regarding the second notion, Ahmadi-Nejad insisted that Iran could have risen to be a great nation, exactly as it had been in ancient times. The problem does not lie among Iranians but in the outside world, which decisively hinders Iran's drive to become a serious competitor in the international arena. The professional politicians – 'those who ruled since the revolution' – could not comprehend this basic fact. They were far from realities on the ground and could not see eye to eye with the common people and listen to what they had to say. They spent more time with foreign diplomats and leaders than with their own people.

These two themes traded well on the disparities and damage endured by the lower classes as a result of economic reform. Such outcomes were experienced by other developing societies during the course of economic liberalisation. A small segment of society reaped the immediate fruits of modernisation, leaving a sizeable segment of the population lagging behind. Villagers, low-ranking employees and labourers in the traditional sectors could not adapt to the new realities. They saw a sharp rise in the cost of living along with the decrease in direct state subsidies and support. Such a disparity made good grounds for the populist pledges that linked economic difficulties to political reforms, exactly as Rafsanjani predicted a decade earlier.[5]

Ahmadi-Nejad assumed power shortly after the Abadgaran group had claimed the majority in parliament. Both events highlighted a process of regeneration among the political elite of the Islamic Republic. For the first time since 1979, there were no pre-revolutionary activists amongst parliament and cabinet members. Apart from a few notables, the new political elite represented, by and large, the younger generation within the conservative camp. Its push to power came in the middle of disagreements with the traditional leaders of the camp. The new and older generations shared the same ideological platform but differed in their social backgrounds. The latter held an established position in society linked to a long history of social and political activity as well as their involvement in the foundation of the Islamic regime. In comparison, the new elite lacked such credentials. Their majority had made its way into politics through state bureaucracy. Hence the pattern of concerns, interests, relations and pivots of power were different from their elders. In other words, the traditional leaders had their sources of power outside the state; their political and social influence interacted and affirmed each other. While the new elite was a product of the state, the state represented their only source of power and interests. Different loci of interests, inside and outside the state, represented a major factor in informing the two sides' perception of the state, its role and relation with the society. On this basis, the new elite retained a traditional attitude of religiosity referring to their ideological, right-wing platform. Their economic strategies at the same time had an interventionist character, which is usually attributed to the left wing.

With regard to the power structure, the above developments signify the supreme leader's accumulation of all the veins of power in his hands. In May he plainly expressed his delight at 'the resurgence of the value-based (*usulgara*) discourse and the consolidation of state powers after a period of fragmentation.'[6] Since he assumed the office of wilayat al-faqih in 1989, Ayatollah Khamenei has never enjoyed the full obedience of both parliament and government as he does now. The consolidation of state powers will satisfy some conservative elements, at least in the short term, for it helps to enhance state efficiency. But it could also boost an anti-state propensity among alienated forces. We have already seen indications of a growing gap between Khamenei and some religious leaders to whom he owes his ascendance to the office of wilayat al-faqih, despite reservations towards his religious credentials. In Qum, the home of the religious establishment, a number of great Ayatollahs have overtly or covertly expressed discontent with the new elite's tendency to undermine political pluralism. For example, Ayatollah Jawadi Amoli, an eminent authority and influential conservative leader, made a fierce attack on the new group's manipulative attitude:

> Seven years ago I publicly opposed the reformists, yet I have heard not even a single word of disrespect from them all these years. Now you show me all kinds of impoliteness merely because I expressed an opinion different from yours.[7]

A few more words worth noting in this regard: the swap of generations could be viewed as a natural process. Nevertheless there are certain events implying that this process is not really spontaneous but a planned action pursued by the supreme leader personally. This is particularly evident in the case of the clerical elite. In recent years, many of Ayatollah Khomeini's close aids have either retired or been removed from the state system. In a few cases, natural causes, such as personal health, were a good excuse. In others, there is no such explanation. In the early 1990s, Ayatollah Khamenei removed his immediate rivals, i.e. the leftist clerics. In the late 1990s he started replacing the conservative notables with younger clerics and bureaucrats. Most of the newly elevated clerics were trained by Ayatollah Misbah Yazdi, a radical scholar who rose recently to become a major player in the political scene. In a strict religious sense, Yazdi excels the leader Khamenei in his credentials but lacks any revolutionary ones. This is why he kept a low profile during Ayatollah Khomeini's reign. He owes his current rise to the supreme leader's interest in someone with a recognised religious authority, who is ready to work in the shadow of the leader. I have already introduced Yazdi and his views in Chapter Four. He is currently viewed as the principal theorist of the conservative faction. Nevertheless, he does not limit himself to theorising. Yazdi's disciples play a major role within Ahmadi-Nejad's government.[8] The president himself has repeatedly expressed a strong inclination towards Yazdi and the school of thought he propagates.[9] During recent years Yazdi's activities have spanned a wide area from universities to the armed forces. In late 2005 he launched an initiative to buttress his influence among the ordinary people all over the country. In December of that year he chaired a clerical seminar aiming 'to contemplate the upcoming elections of the Council of Experts, the body assigned to select and monitor the performance of the supreme leader. The attendants were urged to have an effective presence in all regions and be closer to the ordinary people. They were also advised to focus principally on the young generation and to provide them with a clear vision of the rightful line in this perplexing time.[10] Yazdi's early inception of his electoral campaign implied an intention to set the rules on how and who would fight the elections in December 2006. Since the Islamic Revolution, the nomination of the conservative candidates for the Council was trusted to the major cleric associations, Rohanion Mubarez and the Professors Association of Qum Seminaries. For some politicians, such as Khatami and Rafsanjani, that movement implied Yazdi's intention to hold sway over the supreme leader and finally take over the office.[11] Another instance of this tendency is seen in the enormous efforts to undermine the position of Hashemi Rafsanjani by Yazdi's followers. Rafsanjani is viewed as the natural successor of the incumbent leader.

Here it is worth noting that Yazdi's ambitions are not expected to materialise easily. His views and behaviour are hard to swallow by either faction. His push for power will likely worsen the divisions within the religious camp and probably undermine the political role of the clergy.[12]

The Increasing Role of the Military

I have noted earlier that Ahmadi-Nejad's electoral victory was indebted, at least partially, to crucial support from the commanders of the Revolutionary Guard. Hence, it was natural that the guard enjoyed a special privilege and influence under the new government. In addition to many high positions entrusted to former guard commanders, service in the force has been designated as a criterion to qualify for state high ranks. The political expansion of the guard has led to security concerns becoming paramount and decisive. On the other hand, the guard has taken the opportunity to expand in the business sector, even to remove its competitors on some occasions. For example, a contract for a second mobile phone network with the Turkish firm *Turk Cell* was cancelled in 2005 after the latter refused to give up control over the project to its local partners. Another deal to operate the newly built Tehran Airport was cancelled over national security concerns and transferred to a local company. In both cases the decisions were made to favour companies owned by the Revolutionary Guard. In June 2006 *Khatam al-Anbia* Headquarter, the engineering section of the guard, was given a US $1.3 billion contract to build 900 kilometres of gas pipeline between the Persian Gulf and the southeastern city of Iranshehr. A week later, the firm obtained another major deal worth $2 billion to develop the fifteenth and sixteenth phases of the South Pars oil field. More contracts were also given to other companies owned by the guard during 2006, including a $2.5 billion deal to extend the Tehran underground lines and a comprehensive contract to modernise the whole water and electricity networks of the western regions.

The Model of Ruling Pursued by the New Government

An Economic Perspective: the 'Chinese Model'

The new ruling elite apparently embraces the so-called 'Chinese Model of Development' as the most suitable for the particular conditions of the Islamic Republic. It was around the middle of 2001 when the so-called 'Chinese Model' started to float around Iran's conservative circles. According to early 2004 Reuters reports, the idea became 'the new buzzword in Iranian politics'.[13] Except for the name, the idea was not novel. Many of its implications were already in action since the early 1990s in the frame of the Policy of Economic Adjustment adopted by the former president Hashemi Rafsanjani. To explain why the Iranian conservatives have found an interest in that model, one can point out the amazing performance of the Chinese economy during the last two decades, given that the power and role of the communist elite remained by and large intact.

The 'Chinese Model' refers to the programme of economic reforms adopted by Deng Xiaoping, the former leader of the Chinese Communist Party, with the aim of raising the gross domestic product from US \$250 per capita in 1978 to \$1,000 by 2000. In this model, the political and economic aspects of development are dealt with on different bases. It opts for a gradual liberalisation of the economy, maintaining a decent distribution of material goods favouring the low-income groups, and emphasising self-sufficiency and independence as the major objectives of economic strategies. Thus, it welcomes foreign aid in terms of finance and know-how but opposes political and cultural influence. On the political side, it stresses the sovereignty of law, a degree of representation and limited civil rights but reserves the crucial powers to the upper echelon of communist elite.

Contrasting with the model of 'Shock Therapy' promoted by the US administration or even the Structural Adjustment Programme designed by the International Monetary Fund for sub-Saharan Africa, China has taken a gradualist approach based on an experimental rationality: start small, test, assess and then generalise.[14] This approach is said to be inspired by an ancient Chinese wisdom: '*Mo zhe shi tou guo he*', or cross the river by groping for the stone under your feet. Through this approach, the communist leadership was able to avoid the destructive impacts of the shock therapy that led to social unrest and chaos in other countries such as Russia and

Egypt. Social frustration is said to be an outcome of unduly mixing up the political and economic factors of development. Political transformations release a high tide of expectations and aspirations that cannot be fulfilled while the economic system is being modernised. The Chinese leaders acknowledge that democratisation is crucial for sustainable development. Nevertheless, democracy has to be advanced step by step, certainly after a responsive economy is established. China's priority was to set up a safety net ahead of any political transformation. The development strategy considers different rates of growth for the well-off and impoverished regions. Foreign and export-oriented investments were directed to the coastal and potentially well-off areas, which were considered ready for a fast growth. On the other hand, the rural and potentially vulnerable regions were given more reserved and somewhat slow programmes of development. The aim was to protect the poor from the aggressive forces of the changing market during the transition to a free economy. The philosophy behind this approach is simple. As put by a Chinese writer: sustainable development requires a 'national consensus on modernisation and ensuring overall political and macroeconomic stability in which to pursue wide-ranging domestic reforms'. Thus he argues that:

> The paramount task for most developing countries is how to eradicate poverty, a root cause of conflicts and various forms of extremism. What they usually need is not a liberal democratic government, but a good government capable of fighting poverty and delivering basic services and basic security.[15]

Despite a pile of difficulties and of course reservations on the Chinese strategies,[16] its actual outcomes have been miraculous. Between 1979, when the reform programme was launched, and 2003 the gross national product (GNP) has increased from US$44.2 billion to US$1,425.6 billion. An annual growth rate in GNP of 9 per cent is far higher than in any other country in the same period. Poverty reduction is also amazing: official figures estimate a decline in the rural poverty rate from roughly one-third of the population (some 260 million people) in 1978 to only about 3 per cent at the end of 2000 (some 30 million people). World Bank estimates, based on the higher international poverty line of US$1a day per person, show the rural poverty rate falling from 42.5 per cent of the rural population in 1990 to 24.9 per cent by 2000.[17] The expansion of export-oriented industry has made it possible for China to multiply its foreign trade by around 22-fold in the last two decades.[18]

Economic prosperity has provided for the stability and strength of the regime concurrent with a rising influence upon international affairs. The success of the Chinese model of development has attracted wide attention among the Third-World elites, given the fact that the great achievements were made within the framework dictated by the ruling communist party, which remained, by and large, in full control. This point is particularly interesting for a wide range of politicians who aspire to modernisation but are not ready to exchange it for their own power. The Iranian conservatives are certainly one of these elites. They are honestly keen to build a strong and prosperous nation, without damaging the regime's bedrock.

Since the mid-1980s at least, the preservation of the religious character of the Islamic regime has been elevated to the paramount concern of the ruling elite. As a grounding principle, the idea was defined strictly in the form of the political clergy retaining an overall domination. Rafsanjani's Policy of Adjustment, designed in the early 1990s, meant to handle the economic difficulties ensuing from the eight-year war with Iraq as well as the quasi-socialist model that was adopted in the aftermath of the Islamic Revolution. This policy meant to redirect the Iranian economy in line with global free-market trends without structural changes in the power arrangements. As explained in the previous chapters, this policy could not avert some political by-products, however undesired.

Apart from the general inclination towards economic modernisation, inclinations towards that particular model of development are certainly motivated by political factors. The strong advancement of the Reformist model led by President Khatami was a real source of worry for the conservatives and the clerical elite. His praise for liberal democracy, religious pluralism, civil society, sovereignty of law and the like were viewed as an attempt to undermine the religious domination from within.

Throughout Khatami's first four-year term in office, the conservatives made enormous efforts to undermine his discourse and proposals. They also tried to force him away from the Reformist camp. Yet he was able to survive and win a second term with even more votes. His rising popularity has prompted the conservatives to seek an alternative model on a par with the Reformist one. The models of Malaysia and China have been considered. Nonetheless, the latter seems to have satisfied the concerns of the conservative elite more than the quasi-liberal model of Malaysia, notwithstanding its Islamic flavour.

In 2002 the supreme leader sent two of his close aides to China to study its model of development.[19] It is widely known that three of his advisors at least favoured that model: Mohsen Reza'ei, the secretary general of the

Expediency Council, the advisory board of the leader, Ali Akbar Velayati, the leader's special advisor on international affairs, and Abbas Maleki, the former deputy minister of foreign affairs. The supreme leader himself has denied his favour to any foreign model, stressing that a locally formulated model of development would be more satisfying for Iran's peculiarities.[20]

The grounding principles of the Chinese model are obvious in *Sanad-e Chashm-andaz* (the Twenty-Year Perspective Deed), which was adopted by the Expediency Council and endorsed by the supreme leader in 2004. The deed defines a set of guidelines to be followed by successive governments in order to ensure consistency in the economic and developmental policies. Many of the guidelines keep up with the principles adopted by the former governments of Rafsanjani and Khatami. The deed also opts for a gradual economic liberalisation, inviting foreign investments and reconciliation with the international community. It foresees some structural changes in the political arena as a natural outcome of the economic development, the improvement of public education and mass communication and particularly of the rising of new generations unfamiliar with the revolutionary experience and its values. In a way, the Twenty-Year Perspective Deed can be regarded as the Iranian version of the Chinese Model, albeit on the theoretical level.

In reality things are somewhat different from the plans. According to Rafsanjani, the chairman of the Expediency Council, the aforementioned guidelines are not being carried out as planned.[21] Foreign as well as local investors still face legal and political impediments. I have noted in earlier chapters that the conservative trend is preoccupied with an outside threat. This preoccupation has had a negative effect on foreign investment in recent years. To put it in a different order, the conservative elite is convinced that the Chinese Model of Development satisfies Iran's particular needs. Nevertheless, it is not yet ready to face the challenges imbedded within any developmental model. China has seen the model succeeding after the doors were opened for foreign investors, the market was liberated, and the private sector was given a decisive role. The improvement of relationships with the other nations as well as the international financial institutions was also crucial.

In comparison, Iran does not seem ready to take a similar course. Robust development requires stable relationships with the outside world, the rule of law and flexible market regulations. In addition, economic development yields certain by-products – political and otherwise – which have to be dealt with in a positive manner. Without a serious readiness to take up such a challenge, even a good model of development cannot make a meaningful difference.

An International Perspective

In sharp contrast to Khatami's policy of 'tension-defusing', which earned him international respect and improved Iran's foreign relations, Ahmadi-Nejad started his presidency with a number of inflammatory declarations, followed by taking a hard line on Iran's nuclear ambitions. The latter has apparently boosted the president's popularity. Nevertheless, it has worried the business sector and a good segment of the elite, especially those who believe that a robust economy depends very much on friendly relations with the outside world.

Apart from his personal propensity, Ahmadi-Nejad's hard line could be referred back to a general tendency of the supreme leader Ayatollah Khamenei as well as the new elite, which rose to power through the legislative elections of 2004. The general view as voiced by Khamenei suggests that Iran has given a lot to calm down the international concerns over its policies but gained nothing. It kept an open door with the US, UN and European Union on many issues including the nuclear programme and the anti-terrorism campaign. It has also provided direct support for Western efforts in Afghanistan and Iraq. Contrastingly, Europe and the US kept raising their demands accompanied by constant threats and pressure. The poor response to President Khatami's policy of 'tension-defusing' implies that Iran is not welcomed as an equal partner in a US-led international order.[22]

Obviously the Iranians understand that a hard-line policy would be responded to in kind by their world partners. In addition, it would inescapably fuel more differences among the national elite. We know that a good segment of the elite from both factions, the conservative and Reformist, favours normal relations with Europe and the US. Nevertheless, the ruling group is adamant that the worsened situation in Iraq since the US invasion in 2003 provides for a better position in any future negotiation with Western governments. After a seemingly easy victory, the US army sees its losses rising steadily while unable to stop the country from slipping down into quasi-civil war. The White House is being pressured to consider Iranian support in bringing peace in the embattled country. Tehran holds some decisive keys in Iraq that can be used for or against the US policies. For the Iranians, the more the US forces become embroiled in the Iraqi crisis the less threat is directed at them, which offers them a better opportunity to carry on with their agendas.

On the other hand, rocketing oil prices since 2003 made it impossible for Washington to risk another crisis in the Middle East. Another crisis in the region would take the price of oil beyond US $100 per barrel resulting, as many analysts predict, in global economic chaos, particularly in the United States.

Under Ahmadi-Nejad, Iranian foreign policy is carried out through a two-fold strategy: it pushes to the utmost possible limits but avoids direct engagement with its rivals. Accordingly, it has resisted international pressure to stop uranium enrichment while stressing full compliance with the international convention on nuclear proliferation. In Iraq and Afghanistan, it has offered a helping hand to the United States but without a clear recognition of the US arrangements in the two countries. This policy presumes that Iran has the potential to be a strong and competent nation. Recognition and respect can be achieved by developing high-tech sectors, including nuclear, petrochemical, engineering and weapon industries.

The Nuclear Programme

In 2003 international attention was attracted to the claim that Iran was developing a nuclear capability for military use. An opposition group revealed the existence of two secret facilities, apparently supervised by the Revolutionary Guard. These previously unknown activities include a plant for heavy-water production at Arak, near Tehran, and a uranium-enrichment plant at Natanz, near Isfahan. The International Atomic Energy Agency (IAEA) held Iran in violation of its safeguard agreement with the agency as well as its commitments within the Nuclear Non-Proliferation Treaty (NPT). Despite Tehran's insistence on the peaceful nature of its programme, the international community has never felt that the situation has been satisfactorily resolved. The European Union has assigned the foreign ministers of France, Germany and Britain (known as the EU-3) to broker a new deal resolving these international concerns. In October the two sides reached an agreement (known as the Saad-Abad Understanding). In this agreement Iran has promised more transparency and compliance with the IAEA rules of control. It has also committed itself to voluntarily suspension of all activities related to uranium enrichment. In return, Iran was promised financial and technical help, including support for new light-water nuclear plants. As a gesture of goodwill, Iran has signed the Additional Protocol on nuclear non-proliferation. The United States, however, remained sceptical. Its doubts were further confirmed after additional undeclared activities were revealed in 2005, including the drawing up of secret designs for an advanced

P2 centrifuge and the apparent acquisition of components from Pakistan. As expected, Iran came under intense pressure from the Western states and media. In return, Tehran took a challenging position and decided to resume all activities previously put on hold. In November the EU-3 ministers were able to bring Iran back to its previous commitments. But the agreement could not gather momentum, mainly because of the political chaos that prevailed in the Middle East at the time.

In my opinion, Iran's changing positions on the nuclear issue are highly influenced by the US military presence near its borders, notably in Afghanistan and Iraq. When the US forces toppled Saddam Hussein's regime in 2003 the feeling was that Iran would be America's next target. Thus, Tehran took a conciliatory position and agreed to suspend its worrying activities. With the change of situation in Iraq, notably the rise of military resistance against the American forces, the Iranians came to the conclusion that they were not facing an imminent threat. The apparent failure of the US army to contain the Iraqi resistance would deter any plan to push into Iranian territory. Hence Iran found it a good time to cross the last barrier before elevating itself to the status of a nuclear nation: the acquiring of uranium-enrichment technology. This explains why Iran has taken the risk of facing an international embargo and endangering its relations with Europe and its neighbouring countries.

A Political Perspective

Tough politics are naturally segregationist. The further you go towards the extreme, the more friends you lose. During the last decade Iran was about to reach a new consensus over the major principles grounding its political system. Openness, plurality and participation have been major themes in that movement. The economic applications of such principles have been a point of agreement by almost all parties, unlike their political applications, which were disputed by a good segment of the conservatives. Nevertheless, the Reformist initiatives by the former president Muhammad Khatami have deeply affected the political environment. The structure of Iran's politics has changed to a considerable extent, whereby a major retreat to revolutionary politics became almost impossible.

Apart from a minor group supporting a radical model similar to that of North Korea, the mainstream political elite prefers moderate and participatory politics but to different extents. Bearing this in mind, one can predict that the overwhelming support given earlier to Ahmadi-Nejad by the conservative trend would not last very long. We have already seen indications to the aforementioned change in the elections of the local councils and the Council of Experts held in December 2006. In these elections Ahmadi-Nejad's supporters and the mainstream conservative alliance had contended with each other. In some cases the moderate conservatives joined the Reformists against the president's group. As a result, the latter came out of the elections almost empty-handed. The Reformists won around 40 per cent of the votes, the conservatives got 50 per cent, while the share of the president's supporters was limited to 3 per cent. Many analysts and politicians explained this result as 'an indication of the people's distrust of the radicals'.[23]

At the beginning of his term in office, Ahmadi-Nejad and his team enjoyed the apparent backing of the conservative trend. Under the surface there was a different story. The dissension over personal and political issues grew even worse after the Reformists were removed from power. As noted earlier, Ahmadi-Nejad rose as a representative of the new conservative generation who plainly seek to push aside their elders.[24] The definition of the latter group became a point of contention given the majority of conservative leaders were in their sixties or seventies.

The Outcome of Risky Politics

The radical line pursued by the Ahmadi-Nejad government has already produced bitter fruit on various levels. On the economic level, for example, the initial pledges to carry on the policy of economic liberalisation have not been fulfilled. The state-owned companies keep expanding, most of the publicly financed projects are given to the public sector, and certain organisations (such as the Revolutionary Guard) are shown extra favour.[25] This tendency was publicly criticised by the Chamber of Commerce,[26] the contractors associations[27] and many economists. In June 2006 fifty economists and university professors condemned the government's economic policies as inconsistent and lacking scientific justification. Their communiqué spells out ten points involving a 'plain diversion from the framework of the Fourth Development Plan and the Twenty-Year Perspective Deed' adopted under the former government.[28]

The plans to use foreign know-how and finance to develop the oil industry have sustained the worst damage. A deal with the Japanese firm Inpex to develop the massive oil field of Azadegan was put on hold because of political concerns. Another major project to pipe Iranian gas to India and Pakistan is facing difficulties, apparently because of the US pressure on India. The two deals are worth two and four billion US dollars respectively.

Other than their direct benefits, foreign investments are viewed as crucial to encourage the local private sector to invest. Historically the Iranian wealthy class takes foreign investment as a sign of security: when it comes in a large size they take the risk, when it goes away they hold back. Doubts about foreign and local investments have already damaged the financial market. Tehran Stock Exchange saw the worst effect. From October 2004 to June 2006 the market index fell by 30 per cent as it lost roughly 68 per cent of its dealers.[29]

The government's welfare policy is also accused of being inconsistent with the Twenty-Year Perspective Deed. In late 2005 the Parliament considered a set of bills aiming to improve the livelihood of the impoverished strata. The package included new state funds to help young married couples, cancelling the public debts of low wage earners, increasing housing credits and raising the wages of the low-ranking state employees. In addition, the underdeveloped regions were promised extra funds to enhance their economy. The president has pledged a personal commitment and visited several regions to look closely into their immediate needs.

Most of the Reformist and moderate conservative politicians turned a sceptical eye on the above policies, for they recalled the leftist strategies of the 1980s. I have noted in Chapter Three that the idea of direct support was abandoned in the early 1990s. As the then president Rafsanjani put it, 'only through a systematic and comprehensive enhancement of the economic output, Iranian economy can develop an egalitarian character and ensure a fair distribution of resources throughout the nation.'[30]

In late 2006 there were signs of economic slowdown. On the one hand, welfare policies were blamed for pushing up the rate of cash supply and thus inflation. On the other hand, the decline in private and foreign investments had to be compensated for by raising government expenditure. According to the guidelines of the Fourth Development Plan (2005–8), the government was to gradually decrease its budget's dependence on oil income in order to reduce the role of the state and give the private sector a wider role in the economy. For the fiscal year of 1385AH (from April 2006 to March 2007), the oil income contribution to the budget was to be limited to US $15 billion. Contrastingly, this share was raised to US $50 billion. Rising state expenditure could push up inflation. According to official reports, the circulating cash supply rose to a record figure of IR1.06 trillion (US $114 billion) in 2006, 35 per cent more than the previous year.[31] A report by the parliament research centre warns that uncontrolled expenditure by the state could worsen inflation. There has already been a worrying rise in consumer prices from housing to basic foods, fuel and so forth.[32]

On the international level the picture is even worse. The great efforts made by former president Muhammad Khatami to improve Iran's international and regional relations are being wasted by the incumbent government. In December 2006 the UN Security Council imposed a package of punishments on the country. Shortly afterwards the European Union made clear that its members were committed to the resolution.

The alleged interference in Iraq has also damaged Iran's relations with its Gulf neighbours. As a result, the country became less attractive to foreign trade and investment. And the hope of continuing the annual growth rate of 7 per cent, which had been achieved under the previous government, completely vanished. Foreign investments were furnished by the Fourth Development Plan as 'essential for a steady growth' and a 'key factor to generate new jobs'.

In January 2007 President Ahmadi-Nejad looked increasingly isolated within Iran itself. Some notable politicians and religious leaders hold the supreme leader responsible for the problems ensuing from the president's policy. The feeling is that Ahmadi-Nejad would not go so far without the leader's support. As a matter of fact, Ayatollah Khamenei made an attempt to make Iran's foreign policy more balanced. In July 2006 he appointed an advisory board on international affairs, consisting of five moderate figures, three of whom have served in Khatami's cabinet. The move came days after he issued a decree on 2 July, reaffirming the policy of privatisation adopted under the former government. These two steps were not taken seriously by the political elite because the overwhelming tendency within the government leans in a different direction.

In general it could be said that the leader is being questioned over the damage done so far. In January 2007 Mahdi Karroubi, the ex-parliament speaker, started a series of activities aiming to build up domestic pressure against the president. In a rare meeting with a number of Reformist ex-ministers, MPs, notable journalists and politicians, he spoke of a new initiative to bring back normal politics to the country. He also implied an endeavour to form a united front under the leadership of the former presidents Rafsanjani and Khatami.[33] Three days later, Rafsanjani held a meeting with a hundred MPs, half of whom belonged to the conservative camp. Apparently the meeting aimed to discuss the bill of the government budget for the fiscal year of 1386AH (from April 2007 to March 2008). Rafsanjani talked plainly against the government proposal and described it as inconsistent with the general guidelines agreed by the regime's leaders. He also criticised the 'poorly-calculated policies' which brought the country to the verge of a crisis.[34] This unprecedented meeting was a stark sign of the president losing support within parliament and the conservative camp in general.

Conclusion

The elevation of Ahmadi-Nejad to president of the Islamic Republic signifies a shift towards radicalism. However, this tendency should be taken with some reservations. His electoral victory could be attributed to the economic difficulties ensuing from the Reformist strategy of market liberalisation. Nevertheless, many politicians believe that Ahmadi-Nejad would not have won without the support of the Revolutionary Guard, in which case the fairness and legality of the elections are questioned. At any rate, the rise of Ahmadi-Nejad represents, on the one hand, the supreme leader accumulating all the state powers within his hands, and on the other, the shift in the political leadership within the conservative camp to the new and younger generation.

The radical tendencies of the president can be explained on the basis of personal or social background. It can also be linked to a general tendency of the supreme leader Ayatollah Khamenei and the new conservative elite, which has risen to power since 2004.

The new elite believes in the so-called 'Chinese Model of Development' which opts for a gradual remodelling of the economy in line with the free market but without a parallel change in the political structure as proposed by the classic (Western) theory of development. On international relations, the new elite believes that once Iran becomes a strong nation it will receive a fair and respectful treatment from the international community. This belief is manifest in its attempts to join the world nuclear club as well as the national celebration of the weapon industry.

The radical policies of Ahmadi-Nejad have so far yielded some bitter results on the economic and political fronts as well as in foreign relations. Foreign and domestic private investment has dropped sharply. Government expenditure went higher than ever, while signs of inflation and economic slowdown are looming.

Iran in 2007 seems very close to international isolation. President Ahmadi-Nejad seems increasingly isolated within the country. A part of the blame is being put on the supreme leader, whose authority amongst the elite and the public is also being questioned.

As a final word, one can say that Iran is at a crossroads. It has to choose between isolation similar to the situation of North Korea or giving some concessions to rebuild the damaged trust of its world partners. Rumours about a possible attack by the US air force on Iran's nuclear facilities add more fuel to the concerns within the country itself and in the region. Such a threat will probably bring Tehran back to the negotiating table over its nuclear programme and other issues. This will probably give rise to the moderate trend within the elite. However, everything depends on a decision by the supreme leader to carry on with radicalisation or to return back to the strategy of 'tension-defusing' pursued by the former presidents Hashmi Rafsanjani and Muhammad Khatami.

Conclusion

For some researchers, the rising trend of political reform in Iran signifies a reversal of the religious-political model that has prevailed since the Islamic Revolution of 1979. The tendency of the Islamic Republic in recent years to come into line with the universal standards of politics and administration is explained by this group of researchers as evidence of the failure of religion to meet the demands of a changing world. There is nothing novel in this assumption since it affirms a common theme in the study of development that suggests religion will inevitably give up in the face of the compelling realities produced through the process of modernisation.

While appreciating the aforementioned argument, this study seeks to develop a different hypothesis on the possibility of formulating a model for the relationship between religion and modern politics capable of fostering a viable democracy. The thesis puts forward two major arguments: the first concerns the adaptability of religious principles, particularly those that concern public affairs, to modern demands. The second emphasises the crucial role of religion in bringing about a consensual and participatory political system. The two arguments have been advanced through a three-fold scheme of analysis, including a historical analysis of the evolution of the Shi'i political worldview, an analysis of the present debate over the correspondence between Islam and modernity in Iran, and an empirical assessment of the achievements and failures made during the ongoing experience of the Islamic Republic.

Adaptability

Throughout the long history of Shi'a, the changing realities of the community's life have been mirrored by a reciprocal change in their religious worldview. The latter change took the form of a continuous reinterpretation of the basic principles of religion, signifying its disposition to free itself from the contextually conditioned relations and interpretations. The adaptive character of the religion is explained on four bases.

First: there is a relatively clear distinction between two scopes of religiosity, the scope of worship or the pure relation between man and God (*i'badat*), and the scope of mutual relations between the people (*mu'amalat*). In the latter scope, religion offers mainly general principles, most of which are in line with common rationality. Thus it leaves more room for reasoning with reference to society's collective rationality and changing needs.

Second: the absence of a formal religious establishment, hence a single authority to interpret and enact the religious rules, allows the religious scholar to review his peers' interpretations in the light of the new demands and realities of life.

Third: the production of ideas by the religious scholars and thinkers is highly influenced by their relations with the intellectual and social trends outside the religious realm. Thus we can find among the religious trends groups leaning towards socialism or liberalism, nationalism or internationalism, traditionalism or modernity, authoritarianism or democracy and so on. All these groups ground their claims on a religious basis. Nevertheless, they can be properly understood only by locating them within the broader variety of ideologies and trends on a global level.

Fourth: the above process also highlights an inherent tendency among religious leaders to ensure religion's responsiveness to the varying concerns of the community. This tendency is meant to preserve the basic threads that tie the believers to their basic beliefs. Therefore the religious leaders tend not to be too rigid about the change of attitudes and lifestyles as long as they stop short of damaging the bedrock of religious association.

From the historical experience of the Shi'i community, we learn that the evolution of its political worldview has been profoundly influenced by the degree of its political engagement. Thus I have argued that the more religion engages in the political process the more it evolves. The direction of this evolution is determined by factors outside the religious realm. An accurate judgement of the capacity of religion to adapt to the modern patterns of politics and socialisation has to consider the sociological dimension, i.e. the compelling imperatives of the society in question.

The Role of the Religion

This study appreciates the argument that religious traditions are inherently unhelpful to the process of democratisation. Nevertheless, it does not view secularisation as a viable answer to the problem. The major reservation on the public role of religion is related to its emotional effect, which hinders the individual from grounding his intentions and actions on a rational basis. It is also argued that the organic relationship within the community of believers downgrades individuality and lures the individual into accepting the status of subject rather than an equal citizen. As a result, a religious-based power will likely justify a kind of dictatorship in the guise of a virtuous authority.

While this thesis is not aiming to refute these assumptions, it tries to expand the scope of investigation, hence probabilities, by redefining the core of the religion-politics problem on the one hand and assessing the function of the religion from a sociological point of view on the other hand.

Religion-State Antipathy

This study has argued that the religion-democracy aversion is an offshoot of a historical antipathy between Shi'ism and state. This antipathy, which ensued from the hostility of the state, has been a residual element in the Shi'i system of thought. After the rise of the Pahlavi regime in the early twentieth century, this antipathy was reaffirmed by the tendency of the Iranian state to secularise society through the course of modernisation. The strategy of removing religion from the public sphere was reacted against by the religious community alienating themselves from the political process and denying the legitimacy of the state and its eligibility to represent them. In this light, I argue that democratisation in Iran has not been hindered by the individual giving up his individuality or the community surrendering its choices to the religious leaders. It was rather that a secular state could not win the hearts and minds of the people as the state of their own.

Accordingly, the reconciliation between the religion and democracy had to be preceded with a reconciliation between Shi'ism and the state in order to bring about a sense of consensus among the people themselves on the kind of political system which would meet their ideals and wants. Such a consensus is crucial to revitalise the public willingness to come out of their cognitive confinements – i.e. the traditions of self-alienation – and take part in the process of change. If the course of democratisation is destined to advance vigorously, it has to expand on a renewed willingness on the part of the population to prefer democracy over all other alternatives. Given that religion remains an agent of social solidarity and its long-established contribution to the national identity of Iran, the stipulation of secularism for democracy, particularly in the sense common in the Western world, is hardly helpful to the course of democratisation in Iran. It basically hinders the evolution of a new political culture in a society capable of fostering an active participation in political affairs.

Religion and Democracy

Whether religion functions in favour of democracy or otherwise depends on factors outside the religious realm. In the modern history of Iran the change of lifestyle, roles and institutions has instigated a parallel transformation in the culture, including the religious worldview. In this light, we have noticed, for example, that the wide popular participation in the revolution of 1979 served to affirm the role of the people both as a source of authority and as force of political reform. This is significant particularly because the hitherto-established religious doctrine of authority does not ground authority in the popular will, nor does it sanction the people's preferences. Since the revolution, the religious doctrine of authority has undergone profound and constant revisions aiming to get it in tune with the compelling requirements of a modern state. These modifications have undoubtedly been the fruit of the structural transformations and particularly their reflections on the tendencies and ideals of the Iranian society.

The Process of Reconciliation

The reconciliation between religion and democracy involves modifications in the religious worldview as well as in some of the principles of democracy. This is seen as essential in facilitating a model of governance that concurrently honours the major principles of democracy and the ideals of society. This is rather a complex process. The current debates over the issue in Iran show that, although a promising advance is being made, complete harmony between the two is contingent upon resolving a considerable number of issues, none of which are negligible or easy to skirt around. Questions like the source of sovereignty, the state's role with regard to religion, constitutional rights and so forth are new to religious thinking. Some important answers have been given. Although Ayatollah Khomeini covered the first, most critical, mile on that long road, more theoretical work still needs to be done before new notions are established within the religious school of thought. Interestingly, the challenge of modernity has brought a renewed tendency within religious scholarly circles to question many of the assumptions that were hitherto taken for granted. It has also boosted the interest in philosophy, sociology, economics and other disciplines related to political theorisation, which remained by and large at the margin of scholarly interest until recently.

The course of reconciliation between Shi'ism and democracy in post-revolutionary Iran can be divided into two phases. The first phase was carried out in the aftermath of the Islamic Revolution and aimed to integrate religion into state institutions. In this phase, the state was endowed with religious value providing the possibility of modifying religious rules in relation to the state's imperatives. The second phase, which is still carrying on, has been undertaken by a reforming trend seeking to bring about a democratic political system on a religious platform. Its aim therefore is to reconcile the religious state with democracy through a broader modification of the religious framework.

The first phase was led by religious leaders with a traditional-revivalist background. The second phase is driven by modernist intellectuals and activists and advanced by the civil activities of the middle class and the younger generations. The Reformist trend was instigated by the failure of the revolutionary paradigm to cope with changing conditions on both the local and international levels. On the local level, the study has highlighted the social transformations brought about by the revolution and the war with Iraq, especially the emergence of a new generation dissatisfied with the post-revolutionary ideology of the government. On the international level, the major source of influence has been the collapse of the Soviet Union in 1991, which profoundly discredited the totalitarian and centralised political systems.

The rise of the new paradigm took the form of a spontaneous, cross-sectional movement aiming to put into effect a political agenda which involves a broad deviation from the hitherto established principles of ruling, religiosity and socialisation. The Reformists' rise to power in 1997 was labelled by some researchers as the second republic or second revolution.

After eight years in political power, the Reformists could not claim complete success in conquering the traditional-authoritarian strongholds within the state. The long list of failed attempts to push ahead the course of democratisation brought many analysts to believe that the Reformist project had no chance of continuing. Among the Reformists themselves, some figures and groups started to propagate a different paradigm involving substantial changes to the Constitution of the Islamic Republic. For example, Akbar Ganji, who has been in jail since 2000, published in 2002 his *Manifesto for Republicanism*, calling for a complete separation between religion and state. A similar call was supported by one of the major student associations.

Despite the uncertain progress of democratisation, the Reformist paradigm seems to have achieved a fair proportion of its objectives. In this regard, I would like to draw a clear line between the evolution of the paradigm itself and the success, in the political sense, of the reformist faction. This differentiation is necessary because the latter is usually assessed according to its assumption of political power. By comparison, the advance of the paradigm must be assessed through its various effects on the function of the society at large. Thus we deal with three distinct aspects: the success or failure of the reformist faction to translate the paradigmatic advance into political strength; the effects of the new paradigm on the functioning of the state; and the effects of the new paradigm on the functioning of society.

Success at the first level is obviously limited, compared with achievements at the institutional and structural levels. On the other hand, we know that the Reformist faction does not seek to replace the existing political system. Thus its pursuit of democratisation has to be understood as one of reform, not of replacement. This choice is fairly justifiable from the perspective that the existing regime does not blindly reject democracy nor does it lack the institutions of a democratic system. The Constitution of the Islamic Republic and many of the conventions which have become established throughout the last twenty-five years bear many of the features of other democratic systems. The Reformist mission thus seeks to redefine the principles, roles and institutions within the political system so as to empower the people to choose and set the preferences of their government. In other words, it is a mission to change the position of the state from being a government above the people to a government of the people.[1]

For the particular purpose of this study, I would like to put a special emphasis on the main characteristic of the Reformist paradigm: i.e. its being a religious discourse embracing liberal democracy and producing a range of theoretical formulations seeking to break some of the major deadlocks in the religion-modernity debate. Questions like the religious character of the state, the source of sovereignty, the role of the people and so forth have been addressed from an authentic religious platform but in a close correspondence with their counterparts in liberal thought.

The two phases through which the political thought in Shi'ism has been developing show that the prospect of a religious-based democracy is both realistic and achievable. Such a model provides a practical solution to the impasse of democratisation in many other Muslim societies.

The Way Ahead

Considering both the positive and negative developments, Iran appears at the time of writing to be closer to democracy than it was in the 1970s. The last decade in particular saw tangible progress in this respect, permitting the argument that the course of democratisation, despite all the hurdles, is becoming day by day the most compelling among all other choices. There is nevertheless much work to be done before the Islamic regime can stand alongside other democratic systems. Democracy is not a project to enforce by law, nor is it an overnight change of policies or staff. It is rather a long process that often involves difficulties and setbacks. The process of democratisation in Iran is promising because the foundation is already in place. The study has shown that many of the previously assumed impediments to democracy were already addressed theoretically or practically, including the role of the people and the relevance of modernity to religion. It also highlighted the evolution on the cultural and structural levels as well as the gradual upturn of institutionalisation. The shift from the revolutionary-traditional paradigm to the Reformist one was an embodiment of the society's awareness of its role. Since then, this role became even more effective and compelling in such a way that no political faction could trade on public ignorance or indifference any longer.

Despite the claimed progress, there remain many issues pertaining to the Constitution, culture, elite structure and other institutions that have to be addressed theoretically as well as institutionally. Some of these are addressed below:

The Sovereignty of God

The religious perspective on political participation is considered in relation to the principle of the sovereignty of God over the universe and man. In contrast, democracy is grounded on the idea that sovereignty is naturally oriented in society. The question of sovereignty is crucial because almost all the institutions within the political system function with reference to the particular definition of sovereignty upon which the system is grounded.

Among contemporary Muslim leaders, the legislative application of the idea was emphasised by the Indian scholar Abu'l-A'la al-Mawdudi vis-à-vis the idea of legislation by man, which was advocated by the secular elite after the formation of the state of Pakistan. Sayyid Qutb, the Egyptian theorist, took the idea beyond that certain limit and asserted that the sovereignty of God ought to reflect on every aspect of life and on government actions in particular. Although the earlier views of Khomeini are similar to Qutb's, at least in the outset,[2] his later views and practice lean towards investing sovereignty in society. On 11 October 1981 he ruled that a two-thirds majority of the Majlis's deputies could override the views of the Constitutional Council regarding the compatibility of parliamentary bills with religious principles.[3] He also ruled in 1987 that the government could refer to pure rational justifications to formulate and enforce the executive policies regardless of the views of the ulama. This principle was eventually ratified by the Constitution and institutionalised through the newly formed Expediency Council.

The idea of linking state policies to the common interest on the one hand and to public consent on the other started to attract widening attention among the religious scholars. Nevertheless, it is not yet established on undisputable theoretical grounds. Therefore it is likely to be open to differing interpretations, especially with regard to the powers of the faqih in comparison with those of the directly elected institutions. The current debate has not yet tackled the core question of sovereignty, which is the recognition of the will of the people as the ultimate and unfettered reference for decision making in the public sphere.

The question of sovereignty can be sorted out only if the political role of religion and consequently the function of the state in this respect are redefined. It seems that a good deal of the problem emanates from the perception that the state functions as a guardian and propagator of religion. Due to the notion of free choice not being deeply seated in the Iranian social system, religious propagation does not take the form of a cultural exchange between the various views. It rather unfolds through the imposition of the particular ideology and lifestyle of the hegemonic group over the whole nation, which inescapably infringes their rights as free and equal citizens.

The Role of the Ulama

Clerical hegemony represents an impediment to the evolution of democracy in the Islamic Republic. It involves a kind of discrimination against the majority, it substitutes merit with status and bestows infallibility and holiness upon the rulers which in turn prevents them from being held to account or their authority being contested. In comparison, democracy is basically about restricting the powers of the ruler and enabling the public or their representatives to scrutinise his work. As maintained by Lord Acton: 'The danger is not that a particular class is unfit to govern. [...] Power tends to corrupt, and absolute power corrupts absolutely.'

Clerical domination was brought about by a certain chain of events rather than a predetermined policy; however, it has been substantially aided by a large body of literature claiming the superiority of the ulama, in addition to the natural disposition to power in every group. Emphasis on the clerical hegemony reached a point where Ayatollah Beheshti, a notable revolutionary leader, asserted that the ulama 'will continuously and determinately supervise the political process. All the executives must accept this supervision or surrender their positions to those who accept'.[4]

The role of the clergy is deeply seated in the social culture where adherence to religion symbolises the highest personal credentials. In the early phase of the revolution, people seem to have trusted religious leaders as humble and graceful persons regardless of their ability to deliver on their promises. In traditional societies, and especially during revolutionary periods, persons rather than ideas tend to gain the focus of public attention. Since the mid-1980s, the clerical role took a downturn; the clerical representation in parliament has dropped from 45.4 per cent in the first two terms (1980–8) to 28.7 and 25 per cent in the third and fourth terms.[5] In the 2004 elections the clergy won forty-one seats, or 18 per cent of the total. Field research by Rafi'pour found that, although the belief in religion, in the broader sense, was still strong among the general people, it was no longer associated with a similar trust in the ulama or interest in the lifestyle they propagate.[6] In comparison, the 1990s saw religious intellectuals emerging as an influential group, especially among the youth. According to an official survey in 2004, the religious speeches given on the state TV by lay thinkers attracted more watchers than the ones given by clergy members.[7]

The decline of clerical popularity will certainly affect their political role. However, a major shift in this regard is not likely to occur soon unless the notions of equal opportunities and accountability are firmly institutionalised. Democratisation primarily requires that roles be linked to merit rather than status, and privileges be offset by accountability and responsibility.

Equality

In a democratic system all individuals are potentially equal. It is understood that people are usually different in various respects with the effect that some of them get more opportunities than others. Nevertheless, the law must ensure potential equality and help the less advantaged to achieve the same conditions enjoyed by the average citizens. In the case of Iran, the law restricts the right to assume the highest office in the state not only to the Shi'i citizens who up make the sweeping majority of the population but also to the male ulama, which constitute just a small fraction of the society. In a recent ruling by the Constitutional Council, women were denied the right to contest for the presidency, although the Constitution does not plainly define the gender of the president. The Constitution opts for equal citizen-based rights for all the Iranians, but it has also some elements that directly conflict with this principle. These elements are affirmed by the lack of democratic traditions in society. The treatment of women and ethnic minorities provides clear evidence on the implications of such discriminatory traditions.

Initially, traditional jurisprudence denies women eligibility to hold public authority, or the so-called *wilayah*. One of the interesting things about the Islamic Republic is that, although its leaders promote a kind of sexist society, their strategy of 'Islamising' the universities has unleashed a fresh desire among the rural families to allow their girls to move away from their villages to join the city-based universities. The number of female students tripled during the 1990s, a development that deeply enhanced the feminist movement and undermined the traditional pattern of socialisation.[8] In 2003 the debate over women's rights reached a climax with the predominantly-Reformist Majlis ratifying the United Nations' Convention on the Elimination of all forms of Discrimination against Women (CEDAW). Fierce argument from both factions provided an opportunity to reveal the division within the religious seminaries over such a sensitive issue. As expected, the majority of conservative clergy and politicians stood against the Convention while it was supported by the Reformists.[9] Ratification of the bill was blocked by the Constitutional Council. Nevertheless, the debate continued to attract more participants. Ayatollah Sane'i, an exemplar with Reformist inclinations, made a breakthrough by ruling that woman was eligible to assume all the public offices that were available for man. He also ruled that a woman and a man were equal in blood money (*Diyah*). In his view, the distinction between man and woman in this respect was not indefinite; it was made to meet the particular economic conditions of the early Islamic period.[10]

The debate over women's rights showed promising signals due mainly to the robust activities by the feminist movement. In 2004 the Zainab Association, the main conservative women's organisation, joined the campaign for women's eligibility to assume the presidency, implying a major shift within the conservative trend.[11] Karroubi, the former Majlis speaker,[12] and Zibakalam, a university professor,[13] are of the opinion that reservations in this regard are oriented upon the sexist character of the religious seminaries rather than religious principles in the strict sense. Both are adamant that society shows an increasing tendency to recognise equal rights for women, and sooner or later Iranian women will obtain full rights.

The handling of ethnic diversity represents one of the intrinsic deficits in the Iranian political system. The Islamic Republic bears a responsibility to do away with this defect, not only to meet the criteria of a modern state but also to honour its own commitment as a religious system. Iran's drive to democracy depends to a large extent upon its readiness to ensure equal rights for all citizens, regardless of their communal belongings. The minorities should be given extra attention in order to help them catch up with the average national lifestyle, growth and participation in the public affairs.

Iran is a multiethnic society. Persians represent the majority with nearly 45 per cent. The remainder includes around twelve ethnic groups. Turkish Azeris are the largest minority group with nearly 35 per cent of the total, followed by Kurds with 10 per cent, Arabs 5 per cent, Turkmens and Baluchis with 2.5 per cent each.[14] In respect of religion, Sunni Muslims represent the largest minority with around 10 per cent, Zoroastrian, Jewish, Christians, and Bahais make together nearly 1 per cent. The question of ethnic rights came to the fore first during the Constitutional Revolution as a reflection to the Azeris' significant contribution to that event. The demands of ethnic minorities were recognised by the 1906 Constitution, which adopted the system of regional governments as a means of redistributing power from the central government to the regional ones. In reality, the law of local government has never been implemented, and successive governments could not restrict its tendency to centralise. After the 1979 revolution, the Western regions witnessed insurgencies among the Arabs and Kurds. There were also signals of discontent among the Azeris and the Baluchis, all of which were crushed immediately. The ethnic issue does not represent an imminent threat to national security. Nevertheless, this is no guarantee in the long term; the situation may change in the future, especially with the recent revival of the ethnic identities in the Middle East and Central Asia.

The rights of the ethnic and religious minorities were recognised by the Constitution of the Islamic Republic through Articles 15, 19 and 48. Yet the current situation of the minorities is far from satisfactory. Except for the Azeris, the others are generally underrepresented in the state system, their regions are underdeveloped, and the right to freely express the differences specific to their identities is largely restricted or overlooked. Undoubtedly, this is a symptom of a common deficit in the region. In Iran, like all other Middle Eastern countries, the concepts of a multicultural society and of the state belonging to the whole nation are not deeply seated in the political culture and state structure. Minorities are viewed as 'others' by the majority, and their presence is dealt with as a problem or a possible source of problems rather than an opportunity for enriching the cultural diversity of the nation. To this extent, the secular governments of Turkey, Iraq and Syria do not differ from religious Iran or traditional Saudi Arabia. In all these cases, the national government is exclusively attributed to the majority and all 'the others' are treated as 'different' or second-class citizens.

In addition, there appears to be a correlation between the standard of living of the minorities and the distance of their regions from the country centres. Statistically, the most disadvantaged minorities in Iran are the Kurds, Arabs and Baluchis, all of whom live in peripheral areas. This location involves two damaging implications; on the one hand, the Middle Eastern state is highly centralised and urban-based in the sense that national affairs as well as the allocation of resources are conducted from the centre and by the centre-based elite. On the other hand, and due particularly to the inherent sense of insecurity among the ruling elites, the inhabitants of frontiers are usually seen as a possible conduit of outside problems, especially when it occurs among their fellows on the other side of the border. In the case of Iran, the state's treatment of the Kurds is a reflection of the insurgency of their fellow Kurds in Turkey and Iraq. The same can be said about the Sunni minority in the east and southeast after the rise of the Taliban in Afghanistan, and the Arabs during the war with Iraq.

The rise of the Islamic Republic has produced a sense of optimism based on the presupposition that an Islamic state would likely call off the discrimination which was common under the previous regime. This supposition was not realistic for it disregarded the structural impediments whose removal required more than the rhetoric or even the constitutional acknowledgment of the minorities' rights.[15]

For Bani-taraf, an Arab writer and activist from Khouzistan, culture is the main area of discrimination. He argues that the state's disregard of the minorities' cultures has resulted in them failing to make use of the available resources in such fields as education and economic development. In the Arab regions, for instance, 33 per cent of the pupils in primary schools quit before finishing. The figure reaches 50 per cent in the middle schools and 60 to 70 per cent in the high schools. In 2003, Arab university students comprised 1.5 of every 1,000 students nationwide. This figure is by no means comparable to the one of the Baluchi community, which counts only five in 10,000.[16]

The demands of the minorities were substantially aided by the Reformists' rise, especially with their assertion of the principle: 'Iran for all the Iranians'. Both the Arab and Kurds were represented in the cabinet of President Khatami. The role of the minorities, their concerns and their share of national development were first addressed in a comprehensive and explicit fashion through the Fourth Five-Year Development Plan (2005–9). In the theorising process for the plan, the issue of 'ethnicity and development' was put forward as one of eighteen grounding principles for long-term development. Representatives of the larger minorities participated in the Conference of Country's Theorists and Researchers, which was held in 2002 by the state's Planning Organisation to discuss the major goals that the plan was set to achieve. During the three-day conference, five papers were dedicated to the rights and demands of the minorities.

Recent political advances of the Iraqi Kurds seem to have had a profound impact on their fellow Iranians. In a recent development, a meeting held by one hundred Kurd activists spelled out a set of high-flying demands. The meeting, which was organised by the Reformist faction, urged the Kurdish community to use their voting power in the presidential elections of 2005 to impose their demands. In a speech before the meeting, Abdullah Ramadhan-Zadeh, a Kurdish activist and the cabinet's spokesman, put this argument:

> Kurds have around three million votes to cast in the coming presidential election, which can make a big difference. We should not give our votes for free ... We can exchange them with certain demands, including an appropriate share in the public administration. The Sunni community in particular has to be fairly represented in the cabinet, in the embassies and regional governments. Incomes in the Kurdish regions are the lowest nationally. The presidential candidates have to pledge extra allocations to address this deprivation.[17]

A similar initiative was taken by the leaders of the Balushi community, who held a meeting in Tehran and made extensive attempts to lobby the presidential candidates. In brief, the structural change within Iran and the parallel change of political weight of the ethnic groups in the countries surrounding Iran have both contributed to the revival of ethnic identities in the country. These developments will inevitably undermine the centre-periphery relations and the established domination of one culture. The Islamic Republic will have to redefine its conception of state-society relations so to get rid of the type of majority-minority relations that have prevailed for a very long time. This is necessary not only to boost the process of democratisation but also to maintain the religious credentials of the regime. It is absolutely unthinkable that the claim of religious character runs side by side with discrimination. To deal with this problem, Iran needs more than the rhetoric or even the constitutional acknowledgment of the grievances and rights of the minorities. The problem is so deeply seated in the social and political structure, it can only be cured through a comprehensive and far-reaching strategy aiming to enable the minorities to catch up with the national average of development and participation. Such an objective can be achieved only through recognising the identities and cultures of the minorities and ensuring an appropriate involvement in the state administration, the allocation of economic and other resources, and helping them to have a voice in national politics.

The Islamic Republic has the potential to evolve into a democratic political system. Nevertheless, there is much work to be done to arrive at that point. Firstly, it has to put forward democracy as its ultimate choice. Secondly, it has to redefine the grounding principles and institutions of its political system so as to come in line with the democratic patterns of government and socialisation. Thirdly, it has to make extra efforts to deal with the components of authoritarianism, discrimination and suppression, which are inherent in the social and political structure.

In the Islamic Republic, Islam is at stake. A vigorous push towards democracy will put an end to the contention over the capacity of religion to foster modernity. In contrast, any reluctance, with whatever justification, will damage not only the credibility of the religious establishment but also the credibility of the religion itself. Modernisation and democratisation are long and continuous processes. The complete transformation of a traditional society requires time and enormous efforts. Nevertheless, it would be much easier with the existence of a model of transformation with a strong appeal to the public and viable capacity for producing solutions to the unforeseen problems.

Notes

Introduction
1. Richard Bulliet, 'Twenty Years of Islamic Politics', *The Middle East Journal*, vol. 53, no. 2 (Spring 1999).

Chapter One
1. Abdulaziz Sachedina, *The Just Ruler in Shi'ite Islam* (New York, 1988) p. 231.
2. Etan Kohlberg, 'The Evolution of the 'Shi'a', in Kohlberg, *Belief and Law in Imami Shi'ism* (Hampshire, UK, 1991) article I, p. 4.
3. Montgomery William Watt, *The Formative Period of Islamic Thought* (Edinburgh, 1973) p. 38.
4. David Morgan, *Medieval Persia 1040–1797* (London, 1988) p. 160.
5. For a detailed account on the annual memorial ceremony (*Ta'zia*), see Heinz Halm, *Shi'a Islam: From Religion to Revolution*, translated by A. Brown (Princeton, 1996) pp. 41–85.
6. Yann Richard, *Shi'ite Islam*, translated by A. Nevill (Oxford, 1995) p. 29.
7. J. Welhausen, *The Religio-Political Factions in Early Islam*. ed. R. Ostle, translated by R. Ostle and S. Walzer. (Amsterdam, 1975) p. 116.
8. Kohlberg, p 3.
9. Sachedina, p. 26.
10. Kohlberg, p. 4.
11. Ya'qubi, Ahmad, *Tarikh al-Ya'qubi*, (Qum, 1984) vol. 2, p. 325.
12. Welhausen, p. 165.
13. Hassan Hassan, *Tarikh al-Islam*. (Cairo, 1964) vol. 3, p. 193.
14. Hashim M. al-Hasani, *Sirat al-Ayemmah al-Ithnai 'Ashar* (Beirut, 1990) vol. 2, p. 246.
15. On the works of al-Sadiq and his disciples, and especially the so-called four hundred sources *(a s l)*, see Etan Kohlberg, 'Al-Usul al-arbaumia' (Hampshire, UK, 1991) article VII, pp. 128–66.
16. Abdulhadi al-Fadli, *Tarikh al-Tashri'e al-Islami* (London, 1992) p. 206.
17. Halm, p. 24.
18. 'Allamah Jamal al-Din Hilli, *Al-Alfain* (Kuwait, 1985) p. 200.
19. Ya'qubi, p. 349.
20. Shaikh Muhammad al-Mufid, *Al-Irshad* (Tehran, n.d.) vol. 2, p. 185. See also Abu al-Faraj al-Isfahani, *Maqatel al-Talibyyin* (Beirut, 1987) p. 140.
21. Al-Fadl al-Tabarsi, *I'lam al-Wara* (Najaf, n.d.) p. 279.
22. M. ibn Jarir al-Tabari, *Tarikh al-Umam wa al-Muluk* (Beirut, 1967) vol. 7, p. 601.
23. Montgomery William Watt, 'The Significance of Early Stage of Imami Shi'ism', in N. Keddi (ed.), *Religion And Politics in Iran*. (New Haven, 1983) p. 23.
24. Montgomery William Watt, *The Formative Period*, p. 54.

25. Muhammad bin Yaqub Kulaini, *Al-Kafi* (Beirut, 1990) vol. 2, p. 287.

26. Sachedina, p. 90.

27. Kulaini, vol. 1, p. 430.

28. Bodiur Rahman, 'Responsibility for Action in an Early Historical Document of Islam', *The Islamic Quarterly*, vol. 34, no. 4, 1990, pp. 235–45.

29. Ignaz Goldziher, *Muslim Studies*, translated by C. R. Barber & S. M. Stern, edited by Stern. (London, 1971) pp. 93–4.

30. Al-Sharif 'ali al-Murtada, *Rasael al-Sharif al-Murtada* (Qum, 1984) vol. 2, p. 264. On Shi'i theology of the designated imamate, see 'Allama Tabataba'i, 'The Imams and the Imamate', in Nasr, Dabashi and Nasr (ed.), *Shi'ism: Doctrine, Thought and Spirituality* (New York, 1988) pp. 156–67.

31. Kulaini, vol. 1, p. 433.

32. Sachedina, p. 62.

33. Kulaini, p. 294.

34. Said Arjomand, *The Shadow Of God and the Hidden Imam* (Chicago, 1984) pp. 58–9.

35. Marshall Hodgson, 'How Did the Early Shi'a Become Sectarian', *Journal of the American Oriental Society*, 75, no. 1, January–March 1995, p. 12.

36. Muhammad Tusi, *Al-Iqtisad fima Yata'allaq be al-I'tiqad* (Beirut, 1986) pp. 233–4.

37. This supposition was implied in many rules endorsed by early Shi'a jurists. For instance, religious taxes (*zakat)* and (*khums)* were advised to be reserved until the hidden imam reappeared, and followers were to retain swords to show their readiness to join the imam's army, and so on. See al-Shaykh al-Mufid, *Al-Muqne'ah* (Qum, 1990) p. 286.

38. Jassim Hussain, *The Occultation of the Twelfth Imam*, Chapter Three. (E. edition, retrieved 7 October 2003 from www.yamahdi.com/books/pdf/occultation)

39. Muhammad bin Ali al-Saduq, *Kamal al-Din* (Qum, 1995) the preface, and vol.1, p. 126.

40. Hamid Algar, 'The Oppositional Role of the 'ulama in Twentieth-Century Iran', in N. Keddie, *Scholars, Saints, Sofis* (Berkeley, 1972) p. 232.

41. Tusi.

42. Muhammad H. Najafi, *Jawahir al-Kalam* (Tehran, 1988) vol. 22, p. 182.

43. Murtada Ansari, *Kitab Al-Makasib* (Qum, 1999) vol.3, p. 554.

44. Yousif al-Bahrani, *Al-Hadaeq al-Nazerah* (Beirut, 1993) vol. 25, p. 488.

45. Algar.

46. Kohlberg, 'The Evolution of the Shi'a', p. 14.

47. Kohlberg, p. 15.

48. Shahrough Akhavi, *Religion and Politics in Contemporary Iran* (Albany, 1980) p. 11.

49. Halm, p. 99.

50. Mohammad Moezzi, *Divine Guide in Early Shi'ism* (Albany, 1994) p. 125.

51. 'Abbas al-Qummi, *Al-Kuna wa al-Alqab* (Tehran, 1989) vol. 1 p. 199. Both 'Umani and Iskafi lived in the second half of the tenth century; there is no definite date for their death, yet Tehrani reluctantly puts Iskafi's death at 381AD/991. See: Tehrani, Agha Buzurg, *al-Thari'ah ela Tasanif al-Shi'a* (Beirut, 1983) vol. 14, p. 259. For more information on the two scholars, see Muhsin al-Amin, *A'yan al-Shi'ah* (Beirut, 1986) vol. 2, p. 212.

52. Halm admits that Shi'a scholars were spiritually influential during this period. However, its institutional form has emerged only during the Safavid era (Halm, p. 108). This assumption has also been held by other writers (see for example the account of Arjomand, p. 211).

53. Halm, p. 88.

54. Halm, p. 94.
55. Tusi, *Al-Iqtisad*, p. 297.
56. Al-Mufid, *al-Muqne'ah*, p. 810.
57. Arjomand, p. 63.
58. This treatise was translated into English by Wilferd Madelung: 'A Treatise of the Sharif al-Murtada on the Legality of Working for the Government (*Mas'ala fi 'l-'amal ma'a 'l-sultan*)', *Bulletin of the School of Oriental and African Studies*, vol. 43, no. 1 (1980) pp. 18–31.
59. Arjomand, p. 65.
60. Abu al-Hassan Mawardi, *Al-Ahkam al-Sultaniyyah wa al-Wilayat al-Diniyyah* (Qum, 1986) p. 247.
61. 'Ali Kashif al-Ghita, *Al-Nur al-Sati'* (Najaf, 1961) vol. 1, p. 504.
62. Hussayn Montazeri, *Dirasat fi Wilayat al-Faqih* (Beirut, 1988) vol. 2, p. 259.
63. M. Baqer Sadr, *Al-Ma'alim al-Jadidah li'l-Usul* (Beirut, 1981) p. 62.
64. Halm, p. 101 A.
65. Halabi, Abu al-Salah, *Al-Kafi fi al-Fiqh* (Isfahan, 1983) pp. 420–3.
66. Al-Muhaqqiq al-Hilli, *Sharie' al-Islam* (Tehran, 1990) vol. 1, p. 138. This assertion concerned particularly the authority of the mujtahid to manage the religious taxes (*khums*) in his capacity as deputy of the imam.
67. Arjomand, p. 141.
68. Al-Muhaqqiq al-Hilli, p. 260.
69. Richard, p. 78.
70. Halm, pp. 106–8.
71. 'Ali Karaki, *Jami' al-Maqasid fi Sharh al-Qawa'id* (Qum, 1988) vol. 11, p. 266.
72. Hamid Enayat, 'Iran: Khumayni's Concept of the Guardianship of the Jurisconsult', in James Piscatori (ed.), *Islam in the Political Process* (Cambridge, 1984) p. 161.
73. 'Ali 'Qati'at al-Lijaj' Karaki, in Mahmoud Bustani (ed) *Al-Kharajiat* (Qum, n.d.), p. 56.
74. Arjomand, p. 136.
75. Hassan Romlo, *Ahsan al-Tawarikh* (Tehran, 1978) vol. 12, p. 249.
76. Arjomand, p. 130.
77. Juan R. Cole, 'Imami Jurisprudence and the Role of the Ulema', in N. Keddi, *Religion And Politics*, p. 40.
78. Morgan, p. 159.
79. N. Keddie, 'The Roots of the 'ulama's Power in Modern Iran' in Keddie, *Scholars, Saints, Sofis*, p. 213.
80. Abdulhadi Hairi, 'The Legitimacy of Early Qajar Rule Viewed by the Shi'i Religious Leaders', *Middle Eastern Studies*, vol. 24, 1998, p. 272.
81. Mahdi Radawi, in Mirza Qummi, *Jame'-al-Shetat* (Tehran, 1991) vol. 1, p. 24.
82. Amin, vol. 4, p. 99.
83. Ja'far Kashif al-Ghita, *Kashf al-Ghita* (Isfahan, n.d.) p. 394.
84. Ibid.
85. Ibid.
86. Ibid.
87. Ahmad Naraqi, *'Awaid al-Ayyam* (Qum, 1988) p. 186.
88. Ibid. pp. 190–2.
89. Ibid. pp. 188–9.
90. Ibid.
91. Tawfiq Alsaif, *Nazariat al-Sulta fi al-Fiqh al-Shi'i* (Beirut, 2002) pp. 172–6, 185–91.
92. Ayatollah Khomeini, *Kitab al-Bay'* (Qum, 1985) vol. 2, p. 461. The weakness of

the above narrations was admitted by Khomeini in his study of the principles of jurisprudence. See Ja'far Subhani (ed.), *Tahthib al-Usul* (Qum, 2000), p. 85.

93. Halm, p. 120.
94. Cole, p. 34.
95. Cole, p. 46.
96. Ansari, p. 553.
97. Murtada Ansari, *Kitab al-Qada wa al-Shahadat* (Qum, 1993) p. 47.
98. Akhund M. Khurasani, *Hashiat al-Makasib* (Tehran, 1986) p. 92.
99. Muhammad Bahr al-'Ulum, *Bulghat al-Faqih* (Tehran, 1984) vol. 3, p. 215.
100. Ansari, *Kitab al-Makasib*, vol.3, p. 556–7.
101. Ibid. p. 553.
102. Ibid. p. 560.
103. Ibid. p. 552.
104. On the career of Mirza Muhammad Hassan Shirazi, see Meir Litvak, *Shi'i Scholars of Nineteenth-Century Iraq* (Cambridge, 1988) p. 84.
105. N. Keddie, 'Iran, Understanding the Enigma: A Historian's View', *Middle East Review of International Affairs Journal*, vol. 2, no. 3, September 1998. (Retrieved from www.ciaonet.org/olj/meria/meria98_keddie.html)
106. Jamilah Kadivar, *Tahavule Goftaman Siasi Shi'a dar Iran* (Tehran, 2000) p. 208.
107. For a background on the positions of the clerical groups, see Said Arjomand (ed.), *Authority and Political Culture in Shi'ism* (Albany, 1988) p. 180.
108. Lahidji was among the few researchers who undervalued the role of the clergy in the Constitutional Revolution. He argued they were not the leaders nor were they informedly Constitutionalist. Lahidji, Abdol Karim, 'Constitutionalism and the Clerical Authority' in Arjomand, pp. 133–58.
109. M. Isma'il Mahallati, 'Al-La'ali al-Marboutah fi Wujub al-Mashrutah', in Zargarinajad, G. (ed.), *Rasael Mashroutiat* (Tehran, 1995) p. 525.
110. M. H. Na'ini, 'Tanbih al-Umma wa Tanzih al-Millah' in Tawfiq Alsaif (ed.), *Dhidd al-Istibdad* (Beirut, 1999) pp. 252–9.
111. The treatise of Na'ini (An Admonishment to the Nation and Exoneration of the Faith) was first published in 1908–9 in Najaf, Iraq. On the major elements of the book, see Algar, p. 238.
112. Khurasani, p. 92.
113. Halm, p. 126.
114. Murtada, *Tanzih al-Anbia* (Beirut, 1989) p. 139.
115. Muhammad 'Amili, *Al-Qawa'ed wal-Fawaed* (Qum, n.d.) vol. 1, p. 406. Sayuri, Miqdad, *Nadhed al-Qawa'id al-Fiqhia* (Qum, 1982) p. 492.

Chapter Two

1. This treatise was proposed in the form of thirteen scholarly lectures given in Najaf in January and February 1970. Shortly afterwards, it was published and smuggled into Iran. In 1977 it was published in Iran under the title of *Letters from Imam Mosavi Kashif al-Ghita* without stating the author's name.
2. Ja'far Subhani, *Tahthib al-Usul* (Qum, n.d.) vol. 3, p. 146.
3. Rohollah Khomeini, *Sahifeh Nur.* Compiled by the Institute for Compilation and Publication of the Works of Imam Khomeini (Tehran, 2004). (An e. version is available on the web address: www.ghadeer.org/index.html)
4. Hamid Algar, *The Fusion of the Gnostic and the Political in the Personality and Life of Imam Komeini* (Retrieved from www.khomeini.com/GatewayToHeaven/Articles/PersonalityofImam.html) A list of Khomeini's works is available on www.ghadeer.org/imam/imam.html.

5. On the development of Khomeini's political thought, see S. A. Nabavi, 'Tatavur-e Andishah Imam Khomeini', *Faslnamah Imam Sadiq*, no. 6, (Summer and Autumn 1998). (An e. edition retrieved on 3 June 2004 from www.hawzah.net/Per/ Magazine/IS/006/is00604.htm)

6. Hamid Enayat, 'Iran: Khumayni's Concept of the Guardianship of the Jurisconsult' in Piscatori, *Islam in the Political Process* (Cambridge, 1983) pp. 160–80.

7. Ervand Abrahamian, *Khomeinism: Essays on the Islamic Republic* (Berkeley, 1993).

8. Mohsen Kadivar, *Hukumat-e Walai-e* (Tehran, 2001).

9. Leonard Binder, *Islamic Liberalism*, p. 41.

10. David Held, *Political Theory and the Modern State*, p. 120.

11. David Easton, 'An Approach to the Analysis of Political Systems', *World Politics*, vol. 9, issue 3 (April 1957) pp. 386–7.

12. Taketsugu Tsurutani, 'Stability and Instability', *The Journal of Politics*, vol. 30, no. 4. (November 1968) p. 911.

13. G. Almond, 'A Developmental Approach to Political Systems', *World Politics*, vol. 17, issue 2, (January 1965) p. 192.

14. David Apter, *The Politics of Modernisation* (Chicago, 1965) pp. 66–8.

15. Held, p. 88.

16. G. Razi, 'Legitimacy, Religion, and Nationalism in the Middle East', *The American Political Science Review*, vol. 84, no. 1 (March 1990) p. 72.

17. Andrew Heywood, *Political Ideologies* (New York, 1998) p. 291.

18. D. Eickelman and J. Piscatori, *Muslim Politics* (Princeton, 1996) p. 24.

19. D. Billings and S. Scott, 'Religion and Political Legitimation', *Annual Review of Sociology*, vol. 20 (1994) p. 173.

20. Homa Omid, *Islam and the Post-Revolutionary State in Iran* (New York, 1994) p. 20.

21. For a brief assessment of said programme, see James Bill, 'Modernisation and Reform from Above: The Case of Iran', *The Journal of Politics*, vol. 32, issue 1 (February 1970) pp.19–40.

22. Azar Tabari, 'Shi'i Clergy in Iranian Politics' in Keddie N. (ed.), *Religion and Politics in Iran* (London, 1983) p. 60.

23. Richard Cottam, 'The Islamic Revolution' in N. Keddie, and J. Cole (ed.), *Shi'ism and Social Protest* (New Haven, 1986) pp. 76–7.

24. H. Bashiriyeh, *Mavane' Tawse'ah Siasi dar Iran* (Tehran, 2001) p. 133.

25. L. Binder, 'National Integration and Political Development', *The American Political Science Review*, vol. 58, issue 3 (September 1964) p. 631.

26. S. Arjomand, *The Turban for the Crown* (New York, 1989) pp. 77–8.

27. H. Algar, *The Fusion*.

28. Cottam, p. 78.

29. Misagh Parsa, *State, Ideologies and Social Revolutions* (Cambridge, 2000) p. 140.

30. Carl Brown, *Religion and State: The Muslim Approach to Politics* (New York, 2000) p. 169.

31. Cottam, p. 82.

32. S. Abed, 'Islam and Democracy', in D. Garnham and M. Tessler (ed.), *Democracy, War and Peace in the Middle East* (Indianapolis, 1995) p. 121.

33. See Enayat, p. 172.

34. Khomeini, Rohollah, *Sahifeh Nur*, vol. 21, p. 34.

35. Khomeini, p. 88.

36. Muhammad Shabestar, *Naqdi bar Qara'at-e Rasmi az Din* (Tehran, 2000) pp. 168–71.

37. In comparison, Arjomand argues that no doctrine of illegitimacy of government

during the Occultation can be found in Shi'i legal literature for the entire period of the eighteenth and nineteenth centuries. Said Arjomand, *The Shadow of God and The Hidden Imam* (Chicago, 1984) p. 234.

38. Arjomand, p. 267.
39. S. Akhavi, *Religion and Politics in Contemporary Iran* (Albany, 1980) p. 60.
40. For more details on the topic, see T. Alsaif, *Nazariat al-Sultah fi al-Fiqh al-Sh i'i* (Beirut, 2002) pp. 135–46.
41. M. Momen, 'Authority and Opposition in Twelver Shi'ism', in Burrell, R. M. (ed.). *Islamic Fundamentalism*, a paper read at a seminar held at the School of Oriental and African Studies, 10 March 1988, p. 53.
42. Muhammad B. Sadr, 'Al-Ittijahat al-Mustaqbaliyah le-Harakat al-Ijtihad', *Al-Hadi*, (Qum), vol. 2, no. 3, March 1973. (Retrieved on August 22 2003 from http://209.61.210.137/uofislam/behoth/behoth_isol/06.htm)
43. A. Sachedina, *The Just Ruler in Twelver Shi'ism*, (New York, 1988) p. 26.
44. 'Allama Na'ini, 'Tanbih al-Ummah wa Tanzih al-Millah' in Alsaif, *Dhidd al-Istebdad* (Beirut, 1999) p. 255.
45. Khomeini, *Islamic Government* (Tehran, n.d.) translated by Hamid Algar, p. 25. (Retrieved on 5 March 2003 from http://users.fmg.uva.nl/rsetoe/pdfs/velayat_faqeeh.pdf)
46. Khomeini, p. 19.
47. This argument was held by many scholars including M. H. Najafi, *Jawahir al-Kalam*, vol. 21, p. 397, and M. Ansari, *Al-Makasib*, vol. 1, p. 410.
48. Khomeini, *Kitab al-Bay'* (Qum, 1994) vol. 2, p. 461.
49. Khomeini, *Sahifeh*, vol. 18, p. 181.
50. See for example Najafi.
51. Khomeini, *Kitab al-Bay'*.
52. Sachedina, p. 231.
53. 'Allama Jamal al-Din Hilli, *Al-Alfain* (Kuwait, 1985) p. 65.
54. M. Bahr al-Ulum, *Bulghat al-Faqih*, vol. 3, p. 215.
55. Hilli, p. 200.
56. H. Montazeri, *Dirasat fi Wil a yat al-Faq i h* (Beirut, 1988) vol. 1, p. 527.
57. Na'ini, p. 256.
58. See for example the account of Agha Riza Hamadani on public resources (kharaj) in his *Misbah al-Faqih* (Qum, n.d.) vol. 3, p. 108.
59. Ansari Murtada, *Kitab Al-Makasib*, vol. 3, pp. 553–4.
60. Suroush has made an interesting differentiation between the esoteric and political connotations of the term of wilayah. He argues that the latter connotation is a mistaken derivation from the term. 'Abdol-karim Soroush, *Bast-e Tajrebah Nabavi* (Tehran, 1999) pp. 278–80.
61. Murtada, *Rasael*, vol. 2, p. 90.
62. Khomeini, R., *Misbah al-Hidayah ela al-Khilafat-e wa al-Wilayah*. p. 76. (E. edition retrieved 5 March, 2003 from www.al-kawthar.com/kotob/mesbah.zip)
63. Khomeini, *Islamic Government*, p. 35.
64. For an esoterically oriented definition of existential authority, see Khomeini, *Misbah*, pp. 84–90.
65. Khomeini, *Kitab al-Bay'*, vol. 2, pp. 466–7. In this argument, Khomeini elaborates on a narration attributed to the first Imam, 'Ali ibn Abi-Talib. See Shareef Al-Radi, *Nahj al-Balaghah*, p. 80.
66. Ibid.
67. For details on the topic and the various opinions of Shi'a scholars, see Alsaif (2002), p. 273.

68. Khomeini, vol. 3, pp. 13–6.
69. Khomeini, *Sahifeh*, vol. 20, p. 170.
70. Cited in Arusta, M., Ehtemam beh Aray-e 'Umumi, *Hukumat-e Islami*, no. 17, Autumn 2000.
71. Qaemmaqami, 'Abbas, *Qudrat wa Mashrou'iat* (Tehran, 2000) p. 116.
72. Khomeini, p. 170.
73. Hall, S., 'The State in Question', in Hall, S., Held, D. and McLennan, G., *The Idea of Modern State* (London, 1984) p. 7.
74. Bendix, Reinhard, 'Reflections on Charismatic Leadership', *Asian Survey*, vol. 7, no. 6 (June 1967) p. 343.
75. Claude Ake, 'Charismatic Legitimation and Political Integration', *Comparative Studies in Society and History*, vol. 9, no. 1 (October 1966) p. 2.
76. Cited in Ake, p. 1.
77. S. Hajjarian, *Az Shahed-e Qudsi ta Shahed-e Bazaari* (Tehran, 2001) pp. 113–4.
78. Khomeini, *Islamic Government*, p. 23.
79. Khomeini, *Sahifah Nur,* vol. 13, p. 9.
80. Khomeini, *Islamic Government*, p. 86.
81. Cited in 'Fatawa-ye Imam', (editorial) *Hawzah*, issue 23 (December 1987).
82. 'Aliakbar Kalantari, *Hukm Thanavi dar Tashri'e Islami,* Chapter Two. (E. edition accessed 8 February 2004 from www.balagh.org/lib/farsi/08_feqh/01/hokm-i%20 thanavi%20dar%20tashri-i%20islami/04.htm)
83. Hajjarian, p. 120.
84. Enayat, p. 168.
85. On the jurisprudential implications of legislation by fallible man, see Sachedina, p. 25.

Chapter Three
1. Thomas Kuhn, *The Structure of Scientific Revolutions* (London, 1970) p. 160.
2. Ibid. p. 80.
3. Ibid. p. 84.
4. Ibid. p. 150.
5. Ibid. p. 98.
6. Ibid. p. 160.
7. Mark Smith, *Social Science in Question* (London, 1998) p. 198.
8. John Esposito, *Islam and Politics* (New York, 1987) p. 194.
9. Mohammad Mohaddessin, *Islamic Fundamentalism: The New Global Threat* (Washington, 1993) p. 19.
10. Esposito, p. 195.
11. A. Nikpay, 'Ideology, Din, va Enqelab-e Iran', *Matin*, nos 3 & 4 (Summer 1999). (Retrieved on 10 March, 2003 from: www.hawzah.net/Per/Magazine/mt/003/ mt00316.htm)
12. See, for example, H. Bashirieh, *Mavane' Tawse'ah Siasi dar Iran,* p. 133.
13. Renani, 'Tathir-e Qanun-e Asasi bar Sakhtar-e Eqtesad-e Siasi-e Iran', *Iran* (5 May 2004).
14. Mehran Kamrava, *Revolutionary Politics* (London, 1992) p. 67.
15. Sehabi, E., in Amavi, B., *Ektesad-e Siasi-e Jumhouri-e Islami* (Tehran, 2003) 9–58, pp. 42–6.
16. Sehabi, p. 51.
17. H. Dabashi, 'The End of Islamic Ideology', *Social Research,* vol. 67, no. 2 (Summer 2000) (Retrieved on 5 March, 2003 from www.findarticles.com/p/articles/mi_ m2267/is_2_67/ai_63787340)

18. R. al-Sayyid, *Al-Jama'ah wa al-Mujtama' wa al-Dawlah*, p. 364.
19. A. Al-Sharafi, 'Mushkelat al-Hukm fi al-Fikr al-Islami al-Hadith', *al-Ijtihad*, no. 14 (Winter 1992) p. 70.
20. H. Montazeri, *Dirasat fi Wilayat al-Faqih*, vol. 2, p. 300.
21. Hassan Turabi, *Hewarat fi al-Islam, al-Dimuqratiyya, al-Dawlah, al-Gharb* (Beirut, 1995) p. 151.
22. Al-Sayyid, p. 412.
23. Khomeini, *Islamic Government*, p. 88.
24. Ibid. p. 86.
25. Ibid. p. 29.
26. Ibid. p. 31.
27. Ibrahim Yazdi, *Seh Jumhouri*, p. 404.
28. Hashemi Rafsanjani, *'Ubur az Buhran* (Tehran, 1999) p. 60.
29. M. Shabestari, *Naqdi bar Qaraat-e Rasmi az Din*, p. 65.
30. Muhammad Hakimi, Muhammad 'Ali, *Al-Hayat* (Qum, 1987) vol. 2, p. 356.
31. Kamrava, p. 27.
32. Kamrava, p. 35.
33. Kamrava, p. 73.
34. Mohsen Nourbakhsh, in Amavi, p. 62.
35. Rafi'pour, *Tavse'ah va Tazadd*, p. 124.
36. Yazdi, p. 421.
37. Wilfried Buchta, *Who Rules Iran*, (Washington DC, 2000), p. 11.
38. S. Hunter & D. Newsom, *Iran after Khomeini* (New York, 1992) p. 63.
39. This phrase and all the coming phrases between brackets and the quotation are from the Constitution's preamble. For more details, see Amuzegar, Jahangir, *Iran Economy under the Islamic Republic* (London, 1993) p. 26.
40. The whole clause is a summarised text of Article Three of the Constitution of the Islamic Republic.
41. David Miller, *Social Justice* (Oxford, 1979) p. 17.
42. Demetrius Iatridis, *Social Justice and the Welfare State in Central and Eastern Europe: The Impact of Privatization* (London, 2000) p. 8.
43. Miller, p. 255.
44. Ibid. p. 40.
45. John Rawls, *Political Liberalism* (New York, 1993) p. 326.
46. The other four are belief in the oneness of God, the Prophethood, Imamate and the Resurrection.
47. Murtaza Motahhari, *'Adl-e Elahi* (Tehran, 1993) p. 37.
48. Ayatollah Khamenei, communiqué on the first anniversary of the death of Ayatollah Khomeini (31 May 1990). (Retrieved on 2 November, 2004 from www.wilayah.net/pr/bayanat/speeches/68-69/bayan342.htm#link1439)
49. Ayatollah Khamenei, Friday Prayer Speech, (27 March 1980). (Retrieved on 2 November 2004 from www.hwzah.net/per/e/ef/efc/efcb/efcbw/efcbw.htm)
50. Hossein Bashiryeh, *The State and Revolution in Iran* (London, 1984) p. 174.
51. Misagh Parsa, 'Economic Development and Political Transformation', *Theory and Society*, vol. 14, no. 5 (September 1985) p. 668.
52. A. N. Khamushi, (President of Iran Chamber of Commerce and a former MP), interview, *Iran*, 3 August 2002.
53. Zanjani, in Amavi, p. 144.
54. Cited in Bashiryeh, p. 72.
55. M. Sadri, 'Dastan-e Degarguni dar Iran-2', *Donya-e Eqtesad*, (19 September 2004). (Retrieved from www.donya-e-eqtesad.com/83-06-29/070629.htm)

56. Al-Sharif al-Radi, *Nahj al-Balaghah,* edited by S. al-Saleh (Qum, 1975) p. 533.

57. Mosavi Tabrizi, 'Jiegah-e Hukumat dar Andisheh Emam', *Matin,* (Winter 1998). (Retrieved on 10 March 2003 from www.hawzah.net/Per/Magazine/MT/001/mt00116.htm) See also Khomeini, *Sahifeh Nur,* vol. 18, p. 186.

58. Hajjarian, *Az Shahed-e Qudsi,* p. 296.

59. 'Ali Rashidi, *Eqtesad-e Mardum-salar* (Tehran, 1997) pp. 58–63.

60. Ibid. p. 69.

61. M. Jenan-sefat, 'Sun'at-e Iran pas az Bahman 57', *Hamshahri,* 20 May 2002. (Retrieved from www.hamshahri.net/hamnews/1381/810230/econw.htm)

62. Ibid.

63. Amir Madani, *Mavane' Tavse'ah Eqtesadi Iran* (Tehran, 1995) p. 142. In 2003, the assets of Buniad Mostaz'afan included 384 firms active in industry, transport, civil engineering, tourism, agriculture, trade and finance, with a workforce of 60,000 employees. Al-Ishaq, the director of the corporation, cited in *Iran.* (4 January, 2003).

64. Jenan-sefat.

65. 'Ali Farazmand, *The State, Bureaucracy, and Revolution in Modern Iran* (London, 1989) p. 206.

66. Hunter and Newsom, pp. 62–3.

67. The text of the law is available on the official site of the Ministry of Jehad-e Keshavarzi (Agriculture). (Retrieved from www.frw.org.ir/fa/saruquz/darbure_suzmun/majmooe_qavunin/1359.htm)

68. *Vaqe'iat-ha va Qazavat-ha,* a book by an anonymous assistant of Ayatollah Montazeri in defence of his position. (Retrieved July 2004 from: www.Montazeri.ws/farsi/vageiat/html/0010.htm#0078)

69. For some details on the related controversy, see Baktiari, Bahman, *Parliamentary Politics in Revolutionary Iran: The Institutionalization of Factional Politics* (Florida, 1996) pp. 84–92.

70. Farazmand, p. 213.

71. The World Bank, *Islamic Republic of Iran: An Agricultural Policy Note,* Report No. 29428-IR (22 June 2004) p. 5.

72. UN HDR 2004, http://hdr.undp.org/statistics/data/indic/indic_10_1_1.html

73. Rusta, M. & Ramazani, M., 'Barrasi Vaz'iat-e Tavzi' Daramad dar Iran', *Ettela'at Siasi Eqtesadi,* no. 177–8, (May–Jun., 2002) 250–63, p. 257. The figures are based on the statistics of the Centre for Statistics of Iran, but disputed by other sources. Compare with Rafi'pour, *Tavse'ah va Tazadd,* pp. 177–9.

74. Cited in Mark Robinson, 'Democracy, Participation and Public Policy: The Politics of Institutional Design', in Robinson, and White (eds), The *Democratic Developmental State: Politics and Institutional Design* (Oxford, 1998) p. 156.

75. Robinson, p. 157.

76. Richard Topf, 'Electoral Participation', in Fuchs, and Klingemann (eds), *Citizens and the State* (Oxford, 1995) p. 29.

77. Kamrava, p. 112.

78. Menasheri, *Post-Revolutionary Politics in Iran,* p. 68.

79. Vanessa Martin, *Creating an Islamic State: Khomeini and the Making of a New Iran* (New York, 2003) pp. 105–6.

80. Makarim Shirazi, *Buhuth Fiqhiah Muhemmah.* (Qum, n.d.) p. 472.

81. Shirazi, p. 476.

82. M. Salehi, *Insurgency through Culture and Religion: The Islamic Revolution of Iran* (New York, 1988) p. 151.

83. Ibid.

84. See in this regard, Homa Katouzian, *The Political Economy of Modern Iran* (New York, 1981).
85. Kamrava, p. 75.
86. For a brief account of the thoughts of Taleghani, see Manochehr Dorraj, *From Zarathustra to Khomeini: Populism and Dissent in Iran* (London, 1990) p. 153.
87. Sehabi, p. 46.
88. For some details on the Neighbourhood Councils, see Bayat, Asef, *Street Politics* (Cairo, 1997) p. 89. The book offers an insightful and first-hand account of the political action of the people, the lower classes in particular, during the formative period of the revolution.
89. Bayat, p. 94.
90. Cited in *Emrooz*, 20 January 2003.
91. Yazdi, p. 380.
92. Kazim Hairi, *Al-Marje'iah wa al-Qiadah* (Qum, 1998) pp. 91–3.
93. Yazdi, p. 344.
94. Hairi, p. 195.
95. Hashemi Rafsanjani, 'Diaries of 1362 (1983)', *Jam-e Jam*, (28 October 2002). (Retrieved from www.jamejamdaily.net/shownews2.asp?n=23061&t=book)
96. Rafsnajani, in Safiri, *Haqiqat-ha va Maslahat-ha*, p. 80.
97. Hashemi Rafsanjani, cited in *Baztab*, 18 January 2003.
98. Kamrava, p. 61.
99. Renani.
100. Amavi, p. 182.
101. Ibid.
102. Edmund Gareeb, 'The Roots of Crisis', in Joyner, Christopher, *The Persian Gulf War: Lessons for Strategy, Law, and Diplomacy* (New York, 1990) p. 22.
103. Ehteshami, p. 30.
104. Stephen Pelletiere, *The Iran-Iraq War: Chaos in a Vacuum* (New York, 1992) p. 141.
105. James Bill, 'Morale vs. Technology: The Power of Iran in the Persian Gulf War', in Farhang Rajai, *The Iran-Iraq War: The Politics of Aggression* (Gainesville, 1993) p. 201.
106. Iran-Iraq Ceasefire: UN Conducts Peace Talks in Geneva, New York, *UN Chronicle*, vol. 25, issue 4 (December 1988).
107. Khomeini, vol. 21, p. 46.
108. Hunter and Newsom, p. 73.
109. Sohrab Behdad, 'Foreign Exchange Gap, Structural Constraints, and the Political Economy of Exchange Rate Determination in Iran', *International Journal of Middle East Studies*, vol. 20, no. 1 (February 1988), p. 3.
110. Bashiriyeh, p. 174.
111. Ayatollah Jawadi Amoli, Friday Prayer speech, Qum, *Iran*, 15 June 2002.
112. Geneive Abdo, 'Re-Thinking the Islamic Republic: A "Conversation" with Ayatollah Hossein 'Ali Montazeri', *The Middle East Journal*, vol. 53, no. 4 (Autumn 1999).
113. Ehteshami, p. 30.
114. Muhammad H. Beheshti, public speech (late 1980), cited in *Kayhan*, 27 June 2004.
115. Homa Katouzian, 'Problems of Political Development in Iran', *British Journal of Middle Eastern Studies*, vol. 22, nos 1/2. (1995), p. 12.
116. Wilfried Buchta, *Who Rules Iran?* (Washington DC, 2000) p. 52.
117. Buchta, p. 11.
118. Hashemi Rafsanjani, *'Ubur az Buhran*, p. 60.
119. Cited in 'Fatawai-e Imam', (editorial) *Hawzah*, no. 23 (December 1987).
120. Robin Wright, *The Last Great Revolution* (New York, 2000) p. 21.

121. Amuzegar, p. 319.
122. Safiri, p. 158.
123. Amuzegar, p. 315.
124. Elton Daniel, *The History of Iran* (London, 2001) p. 230.
125. Amuzegar, p. 341.
126. Rashidi, p. 72.
127. M. Jenan-Sefat, 'Sun'at-e Khodro', *Hamshahri* (10 December 2002).
128. Rashidi, p. 161.
129. Statistical Centre of Iran, *Statistical Yearbook 1381*, tables 11.38, 8.16.
130. Ehteshami, p. 115.
131. D. Menasheri, 'Iran', in Ami Ayalon, *Middle East Contemporary Survey: 1993* (Boulder, 1995) p. 332.
132. Rafi'pour, p. 150.
133. Statistical Centre of Iran, *Statistical Year Book (1382)*, tables 17--14 and 17–20.
134. Menasheri, p. 332.
135. Kuhn, p. 206.
136. A. W. Samii, 'Sisyphus' Newsstand: the Iranian Press under Khatami', *MERIA*, vol. 5, no. 3 (September 2001). (Retrieved from: http://meria.idc.ac.il/journal/2001/issue3/jv5n3a1.html)
137. Reporters without Borders (organisation), 'Iran Annual Report 2003'. (Retrieved from www.rsf.org/article.php3?id_article=5382&var_recherche=iran)
138. For some information on the group, see H. Murtaja, *Jenah-haye Siasi dar Iran Emrooz*, p. 163. Also: A. Shadlo, *Ettela'ati darbareyeh Ahzab va Jenah-haye Siasi Iran Emrooz*, p. 179. On its violent propensities and relations with the other conservative factions, see *Iran*, 23 and 24 December 2003 (interview with M. Namaki). Also: *ISNA*, 27 May 2003. Also: *ILNA*, 6 December 2003. (Retrieved from: www.ilna.ir/shownews.asp?code=56176&code1=1)
139. See, for example, the results of the opinion poll regarding the legislative elections (January 2004). The official website of the Constitutional Council. (Retrieved from www.irisn.com/akhbar/1382/13821029/13821029_irisn_00005.htm). Other polls conducted by a conservative faction in March and April 2005, regarding the possible voting in the imminent presidential elections, gave the reformist candidate 16.6 per cent while the support of the conservative candidates have ranged from 13.8 to 5.8 per cent. The polls were contributed to by nearly 55,000 Internet-users inside Iran. *Baztab*, 14 April 2005. (Retrieved from www.baztab.com/news/23294.php)
140. M. Khatami, *Tavse'ah Siasi*, p. 41.
141. United Nations and IRI Plan and Budget Org., *Human Development Report of the Islamic Republic of Iran, 1992*, p. 132.
142. *Iran*, 20 January, 2003.
143. On the 1999 local elections and their implications, see Kian Tajbakhsh, 'Political Decentralization and the Creation of Local Government in Iran', *Social Research*, vol. 67, no. 2, (Summer 2000), pp. 377–404. For a statistical account on women's participation, see 'Women's Participation in Local Councils' in Baquer Namazi (ed.), *Iranian NGOs: Situation Analysis*, (2000). (Retrieved from: www.iranngos.org/reports/SituationAnalysis/009_10WomenPart.htm)
144. *Iran*, 22 August 2004, citing 'Ali Baqeri, GM of political affairs in the Internal Ministry.
145. *Emrooz*, 8 July 2003.
146. Shargh, 17 November 2003.
147. Namazi. (Retrieved from www.iranngos.org/reports/SituationAnalysis/003 Summary.htm)

148. Iran NGO Resource Centre (Hamyaran). (Retrieved from www.hamyaran.org/projs_activs/ngo_community_building.htm)
149. *IRNA*, 6 February 2003, and *ILNA*, 9 July 2004. (Retrieved from http://www.ilna.ir/shownews.asp?code=111738&code1=3)
150. Cited in *MOSNAD*. (Retrieved on 22 January 2005 from www.mosnad.com/News/telexu.htm)
151. *ISNA*, 3 November 2004. (Retrieved from www.isna.ir/news/NewsPrint.asp?id=451748)
152. *Iran*, 10 January 2005.
153. *Hamshahri*, 14 September 2002.
154. 'The Law for Attracting and Supporting Foreign Investment' was passed by the Parliament in March 2002 but rejected by the Council for the Maintenance of the Constitution. In May the Expediency Council rebuked the former council's arguments and endorsed the law. (See: www.gsi.ir/?lang=fa&p=26-06)
155. For details, see *Iran*, 4 August 2004.
156. *IRIB News*, 11 December 2004. (Retrieved from www.iribnews.ir/Full_en.asp?news_id=183904&n=14)
157. *Shargh*, 9 August 2004.

Chapter Four

1. Mohsen Hajari, 'Muqaddamah bar Sinkh-shenasi Rast dar Iran', interview, *Chashm-andaz Iran*. vol. 9 (June 2001) p. 59.
2. H. Shari'atmadari, *Kayhan*, 21 August 2004, p. 2. (Retrieved from www.kayhannews.ir/830531/2.htm)
3. M. Behnoud, 'Mushkel-e namgozari Gurouha dar Daroun Jumhouri Islami', BBC (Farsi service), 4 April 2004. (Retrieved from www.bbc.co.uk/persian/iran/030317_a-mb-iran-factions.shtml)
4. Andrew Heywood, *Political Ideologies* (New York, 1998) p. 69.
5. Mohsen Kadivar, *Daghdaghah-hye Hukumat-e Dini*, p. 165.
6. William Montgomery Watt, 'The Significance of Early Stage of Imami Shi'ism', in N. Keddie (ed.) *Religion and Politics in Iran* (New Haven, 1983) p. 21.
7. Misbah Yazdi, *Negah-e Gozara be Wilayat-e Faqih* (Qum, 1999) p. 53.
8. Alfadl Shalaq, *Al-Ummah wa al-Dawlah*, p. 52.
9. J. B. Skemp, *Plato's Statesman* (London, 1987) p. 40.
10. Paul Stern, 'The Rule of Wisdom and the Rule of Law in Plato's Statesman', *The American Political Science Review*, vol. 91, issue 2 (June 1997) pp. 267–8.
11. Plato, *The Republic*, translated by Desmond Lee (London, 2003) p. 192.
12. Ibid. p. 198.
13. Cited in S. Akhavi, *Religion and Politics in Contemporary Iran* (Albany, 1980) p. 9.
14. Husayn 'Ali Montazeri, *Dirasat fi Wilayat al-Faqih* (Beirut, 1988) vol. 2, p. 102.
15. Muhammad H. Esfahani, *Hashiat al-Makasib*, vol. 1, p. 214.
16. Cited in Sa'eed Hajjarian, *Jumhouriat* (Tehran, 2000) p. 786.
17. Ibn Jarir Tabari, *Jame' al-Bayan* (Beirut, 1995) vol. 5, p. 206.
18. Esfahani, p. 215.
19. Peter Steinberger, 'Ruling: Guardians and Philosopher-Kings', *The American Political Science Review*, vol. 83, issue 4 (December 1989) pp. 1207, 1213.
20. M. Larijani, *Naqd Din-dari va Modernism* (Tehran, 1997) pp. 60–1.
21. Jane Clark, 'Fulfilling our Potential: Ibn 'Arabi's Understanding of Man in a Contemporary Context', *The Journal of the Muhyiddin Ibn Arabi Society*, vol. 30 (Autumn 2001). (Retrieved from www.ibnarabisociety.org/clark.html)

22. Zayn al-Din al-'Amili, (the Second Martyr), *Rasael al-Shahid al-Thani* (Qum, 1989) vol. 2, pp. 138–43.

23. 'Ali, 'Wilayat-e Mutlaqa az Didgah Ibn Wa'ezi, 'Arabi va Mir Haidar Amoli', *Ma'refat* quarterly, no. 49 (December 2001). (Retrieved from www.hawzah.net/Per/ Magazine/mr/049/mr04915.htm)

24. Golamreza Jalali, 'Nazarieh Insan-e Kamil az 'Erfan Ibn 'Arabi ta 'Erfan Imam Khomeini', *Hawzah,* no. 94–5. (Retrieved from www.hawzah.net/Per/Magazine/ HO/094/Ho09412.htm)

25. Larijani, p. 61.

26. Ridwan Al-Sayyid, *Al-Jama'ah wa al-Mujtama' wa al-Dawlah* (Beirut, 1997) p. 386.

27. S. Arjomand, *The Shadow of God and the Hidden Imam* (Chicago, 1984) p. 96.

28. Arjomand suggests that, in Shi'ism, political and religious authority are clearly differentiated from each other to the extent that kingship could be legitimised only as temporal rule. This idea was applicable, however reservedly, until the late 1970s. From then on, Shi'i scholars came to link legitimacy to the faqih rule. See A. Sachedina, *The Just Ruler in Twelver Shi'ism,* (New York, 1988) p. 26.

29. Ibid.

30. David Held, 'Central Perspectives on the Modern State', in McLennan, Hall and Held (ed.), *The Idea of Modern State* (London, 1984) p. 32.

31. Harvey Mansfield, 'Self-Interest Rightly Understood', *Political Theory,* vol. 23, no. 1, (February 1995), p. 52.

32. Stuart Hall, 'The State in Question', in McLennan, Hall and Held, p. 24.

33. John Hall, *Liberalism: Politics, Ideology and the Market* (University of North Carolina Press, 1988) p. 185.

34. Alisa Carse, 'The Liberal Individual: A Metaphyisical or Moral Embarrassment?', *Noûs,* vol. 28, no. 2 (June 1994) p. 185.

35. J. P. Geise, 'In Defence of Liberalism', *The Western Political Quarterly,* vol. 44, no. 3 (September 1991) p. 593.

36. Alisa Carse, pp. 185–6.

37. Harvey Mansfield, p. 54.

38. Misbah Yazdi, *Al-Mujtama' wa'al-Tarikh min Wejhat Nazar al-Quran al-Karim,* translated by M. Khaqani (Tehran, 1994).

39. Heywood, p. 83.

40. Larijani, p. 75.

41. Larijani, p. 192.

42. See J. Locke, (1690) *The Second Treatise of Civil Government,* Chapter II. (Retrieved from: www.constitution.org/jl/2ndtr02.htm) Somers makes a similar argument to support her theory of civil society. She highlights Locke's idea of the pre-political society, especially its claimed capacity to be a self-organised, harmonious and fully functioning commercial community independent of the administrative state. M. Somers, 'Narrating and Naturalising Civil Society and Citizenship Theory: The Place of Political Culture and the Public Sphere', *Sociological Theory,* vol. 13, no. 3 (November 1995) p. 249.

43. M. J. Larijani, 'Islam: Dawlat-e Qadim va Jadid', *Hukumat-e Islami,* (Summer 2000) no. 16. (Retrieved from www.nezam.org/persian/magazine/016/03.htm)

44. Heywood, p. 75.

45. Larijani, *Naqd,* pp. 141–2.

46. M. Yazdi, *Nazarieh Siasi Islam* (Qum, 2001) p. 150.

47. Larijani, p. 150.

48. M. Larijani, 'Islam va Democracy', *Ma'refat,* no. 12, (Spring 1995). (Retrieved from www.hawzah.net/Per/Magazine/mr/012/mr01204.htm)

49. M. Larijani,'Hukumat-e Islami va Marz-hie Siasi', *Hukumat-e Islami*, no. 2, (Winter 1996). (Retrieved from www.hawzah.net/Per/Magazine/he/002/04.htm)

50. Sandel (1984), cited in Daryl Glaser, 'Normative Theory', in Marsh and Stoker (ed.), *Theory and Methods in Political Science* (London, 1995) p. 27.

51. M. Asifi, 'Written Interview', *'Ulum-e Hadith*. (Retrieved on 9 February 2004 from http://www.hadith.net/persian/products/magazine/olum-f/07/002.htm)

52. Larijani, p. 192.

53. Larijani, p. 69.

54. For a brief discussion on the topic, see David Held, *Models of Democracy* (Cambridge, 1997), p. 78.

55. R. Scruton, *A Dictionary of Political Thought* (London, 1996) p. 71.

56. M. Majlisi, cited in M. Nasiri, *Dastour-e Shahriaran* (Tehran, 1994) p. 21.

57. See, for example, the arguments of Fadlullah Nouri: 'Hurmat-e Mashroutah, in Zargari-Najad, *Rasael Mashroutiat* (Tehran, 1995) p. 160.

58. Qaemmaqami, 'Abbas, *Qudrat va Mashro'iat* (Tehran, 2000) p. 112.

59. 'Ali, Khamenei, *'Ebrat-hie 'Ashura: 'Awam va Khawas*, A speech to military commanders (Tehran, 9 June 1996). (Retrieved from www.andisheqom.com/HTM/ Imam%20Hosean/HTM/Ebratha/htm/1.htm. accessed on 13 April 2003)

60. Jamal al-Din al-Amili, *Ma'alem al-Din* (Qum, n.d.) p. 22.

61. Sharif al-Radhi, *Nahj al-Balaghah* (Qum, 1975) p. 496.

62. M. B. Sadr, *Muqaddamat fi al-Tafsir al-Mawdo'ei li'l-Qur'an*, p. 195. (Retrieved from www.rafed.net/ftp/books/moqadamat.zip)

63. See for example Rohani, Ayatollah M. Sadiq, *Nezam-e Hukumat dar Islam*. (Retrieved on 13 April 2003 from www.imamrohani.com/farisi/kotob/hokomat/01. htm#a09)

64. M. Taqavi, 'Sokhani dar Mafhom Jame'ah Dini', *Fiqh Ahl-e-Bait* (Summer 1996). (Retrieved on 14 April 2003 from www.islamicfeqh.org/magazines/Feqh7f/taghav. htm)

65. Misbah Yazdi, p. 311.

66. M. Lankarani, *Theory 'Adalat dar Hukumat-e Islami va wilayat-e Faqih*. (Retrieved on 14 April 2004 from www.lankarani.org/persian/najlehi/teori.html)

67. 'A. Zanjani, *Fiqh Siasi* (Tehran, 1998) vol.1, p. 566.

68. On Khomeini's eight-article communiqué of December 1982 and related declarations, see M. Mehrizi, 'Dawlat-e Dini va Harem Khususi', *Hukumat-e Islami*, no. 12 (Summer 1999). (Retrieved from www.nezam.org/persian/magazine/012/04. htm)

69. On the political implications of the arbitrary supervision, see Habibullah Payman, 'Nezarat-e Estesvabi Mugayer Huquq Mellat' in *Nezarat-e Estsvabi*, compiled and published by Daftar-e Tahkim Wahdat (Tehran, 1999) p. 198.

70. See the arguments put forward by the Council for the Guardianship of the Constitution against the amended bill of election, passed by the parliament. *ISNA*, 1 April 2003.

71. Yazdi, p. 54.

72. S. Freeland, 'Aristotelian Actions', *Noûs*, vol.19, no. 3. (September 1985) p. 397. Aristotle's concept of action has been criticised by Ackrill, for it explains nothing about 'action' as it explains responsibility for motives, and the physiology of action. In addition, his morally based distinction between action and production is incoherent. John Ackrill, 'Aristotle on Action', *Mind*, New Series, vol. 87, issue 348, (October 1987) pp. 595–601.

73. Larijani, p. 65.

74. D. Beetham, *The Legitimation of Power* (London, 1991) pp. 35–6.

75. S. Hall, 'The State in Question' in McLennan, Hall and Held (ed.), p. 19.
76. Ahmad Naraqi, *'Awaed al-Ayyam* (Qum, 1988) p. 188.
77. Zanjani, p. 256.
78. 'Ali Khamenei, 'Speech to the congregation of Friday Prayer' (Tehran, 1 January 1988).
79. Khomeini, *Sahifeh Nur,* (Tehran, 2004), vol. 20, p. 170.
80. For an account of the 1989 amendments, see Sadra, 'Alireza, 'Barrasi Muqayeseh-ei Qanun Asasi', *Hukumat-e Islami,* no. 7 (Spring 1997). (Retrieved from www.nezam. org/persian/magazine/007/07.htm)
81. M. Momen, cited in Haqiqat, S., *Tawzi'e Qudrat* (Tehran, 2002) p. 272.
82. Misbah Yazdi, interview, *Quds* daily (12 May 2001).
83. 'Bunbast-e Qanun Tahqiq va Tafahus va Pishnahadh-ie Namayendegan Majlis' *Hamshahri,* (Tehran, 2 July 2001). A number of the bills rejected on the above basis were published by *Nouruz* on 10, 11, 12, 13 and 20 June 2002.
84. Husayn Hashemian, 'Zarorat-e Tahqiq va Tafahus Majlis dar Umour Keshwar', *Hamshahri,* 26 June 2000. The Council amended the above rule in 2001 and parliament was authorised to carry out the checks with the leader's approval. *Hamshahri,* 12 August 2001.
85. Yazdi, p. 118.
86. Larijani, p. 78.
87. Haqiqat, p. 272.
88. *Shoma,* the weekly organ of Mo'talefeh, no. 7 (10 April 1997) cited in Hajjarian, p. 302.
89. Muhsen Kadivar, *Hukumat-e Wilaei,* Chapter Twelve. (Retrieved from www.kadivar. com/Htm/Farsi/Books/Book03/Chap12.htm)
90. Misbah Yazdi, Hukumat va Mashro'iat', *Kitab-e Naqd,* no. 7 (Summer 1998). (Retrieved from http://www.hawzah.net/Per/Magazine/KN/007/kn00703.htm)
91. M. Garaweian, *Kayhan Farhangi,* vol. 156. (September 1999). Cited in Hajjarian, p. 786.
92. M. Arusta, 'Majlis Khobragan az Didgah-e Nazarieh Wilayat-e Faqih', *Hukumat-e Islami,* no. 8 (Summer 1998). (Retrieved from www.nezam.org/persian/ magazine/008/04.htm)
93. Abu al-Ma'ali Juwaini, *Giath al-Umam* (Alexandria, 1979) pp. 79–89.
94. Yazdi.
95. 'Ali Mishkini, 'Inauguratory Speech Before the Council of Experts' (Tehran, 20 Mach 2001).
96. Makarim Shirazi, *Buhuth Fiqhiyah Muhemmah* (Qum, n.d.) p. 472.
97. Ayatollah Khomeini, *Kitab al-Bay'* (Qum, 1995) vol. 2, p. 461.
98. Ayatollah Jawadi Amoli, *Biramun-e Wahi va Rahbari* (Tehran, 1998) p. 177.
99. Amoli, Ayatollah Jawadi, quoted in *Resalat* (31 March 1998).
100. Sachedina, p. 25.
101. On the application of common rationality in Shi'i jurisprudence, see Fadli, A. *Durous fi Usul Fiqh al-Imamiyah,* (Beirut, 1999) p. 117. Hakim offers a comparative account of the role of the local convention (*'urf*) in defining the frame within which the religious rules apply. M. Hakim, *Al-Usul al-'Ammah li'l-Fiqh al-Muqaran* (Beirut, 1979) p. 417.
102. See for example Ayatollah Golbigani, *Al-Hedayah ela man lahu al-Wilayah* (Qum, 1963) p. 39.
103. Mishkini.
104. Amoli, Jawadi, *Wilayat-e Faqih* (Qum, 1988) pp. 16–20.
105. Arusta.

106. Kazim Hairi, *Wilayat al-Amr fi 'Asr al-Ghaybah* (Qum, 1994) p. 164.
107. Qaemmaqami, pp. 147–8.
108. Qaemmaqami, p. 145.
109. Larijani, p. 68.
110. Qaemmaqami, pp. 71–5.
111. Misbah Yazdi, *Qalamro-e Din*, Kanoone Goftaman (Qum, 2001). (Retrieved on 3 May 2003 from www.andisheqom.com/htm/kanun/24/K24.htm)
112. Shirazi, pp. 392–6.
113. M. H. Ma'refat, 'Pluralism Dini dar Boteh Naqd', *Andishah Hawzah*, no. 16 (Spring 1999). Retrieved from www.al-shia.com/html/far/books/rooz/maqalat_marefat/poloralism/ploral01.htm)
114. In his diaries of 1980, the former president Hashemi Rafsanjani puts the jurisprudential perception of Islam as the major point of disagreement between his camp (the so-called 'line of the Imam') and the liberals (e.g. Nehzat Azadi); 'they do not accept this fiqh, and we see it as the only basis available to run the Islamic state' Rafsanjani, *'Ubur az Buhran* (Tehran, 1999) p. 60.
115. Khomeini, *Sahifeh*, vol. 15, p. 150.
116. Mahamid, 'Fiqh Mustalah Hawzah dar Duniaye Emrooz', *Huzur*, vol. 34 (Spring 2001). (Retrieved from www.hawzah.net/Per/Magazine/hz/034/hz03425.htm)
117. Khomeini, vol. 18, p. 31.
118. M. Ma'refat, 'Fiqh Jawahiri va Vijegihie unn', *Andishah Hawzah* (Summer 1997). (Retrieved from www.balagh.net/persian/feqh/maqalat/koliyat/23.htm)
119. A. Fakhr, "Awamil-e Puya-ie Fiqh', *Qabasat*, nos 15–6 (Spring 2000). (Retrieved from www.hawzah.net/Per/Magazine/QA/015/qa01513.htm)
120. M. Rezaie, 'Deedgah-e Darbarah Tathir 'Unsur-e Zaman va Makan dar Ijtihad', *Huzur*, no. 15 (Spring 1996). (Retrieved from www.hawzah.net/Per/Magazine/HZ/015/hz01508.htm)
121. Shah Alam, 'Conservatives, Liberals and the Struggle over Iranian Politics', *Strategic Analysis*, vol. 24, no. 3 (June 2000). (Retrieved from www.ciaonet.org/olj/sa/sa_jun00als01.html)
122. Khomeini, vol. 20, p. 102.
123. A. Zanjani, 'Nizam Siasi Islam', interview, *Hukumat-e Islami*, no. 1 (Autumn 1996). (Retrieved from www.nezam.org/persian/magazine/001/02.htm)
124. N. Shari'atmadar, 'Karayie Fiqh Siasi', *'Ulum-e Siasi*, no. 14 (Autumn 2001). (Retrieved from www.hawzah.net/Per/Magazine/OS/014/os01403.htm)
125. M. Momen, 'Din va Musharakat-e Siasi', *'Ulum-e Siasi*, no. 7 (Winter 1999). (Retrieved from www.hawzah.net/Per/Magazine/OS/007/os00702.htm)
126. Qaemmaqami, p. 367.
127. Ayatollah Amini, 'Roykard-e Hukumat-e 'Alavi', in Amini, I., *Hukumat-e Alavi: Bunianha va Chalesha*. Chapter One.(Retrieved from www.nezam.org/persian/books/hukoomate-e_alavi_bunyan_ha_va_chalesh_ha/02.htm)

Chapter Five

1. For an empirical assessment of the transformation of values during the early 1990s, see Faramerz Rafi'pour, *Tavse 'ah va Tazadd* (Tehran, 1998). Also: A. 'Abdi and M. Goudarzi, *Tahavulat-e Farhangi dar Iran* (Tehran 1999). Both studies are based on field researches, qualitative and quantitative interviews.
2. A. 'Abdi, 'Hastah Namarei Entekhabat Akhir', in Rezaie and 'Abdi *Entekhab-e Nou* (Tehran, 1999) pp. 97–102.
3. The statistics are compiled from the Statistical Centre of Iran (www.sci.org.ir), High Council for Cultural Revolution (www.iranculture.org) and 'Abdi.

4. Rezaie, 'Nimeh-pur Livan' in 'Abdi and Rezaie, pp. 113–5.
5. P. Piran, 'Seh Sathe Tahlil Vaqe'ah', in 'Abdi and Rezaie, p. 34.
6. Mehrzad Boroujerdi, 'Can Islam be Secularised;' in Esfandiari, Berton and Farhi (eds), *Intellectual Change and the New Generation of Iranian Intellectuals* (Washington, 2000) p. 13. (Retrieved on 2 June 2004 from http://faculty.maxwell.syr.edu/mborouje/Continuities.html)
7. R. Scruton, *A Dictionary of Political Thought* (London, 1996) p. 265.
8. E. Shils, 'The Intellectuals in the Political Development of the New States', *World Politics*, vol. 12, no. 3. (April 1960) p. 332.
9. 'Alireza 'Alavitabar, *Rawshanfikri, Dindari, Mardomsalari* (Tehran, 2000) pp. 25–26.
10. Vahdat, 'Post-Revolutionary Islamic Discourses on Modernity in Iran: Expansion and Contraction of Human Subjectivity', *International Journal of Middle East Studies*. vol. 35, issue 4 (November 2003) pp. 602–3.
11. H. Bashiriyeh, 'Zawal-e Haviat-e Siasi', *Iran* (16 May 2004).
12. On the state policy to restructure the national identity through education, see M. Shorish, 'The Islamic Revolution and Education in Iran', *Comparative Education Review* (February 1988) pp. 58–75. (Retrieved June 2003 from www.ed.uiuc.edu/EPS/people/Shorish_Islamic_Ed.html)
13. Bashiriyeh.
14. Hamid Jalaipour, *Dawlat-e Penhan* (Tehran, 2000) p. 295.
15. 'Ali Ansari, *Iran, Islam and Democracy* (London, 2000) p. 112.
16. S. Arjomand, *The Turban for Crown* (New York, 1988) p. 92.
17. S. Akhavi, *Religion and Politics in Contemporary Iran* (Albany, 1980) p. 143.
18. *Bayan* was published as a monthly magazine by 'Ali Akbar Mohtashemi in May 1990 and closed in February 1992. It was published again as a daily paper, and closed in June 2000. Hadi Khamenei's *Jehan-e Islam* has been in circulation during 1994. *Salam* was published by Mosavi Khoainiha from February 1991 to July 1999. *Kiyan* was shut down in January 2001.
19. For some details on the circle, see: Muhammad Qouchani, *Pedar Khondah va Chap-haye Javan* (Tehran, 2000) pp. 72–9.
20. M. Haidari, 'Matbo'at Siasi az 57 ta 80', *Iran* (27 May 2002).
21. H. Jalaipour, *Pas az Dovum-e Khordad* (Tehran, 1999) p. 292.
22. Abdol-Karim Soroush, *Akhlagh-e Khodayan* (Tehran, 2001).
23. 'Qabz va Bast' was first published in *Kayhan Farhangi*, a respected cultural monthly journal with reformist tendencies (April 1988). A compilation of the articles was published in the following year under the same title.
24. A. Soroush, *Qabz va Bast Theoric Shari'at*, eighth edition (Tehran, 2003) p. 181.
25. Farzin Vahdat, *God and Juggernaut* (New York, 2002) p. 203.
26. Abdol-Karim Soroush, *Bast-e Tajrebeh Nabavi* (Tehran, 1999) p. 276.
27. For a list of Soroush's books, see his website: www.drsoroush.com. The site offers also some of the articles commenting on his works.
28. Ansari, Ali, 'Continuous Regime Change from Within' in A. Lennon and C. Eiss, *Reshaping Rogue States* (Cambridge, 2004) p. 274.
29. Compare with Abedin, who argues that the common characteristic among reformist figures has been their previous career in the intelligence service. Mahan Abedin, 'The Origins of Iran's Reformist Elite', *Middle East Intelligence Bulletin*, vol. 5, no. 4 (April 2003). (Retrieved from www.meib.org/articles/0304_iran.htm)
30. F. Mahmoudi, 'Mafarre Jadid', *Hamshahri* (8 August 2002). (Retrieved from www.hamshahri.org/hamnews/1381/810517/intep.htm)

31. For some details on Khatami's career, see David Menasheri, *Post-Revolutionary Politics in Iran* (London, 2001) pp. 80–3.

32. For an informed comparison between Soroush, Shabestari and Kadivar and its significance to the Iranian context, see Sadri, M. 'Sacral Defense of Secularism: The Political Theologies of Soroush, Shabestari, and Kadivar' in *International Journal of Politics, Culture and Society*, vol. 15, no. 2 (Winter 2001) pp. 257–70.

33. M. Shabestari, *Naqdi bar Qaraat-e Rasmi az Din* (Tehran, 2000) p. 186.

34. Shabestari, p. 192.

35. Akbar Ganji, *Talaqqi Faschisti az Deen wa Hukumat* (Tehran, 1999) p. 34.

36. Francis Coker, *Readings in Political Philosophy* (New York, 1938) p. 684.

37. Ruth M. Elson, *Guardians of Tradition: American Schoolbooks of the Nineteenth Century* (Lincoln, NE, 1964) p. 286.

38. Scruton, p. 476.

39. David Held, *Models of Democracy* (Cambridge, 1997) pp. 90–3.

40. Apparently the argument over the contradiction between the sovereignty of God and that of man was brought to light by Abu al-A'la al-Mawdudi, the Indian scholar. See: A. Mawdudi, 'Political Theory of Islam', in J. Donohue and J. Esposito, *Islam in Transition* (New York, 1982) p. 258. The notion gained more influence after it was adopted by Sayyid Qutb, the theorist of the Muslim Brotherhood. See: S. Qutb, *Ma'alem fi al-Tariq* (Cairo, n.d.) p. 62. (For an online English translation of the book, see : www.masmn.org/Books/Syed_Qutb/Milestones/index.htm)

41. A.'Amid. Zanjani, *Fiqh Siasi* (Tehran, 1998), vol. 1, p. 50.

42. Sa'eed Hajjarian, *Jumhouriat: Afsoun-zedaei az Qudrat* (Tehran, 2000) p. 754.

43. Hajjarian, p. 190.

44. Husayn A. Montazeri, *Nizam al-Hukm fi al-Islam,* section 5, chapter 3 (Qum, 2004). (Retrieved on 20 July 2004 from www.montazeri.ws/Farsi/Nezam/html/0006. htm#0017)

45. Hossein Bashiriyeh, *Jame'ah Madani wa Tawse'ah Siasi dar Iran* (Tehran, 1999) p. 103.

46. Arthur Schweitzer, 'Theory and Political Charisma', *Comparative Studies in Society and History*, vol. 16, no. 2 (March 1974) p. 159.

47. Ibrahim Yazdi, *Seh Jumhouri* (Tehran, 2001) pp. 101–2.

48. Hassan Rohani, 'Daramadi bar Mashro'iat wa Karamadi', *Rahburd*, no. 18 (Winter 2001) p. 27.

49. See Yazdi. Also Khatami, *Tawse'ah Siasi* (Tehran, 2000) p. 43 and Soroush, *Ferbah-tar az Ideology* (Tehran, 1999) p. 282.

50. H. Montazeri, *Dirasat fi Wilayat al-Faqih* (Beirut, 1988), vol. 1, p. 493.

51. Montazeri, p. 527.

52. Montazeri, *Wilayat-e Faqih wa Qanoon-e Asasi,* chapter 3 (Qum, 1998). (Retrieved in October 2003 from www.montazeri.com/html/books/akhar/velayat/velaya01. html#link2)

53. Yousif Sane'i, 'Speech in Faizia School, Qum', *ISNA* (2 June 2003).

54. Shabestari, *Naqdi,* p. 150.

55. Hassan Ashkoari, *Kherad dar Ziafat-e Din* (Tehran, 1999) pp. 110–2.

56. Soroush, *Razdani va Rawshanfikri va Dindari* (Tehran, 2000) p. 68.

57. Na'ini, 'Allama, 'Tanbih al-Ummah wa Tanzih al-Millah', in T. Alsaif, *Zidd al-Istebdad* (Beirut, 1999) p. 254.

58. Na'ini, pp. 301–27.

59. Na'ini, p. 285. Compare with Mesbah Yazdi, who regards the Islamic state as 'the kingdom of God': M. Yazdi, *Nazarieh Siasi Islam* (Qum, 2001) p. 70.

60. The position of the Shi'i grand exemplar in Iraq is a good example of the said trend.

Ayatollah Sistani has openly dismissed any prefixed role for any group, including the clergy, in the Iraqi government. In various communiqués he insisted that only through election can the government secure legitimacy. See: Rory McCarthy, 'The Rise of the Cleric with all the Answers', *The Guardian* (16 January 2004). (Retrieved from www.guardian.co.uk/Iraq/Story/0,2763,1124233,00.html) Another example is the theory of *Wilayat al-Ummah ' ala Nafseha* (The Nation's Self-Government) advanced by Ayatollah Shams al-Din of Lebanon; see Shams al-Din M., *Nizam al-Hukm wa al-Idarah fi al-Islam* (Beirut, 1991) pp. 416–60.

61. M. Khatami, *Tawse'ah Siasi*, p. 81.
62. H. Montazeri, *Khaterat*, chapter 10. (Retrieved in April 2004 from www.montazeri. com/html/books/khaterat/KHATER50.htm#link414)
63. David Beetham, *The Legitimation of Power* (London, 1991) p. 213.
64. Bashiriyeh, p. 89.
65. Huntington takes public mobilisation as the first sign of modernisation but warns that it also develops an 'explosive rise of aspirations' and argues that unless the political system becomes efficiently institutionalised, these aspirations can convert into frustrations and pave the way for the rise of authoritarianism. S. Huntington, 'Political Development and Political Decay', *World Politics*, vol. 17, issue 3 (April 1965) p. 405.
66. Daniel Lerner, *The Passing of Traditional Society* (New York, 1965) p. 51.
67. Hassan Moradi, *Khod-madari Iranian* (Tehran, 2001) p. 202.
68. Sadiq Zibakalam, *Ma Chegounah Ma Shudim* (Tehran, 1996) p. 112.
69. Homa Katouzian, 'The Aridiosolatic Society: A Model of Long-Term Social and Economic Development in Iran', *International Journal of Middle East Studies*, vol. 15, no. 2 (May 1983) p. 270.
70. Katouzian, p. 265.
71. Lerner, p. 362.
72. Lerner, pp. 50–1.
73. Hootan Shambayati, 'The Rentier State, Interest Groups, and the Paradox of Autonomy: State and Business in Turkey and Iran', *Comparative Politics*, vol. 26, no. 3 (April 1994) p. 319.
74. Leonard Binder, *Islamic Liberalism* (Chicago, 1988) p. 5.
75. J. Esposito, and J. Voll, *Islam and Democracy* (Oxford, 1996) p. 64.
76. According to Jalaipour, the conservatives started to use the term 'Islamic democracy' after the events of 11 September 2001 in order to differentiate themselves from the radical trend associated with Bin Laden. Jalaipour, H., 'Democracy Dini Mohafeze-caranah va Islah-talaban', *Yas-e No* (5 February 2004) p. 2.
77. See for example the suggestions made by Ayatollah Khaz'ali, *ISNA*, 5 February 2003.
78. *Aftab monthly*, vol. 22 (February 2002) p. 22.
79. Misbah Yazdi, 'Hukumat va Mashro'iat', *Kitab-e Naqd*, no. 7 (Summer 1998). (Retrieved from www.hawzah.net/Per/Magazine/KN/007/kn00703.htm)
80. Muhammad Khatami, *Ayen va Andisheh dar Dam-e Khodkamegi* (Tehran, 2001) p. 434.
81. Hajjarian, *Jumhouriat*, pp. 726–8.
82. M. Shabestari, 'Mardomsalari Dini Chist?', *Aftab*, vol. 7 (August 2001) 4–9, p. 4.
83. M. Khatami, *Az Dunia-ye Shahr ta Shahr-e Dunia* (Tehran, 2000) p. 285.
84. Ibid.
85. Khatami, pp. 271–283.
86. Khatami, *Tawse'ah Siasi*, p. 44.
87. 'Alavitabar, pp. 124–5. In 1991 Soroush offered his first precise account on the

idea, especially on the correspondence between religion and democracy. It came in the form of a lecture delivered at a seminar on human rights held by the Ministry of Foreign Affairs. An edited version of the lecture was later published in his book *Ferbehtar az Ideology*, pp. 273–283.

88. See for instance, Khashayar Dayhimi, 'Mardomsalari-e Dini Bed'at dar 'Elm-e Siasat', *Aftab*, no. 22 (January 2003) p. 27.
89. Muhsen Kadivar, 'Mardomsalari-e Dini', *Tabarestan Sabz*, vol. 15 (22 September 2001) pp. 5–7. (Retrieved from www.kadivar.com/htm/farsi/papers/paper006. htm)
90. M. Shabestari, 'Mardomsalari-e Dini', p. 4.
91. Soroush, *Ferbeh-tar*, p. 269.
92. Soroush, p. 279.
93. 'Alavitabar.
94. Mohsen Kadivar, *Daghdaghah-hye Hukumat-e Dini* (Tehran, 2000) p. 261.
95. See, for instance, Muhammadi's analysis of Hizbullah as a principal instance of the populist conception of political participation in Iranian politics. Majeed Muhammadi, *Jame'ah Madani Iran* (Tehran, 1999) pp. 101–12.
96. Kadivar.
97. Khatami, *Tavse'ah*, pp. 47--50.
98. H. Jalaipour, *Pas az Dovoum Khordad*, p. 233.
99. Shabestari, *Naqdi*, p. 108.
100. Soroush, *Bast-e Tajrebah*, p. 361.
101. Hajjarian, *Az Shahed-e Qudsi ta Shahed-e Bazari* (Tehran, 2001) pp. 132–4.
102. Shabestari, *Naqdi*, p. 108.
103. Kadivar.
104. Shabestari, *Naqdi*, pp. 112–7.
105. Soroush, *Ferbeh-tar*, p. 280.
106. A. 'Alavitabar, p. 29. For more on the reformative role of the intellectuals in regard of the religious traditions, see: E. Shils, 'Tradition' *Comparative Studies in Society and History*, vol. 13, no. 2 (April 1971) pp. 122–59. On the contextual determinants of their behaviour, see F. Ringer, 'The Intellectual Field, Intellectual History, and the Sociology of Knowledge', *Theory and Society*, vol. 19, no. 3 (June 1990) pp. 269–94.
107. Ansari, (2004) p. 274.
108. Cited in J. Gerring, 'Ideology: A Definitional Analysis', *Political Research Quarterly*, vol. 50, no. 4 (December 1997) p. 958.
109. Gerring, p. 970.
110. Gerring, p. 971.
111. For the major features of the so-called 'pure Islam' from the viewpoint of Ayatollah Khamenei, see 'Islam-nab-e Muhammadi '. (Retrieved on 22 June 2004 from www. hawzah.net/Per/E/do.asp?a=efcbc.hrm) For a counter account, see Ganji, p. 76.
112. Soroush, *Razdani*, p. 124.
113. Ibid. p. 80.
114. In comparison, Hajjarian equates state religion with civil religion and argues that the emergence of such a version of religion is inescapable in such nations as Iran. Hajjarian, *Az Shahed-e Qudsi*, p. 151.
115. On Shari'ati's thought, see Akhavi, 'Shari'ati's Social Thought', in N. Keddie, *Religion and Politics in Iran* (New Haven, 1983) pp. 125–44.
116. 'Ali Shari'ati, *Islamology: the Basic Design for a School of Thought and Action*. (Retrieved in June 2004 from http://shariati.com/islamgy2.html)
117. Soroush, *Ferbeh-tar*, p. 125.
118. Ibid. p. 49.

119. Ibid. p. 53.
120. Ibid. *Razdani*, p. 51.
121. Shabestari, *Naqdi*, p. 31.
122. Ibid. p. 100.
123. Paul Achtemeier, *An Introduction to the New Hermeneutic* (Philadelphia,1969) p. 11.
124. T Seung, *Semiotics and Thematics in Hermeneutics* (New York, 1982) p. 173.
125. Cited in Seung, p. 189.
126. Shabestari, *Hermeneutics, Ketab va Sunnat* (Tehran, 2000) p. 48.
127. Ibid. p. 66.
128. Shabestari, *Naqdi*, p. 65.
129. Shabestari, *Hermeneutic*, p. 88.
130. Shabestari, *Naqdi*, p. 150.
131. Kadivar, 'Mardomsalari-e'.
132. 'Alavitabar, p. 25.
133. 'A. Qaemmaqami, *Qudrat va Mashro'iat* (Tehran, 2000) p. 55.
134. Hajjarian, *Az Shahed-e*, p. 89.
135. Hajjarian, p. 87.
136. The article 'Faraiend 'Urfi-shodan-e Fiqh-e Shi'i' was first published in *Kiyan*, no. 24 (April 1996) and then in his *Az Shahed-e Qudsi*, pp. 69–91.
137. Ibid. pp. 96–108.
138. Khomeini takes religion and politics to be one and the same. He often reiterated a phrase attributed to Sayyid Hassan Mudarres, a religious leader and politician murdered by Reza Pahlavi in 1937, stating that 'our politics is exactly our religion and our religion is exactly our politics'.
139. Hajjarian, pp. 94–5.
140. Shabestari, *Naqdi*, p. 227.
141. The notion of 'civil religion' refers to a 'religion that serves secular as opposed to transcendent or otherworldly ends'. See Sanford Kessler, 'Tocqueville on Civil Religion and Liberal Democracy', *The Journal of Politics*, vol. 39, no. 1 (February 1977) pp. 119–46.
142. S. Hajjarian, 'Henjar-haye bi-Arzesh, Arzesh-haye bi-Henjar', *Nourooz* (7 March 2002).
143. Soroush, *Bast*, p. 162.
144. Ibid. p. 364.
145. Mahmood Monshipouri, *Islamism, Secularism and Human Rights in the Middle East* (London, 1998) p. 10.
146. S. Hajjarian, *Tavan-e Islahat* (Tehran, 2001) p. 65.
147. S. Hajjarian, *Az Shahed-e*, p. 88.
148. Alavitabar, p. 192.
149. For details on this topic see D. Muhebbi, 'Nazarieh Din Hadde Akthar', *Naqd va Nazar*, vol. 6, issues 1and 2 (Winter 1999–Spring 2000). (Retrieved from www. hawzah.net/Per/Magazine/NN/021/nn02107.htm) Ayatollah Subhani offers a critical account of the notion of minimal application, see: J. Subhani, 'Vijegeehye Elm Fiqh'. (Retrieved from www.balagh.net/persian/feqh/maqalat/koliyat/29.htm)
150. Soroush, *Bast*, pp. 83–112.
151. Ibid. p. 361.
152. Khatami, *Bim-e Mawj* (Tehran, 1992) p. 148.
153. Shabestari, *Naqdi*, p. 31.
154. Ibid. p. 50.

Chapter Six

1. Bahman Baktiari, *Parliamentary Politics in Revolutionary Iran: The Institutionalisation of Factional Politics* (Florida, 1996) p. 221.

2. See, for example, *Ahzab va Tashkilat-e Siasi Iran*, compiled and published by the research centre of the Islamic Revolutionary Guard (Qum, n.d.). (Retrieved 16 August 2004 from www.tooba-ir.org/siyasi/ahzab/kargo/fehrest.htm)

3. Baktiari, p. 84.

4. For a comparative account on the approaches to the role of bureaucracy, see Gerald Heeger, 'Bureaucracy, Political Parties, and Political Development', *World Politics*, vol. 25, issue 4, (July 1973) pp. 600–7.

5. Blondel, Jean, *Comparative Government* (New York, 1995) p. 133.

6. Lester, Seligman, 'Elite Recruitment and Political Development', *The Journal of Politics*, vol. 26, issue 3 (August 1964) p. 618.

7. Heath, Graaf, and Nieuwbeerta, 'Class Mobility and Political Preferences', *American Journal of Sociology*, vol. 100, no. 4 (January 1995) p. 999.

8. 'Alavitabar, 'Alireza, interview with *Bahar*, (16 July 2000). (Retrieved from www.netiran.com/Htdocs/Clippings/DPolitics/200716XXDP01.html)

9. Barviz Beeran, 'Junbush-e Ejtema'i Shahri', *Aftab*. vol. 20 (October 2002) pp. 34–5.

10. Huma Katouzian, 'Problems of Democracy and Public Sphere in Modern Iran', *Comparative Studies of South Asia, Africa and the Middle East*, vol. 18, no. 2 (1998) p. 31.

11. Heath *et al.*

12. Hossein Bashiriyeh, *Mavane' Tavse'ah Siasi dar Iran* (Tehran, 2001) p. 133.

13. J. Eta'at, 'Shekafhay-e Ejtema'i va Gurouh-bandi Siasi dar Iran', *Aftab*, vol. 19 (September 2002) p. 10.

14. David Menasheri, *Post-Revolution Politics in Iran*, p. 49.

15. Muhammad Reza Tajik, 'Ahzab: Furobashi Haviat-e Sunnati', *Baztab* (5 January 2003).

16. Shah Alam, 'Conservatives, Liberals and the Struggle over Iranian Politics'. *Strategic Analysis*, vol. 24, no. 3 (June 2000). (Retrieved from www.ciaonet.org/olj/sa/sa_jun00als01.html)

17. Cited in Mas'oud Safiri, *Haqiqat-ha va Maslahat-ha* (Tehran, 1999) p. 81. The same suggestion was made by Asadullah Badamchian, who was a member of the party central committee, cited in Shah Alam.

18. Cited in Muhammad Haidari, 'Hezb-e Jumhuri Islami: Tashakol-e Siasi dar Rohaniat', *Iran* (24 June 2002).

19. Mehran Kamrava, *The Political History of Modern Iran: From Tribalism to Theocracy* (Westport, 1992) p. 87.

20. Baktiari, p. 55.

21. Frank Tachau, *Political Parties of the Middle East and North Africa* (Westport, 1994) p. 139.

22. Cited in Safiri.

23. Safiri, p. 83.

24. For some details, see Baktiari, p. 80.

25. Shah Alam.

26. *Khorassan* (30 July 2000) p. 4. (Retrieved from: www.netiran.com/Htdocs/Clippings/DPolitics/200730XXDP01.html)

27. Mohsen Hajari, 'Muqaddameh bar Sinkh-shenasi Rast dar Iran', *Chashmandaz Iran*, vol. 9 (June 2001) p. 59.

28. Hamid Zarifinia, *Kalbud-shekafi Jenah-haye Siasi Iran* (Tehran, 1999) pp. 97–8.

29. For some details on the Baha'i faith and community, see Douglas Martin, 'The Case

of the Baha'i Minority in Iran', *The Baha'i World* (1992–3) pp. 247–71. (Retrieved from www.bahai.org/article-1-8-3-7.html) Also Moojan Momen, 'The Baha'i Community of Iran: Patterns of Exile and Problems of Communication' in A. Fathi (ed.), *Iranian Refugees and Exiles since Khomeini* (1991). (Retrieved from www.northill.demon.co.uk/relstud/Iran-patterns.htm)

30. Taher Ahmedzadeh, 'Anjoman Hojjatiyeh dar Bastar-e Zaman', *Chashmandaz Iran*, vol. 5 (May 2000).

31. Ibid.

32. H. Razavi, 'Bazkhuni Parvandeh Anjoman Hojjatiyeh', *Hamshahri* (23 October 2002).

33. Muhammad Tawakkul, 'Bazaar Sunnati Iran dar Seh Dawreh', *Chashmandaz Iran*, no. 16 (October 2002) p. 42.

34. Hassan Khiyati, 'Siasatgorizi va Tarvij Jedayi din az Siasat', *Jumhuri Islami* (31 October 2002).

35. Abol-Qasim Khaz'ali, cited in *Kayhan* (2 December 2002) p. 12.

36. Baktiari, p. 81.

37. Murtaja states the names of twelve groups comprising the affiliates of Rohaniat Mobarez. Murtaja, Hujjat, *Jenah-haye Siasi dar Iran Emrooz* (Tehran, 2000) p. 14. I add here the groups that remained outside this frame, notwithstanding their sharing the ideals and political positions of the conservative camp.

38. Zarifinia, p. 89.

39. Ibid. pp. 90–1.

40. Safiri, p. 186.

41. Cited in 'Abbas Shadlo, *Ettela'ati darbareh Ahzab va Jenah-haye Siasi Iran Emrooz*, (Tehran, 1999) p. 62.

42. Ibrahim Yazdi, *Seh Jumhouri* (Tehran, 2001) p. 296.

43. Shadlo, p. 157.

44. F. Gholami, 'Kalbud-shekafi Mo'talefeh-1', *Baztab* (4 February 2003). (Retrieved from www.baztab.com/index.asp?ID=2525&Subject=News)

45. Shadlo, p. 160.

46. Ibid. p. 170.

47. Ibid. p. 167.

48. Ibid. p.168.

49. F. Ghulami, 'Kalbud-shekafi Mo'talfeh-2', *Baztab* (8 February 2003). (Retrieved from www.baztab.com/index.asp?ID=2649&Subject=News)

50. J. Deliri, 'Shekl-giri Dou E'telaf va Chahar Fraxion dar Majlis Haftum', *Iran* (24 May 2004).

51. *ISNA* (8 February 2004).

52. Kian Tajbakhsh, 'The Fate of Local Democracy in the Islamic Republic', *Iran Analysis Quarterly*, vol. 1, issue 2 (Fall 2003) p. 7.

53. *Iran* (25 February 2004).

54. For some details on the incident and the immediate reactions, see *Hamshahri* (11 July 1999). (Retrieved from www.hamshahri.org/hamnews/1378/780420/Index. htm)

55. M. Roh, 'Mo'talefeh Hezb Shod', *Shargh* (10 January 2004). (Retrieved from www.sharghnewspaper.com/821020/index.htm)

56. M. J. Larijani, 'Zohd-e Siasi', *Jam-e-Jam* (6 September 2004). (Retrieved from www.jamejamdaily.net/shownews2.asp?n=63602&t=pol)

57. Ibid.

58. Shadlo, p. 315.

59. Ibid. p. 314.

60. 'Ali Darabi, interview with *ISNA* (2 January 2004). (Retrieved from http://www. isna.ir/news/NewsContent.asp?id=326823&lang=P)

61. The final communiqué of the second congress of Esargaran Society, *ISNA* (24 January 2004).

62. Cited in *Shargh* (3 January 2004) (Retrieved from www.sharghnewspaper. com/821013/polit.htm)

63. The final communiqué.

64. Cited in *Shargh* (3 January 2004). (Retrieved from www.sharghnewspaper. com/821013/polit.htm)

65. Mujtaba Shakeri, a member of the central committee. Cited in *Jumhuri Islami* (20 October 2003). (Retrieved from http://www.jomhourieslami. com/1382/13820728/)

66. Mujtaba Shakeri, cited in *ISNA* (1 October 2003).

67. M. Bahonar, interview with *Iran* (22 August 2004). (Retrieved from www. iraninstitute.org/iran/1383/830601/dialog.htm)

68. Cited in *Kayhan* (25 February 2004) p. 14.

69. A. Tavakkuli, interview with *Hamshahri* (7 September 2004). (Retrieved from www. hamshahri.org/hamnews/1383/830617/world/econw.htm)

70. M. Quchani, *Pedarkhondeh va Chabhaye Javan* (Tehran, 2000) p. 115.

71. M. Quchani,'Dou Jenah-e Rast', *Shargh* (8 April 2004). (Retrieved from www. sharghnewspaper.com/830120/index.htm)

72. Ibid.

73. *Jomhouri Islami* (6 April 2004). (Retrieved from www.jomhourieslami. com/1383/13830118/13830118_jomhori_islami_02_jahat_ettela.html)

74. A. Rezaie, 'Technocrat-haye Mohafezeh-kar' *Shargh* (10 April 2004). (Retrieved from www.sharghnewspaper.com/830122/econom.htm)

75. 'Ariesh Gurouhha dar Entekhabat', *Hamshahri* (18 February 2004). (Retrieved from www.hamshahri.org/hamnews/1382/821129/world/siasatw.htm)

76. M. R. Bahonar, cited in *Kayhan* (25 February 2004) p. 14.

77. N. Ibrahimi, 'Purojeh Yak-dast Shodan', *Shargh* (18 April 2004). (Retrieved from www.sharghnewspaper.com/830130/polit.htm)

78. Zibakalam, *Sadiq, Moqaddameh bar Enqelab-e Islami* (Tehran, 1999) p. 262.

79. Baktiari, p. 217.

80. Cited in Murtaja, p. 18.

81. Shadlo, p. 104.

82. Shah Alam.

83. J. Deliri,'Farzandan-e 'Asr-e Enghelab va Islahat dar Reqabati Tazah', *Iran* (11 January 2004).

84. Sa'id Barzin, *Jenah-bandi Siasi dar Iran* (Tehran, 2000) p. 60.

85. M. Quchani, *Yeqeh-Sefidha* (Tehran, 2000) p. 86.

86. Shadlo, p. 110.

87. Barzin, p. 59.

88. Cited in Shadlo, p. 110.

89. Cited in *Hamshahri* (3 September 2000). (Retrieved from www.hamshahri.org/ hamnews/1379/790613/siasi.htm)

90. Shadlo, p. 122.

91. Cited in Sepah Islamic Research Centre, *Ahzab va Tashkilat-e Siasi Iran* (Qum, n.d.). (Retrieved on 16 August 2004 from www.tooba-ir.org/siyasi/ahzab/kargo/fehrest. htm)

92. M. Quchani, *Yeqeh-Sefidha*, p. 78.

93. Quchani, p. 126.

94. Barzin, p. 58.
95. Cited in Shadlo, p. 110.
96. Miguel Centeno, 'The New Leviathan: The Dynamics and Limits of Technocracy', *Theory and Society*, vol. 22, no. 3 (June 1993) p. 309.
97. Robert Carlisle, 'The Birth of Technocracy: Science, Society, and Saint-Simonians', *Journal of the History of Ideas*, vol. 35, no. 3 (July–September 1974) p. 449.
98. Centeno.
99. Ibid.
100. See, for example, the speech of Ayatollah Khamenei on the eve of the 1996 elections in Sarjouei and Sadatian, *Entekhabat-e Majlis Panjom dar Ayeneh Matbo'at* (Tehran, 1999) p. 259.
101. M. R. Bahonar, cited in Zarifinia, p. 102.
102. Cited in Sepah Islamic Research Centre.
103. Barzin, p. 59.
104. Cited in Shadlo, p. 116.
105. *BBC News* (25 January 2000). (Retrieved from http://news.bbc.co.uk/2/hi/middle_east/618351.stm)
106. 'Ata'ollah Muhajerani, *Hekayat Hamchenan Baqiest* (Tehran, 1999) and *Estizah* (Tehran, 1999).
107. *ISNA* (17 November 2004).
108. A. Muhajerani, interview with Iran (3 June 2002).
109. Quchani, *Yeqeh-Sefidha*, p. 88.
110. 'Ali Darabi, cited in *Mehr News Agency* (9 February 2004).
111. For some details, see Quchani, *Pedar-khondeh*, p. 30.
112. *Iran* (3 June 2002).
113. Mohsen Rezayi, cited in *Kayhan* (8 February 2000).
114. M. Haidari,'Enqelab-e Islami dar 'Asr-e Ma', *Iran* (20 May 2002).
115. Murtaja, p. 22.
116. M. Haidari.
117. Ibid.
118. Shadlo, pp. 247–58.
119. *ISNA* (9 July 2002).
120. The sentence was later quashed by the Supreme Court of Justice, and Aghajari was released in the early 2005. An English translation of the lecture upon which Aghajari was arrested, is available in *Faith*. (Retrieved from http://ilrs.org/faith/aghajaritext.html)
121. Amir Mohebian, cited in *Resalat* (23 December 2002) p. 2.
122. Quchani, *Yeqeh-Sefidha*, p. 109.
123. Haidari.
124. Murtaja, p. 108.
125. R. Rahimi, 'Kongereh Haftom ya Kongereh Avval', *Shargh* (1 May 2004). (Retrieved from www.sharghnewspaper.com/830212/polit.htm)
126. Shadlo, p. 70.
127. Murtaja, p. 16.
128. Safiri, op. cit. p. 84.
129. See the final communiqué of the group's congress, *ISNA* (12 January 2004).
130. See the speeches delivered in and about the first congress of the group, *ISNA* (4–7 December 2003).
131. N. Ebrahimi, 'Unha Sherkat Kardand' *Shargh* (17 February 2004).
132. Geneive Abdo, 'Electoral Politics in Iran', *Middle East Policy*, vol. 6, no. (4 June 1999). (Retrieved from www.mepc.org/public_asp/journal_vol6/9906_abdo.asp)

133. In the 2000 parliamentary elections, Mosharekat won eighty seats, Rohanion sixty, Kargozaran fifteen, Hambastagi thrity, the conservative faction fifty out of a total of 290 seats. Z. Ibrahimi, 'Jenah-bandihaye Siasi Majlis Sheshum', *Hamshahri* (9 September 2000). According to Na'imipour, the head of the Mosharekat parliamentary faction, his faction consists of 120 MPs among which thirty are committed members of the party. *Nouruz* (2 June 2002) p. 7.
134. Shadlo, p. 127.
135. Jebhe Mosharekat Iran Islami, *Bayanat va Mavaze' ta Congereh Avval* (Tehran, 2001) p. 222.
136. 'Eslahat dar Mosharekat', *Hamshahri* (22 August 2002).
137. Hamid Jalaipour, *Dawlat-e Penhan* (Tehran, 2000), p.205.
138. Amir Muhebian, cited in Jebhe Mosharekat, p. 194.
139. 'Kongereh Sevom Mosharekat dar Astaneh Tahavul' (Report on the third annual conference of the party) *Iran* (22 July 2002).
140. *Hamshahri* (27 June 2002).
141. 'Ali 'Alavitabar, 'Mosharekat va Mojahedin Enghelab Dou Hasteh Asli Dovom Khordad', *Nourooz* (11 July 2002).
142. The official website of the Council for the Maintenance of the Constitution. (Retrieved 18 January 2004 from www.irisn.com/akhbar/1382/13821029/13821029_irisn_00005.htm)
143. See the party agenda for the legislative elections of 2000 in: Jebhe Mosharekat, p. 229.
144. Jebhe Mosharekat, pp. 222–8.
145. Khatami, M. Reza, 'Inauguratory Speech of the Party's Fifth General Congress' (16 October 2003). (Retrieved from http://news.gooya.com/politics/archives/000487.php)
146. The final communiqué of the party's fifth general congress (17 October 2003). (Retrieved on 8 January 2004 from www.ardekan.com/msh_bayaniejebhe.htm)
147. Ibid.
148. See for instance the list of the bills passed by the Majlis but rejected by the constitutional council published by *Nouruz* (10, 11, 12, 13 and 20 June 2002). The list covers the first year of the sixth Majlis works.
149. M. Reza Khatami, 'Inauguratory Speech of the Party's Fifth General Congress'.
150. The final communiqué of the party's seventh general congress, *Emrooz* (4 August 2004). (Retrieved from www.emrooz.ws:81/ShowItem.aspx?ID=4980&p=1)
151. Jebhe Mosharekat, p. 222.
152. M. Reza Khatami, Inauguratory Speech of the Party's Seventh General Congress, *ISNA* (23 July 2004). (Retrieved from www.isna.ir/news/NewsContent.asp?id=409466&lang=P)
153. Jebhe Mosharekat, p. 222.
154. *Salam Iran* (7 December 1998). (Retrieved from www.salamiran.org/Media/IranNews/981207.html)
155. M. J. Roh, 'Moze' Mosharekat darbareh Namzadi Mosavi' (Report on the seventh congress of the party), *Shargh* (22 July 2004). (Retrieved from www.sharghnewspaper.com/830503/index.htm)
156. Kiyan, 'Alireza, 'Ustad wa Shagerdanesh', *Hamshahri* (*Nauruz* special edition), (20 March 2003).
157. H. Razavi, 'Saff-aray-e Tazeh', *Hamshahri* (12 May 2003). (Retrieved from www.hamshahri.org/hamnews/1382/820222/world/intep.htm)
158. Baktiari, p. 235.
159. Schlesinger, p. 374.

160. See, for instance, M. Amin, 'Iran Politics Turns to Right?', *The Washington Times* (28 May 2004). (Retrieved from http://washingtontimes.com/upi-breaking/20040528-035422-8502r.htm)

Chapter Seven

1. Hooshang Amirahmadi, 'Iran's President on Israel and the Holocaust', *American Iranian Council*, 9 January 2006.
2. *Baztab*, 27 November 2005 (www.baztab.com/news/31076.php). See some reactions to these claims by Iranian politicians at: BBC News, 22 November 2005. (www.bbc.co.uk/persian/iran/story/2005/11/051128_sm-ahmadinejad.shtml)
3. *Emrouz*, 23 August 2005. (Retrieved from http://66.98.198.102/archives/2005/08/00003.php)
4. See in this regard the message of Karroubi and Moein's supporters to the supreme leader, ibid. Also the message of Karroubi to President Khatami, *Iran*, July 2005. Also Rafsanjani's communiqué, *ISNA, 25* June 2005.
5. Mas'oud Safiri, *Haqiqat-ha va Maslahat-ha* (Tehran, 1999) p. 158.
6. Ali Khamenei, 'A Speech to the Cabinet and Parliament Members', *ISNA*, 28 May 2006.
7. *Shargh*, 22 June 2005.
8. *Baztab*, 13 September 2005. (Retrieved from www.baztab.com/news/28963.php)
9. *Baztab*, 27 December 2005. (Retrieved from www.baztab.com/news/32651.php)
10. *Khedmat* website. (Retrieved on 20 December 2005 from www.khedmat.info)
11. See, for instance, President Khatami's declarations in this regard, *Iran*, 2 January 2006.
12. See *Jumhoiri Islami*, 6 July 2005, also *Shargh*, 30 January 2006.
13. *Reuters*, 25 February 2004.
14. See in this regard, Joshua Cooper Ramo, *The Beijing Consensus* (London, 2004) The Foreign Policy Centre.
15. Wei-Wei Zhang, 'The Allure of the Chinese Model', *International Herald Tribune*, 1 November 2006.
16. See, for example, Arif Dirlik, 'Beijing Consensus: Beijing "Gongshi." Who Recognises Whom and to What End?', *Globalisation and Autonomy Online Compendium*. (Retrieved on 2 December 2006 from http://www.globalautonomy.ca/global1/position.jsp?index=PP_Dirlik_BeijingConsensus.xml)
17. Nathalie Bouché and Carl Riskin (eds), *The Macroeconomics of Poverty Reduction: The Case of China*, United Nations Development Programme (Beijing, 2004) p. 1.
18. Yu Keping, 'Globalisation and Autonomy in China', paper presented at the Fourth MCRI Globalisation and Autonomy Team Meeting at the Munk Centre for International Studies, University of Toronto, pp. 23–5, September 2005.
19. *Reuters*.
20. Khamenei official website. (Retrieved on 16 June 2004 from www.Khamenei.ir/fa/speech/detail.jsp?id=830327a)
21. *ISNA*, 26 November 2006.
22. Ali Khamenei, A Speech to the Conference on Islamic Unity (Tehran, 21 August 2006).
23. *Kargozaran*, 25 December 2006.
24. *Iran*, 17 January 2007. (Retrieved from www.iran-newspaper.com/1385/851027/html/politic.htm)
25. Among the stark examples of this tendency, one can indicate the increasing involvement of the Revolutionary Guard in economic activities such as the oil industry. See in this regard *Shargh*, 26 June 2006.

26. *Shargh*, 28 June 2006.
27. In a plain message to the heads of state, the associations of builders and engineering contractors claimed that the government's new policies had profoundly undermined the building sector, which makes up to 30 per cent of the GDP. These associations represent ten thousand firms, 60 per cent of whose capacity is said to have been left unfilled during recent months. *ISNA*, 4 July 2006.
28. *Shargh*, 6 June 2006.
29. Ibid.
30. Safiri, p. 158.
31. *BBC News*, 3 January 2007. (Retrieved from www.bbc.co.uk/persian/business/story/2007/01/printable/070103_mf_ka_budgt.shtml)
32. *Aftab*, 20 January 2007. (Retrieved from www.aftabnews.ir/vdchkin23kn-m.html)
33. *Etemad-e Melli*, 24 January 2007.
34. *Aftab*, 25 January 2007. (Retrieved from http://www.aftabnews.ir/vdcd9s0yt509k.html)

Conclusion

1. M. Khatami, *Tavse'ah Siasi*, p. 88.
2. Roxanne Euben, *Enemy in the Mirror* (Princeton, 1999) p. 118.
3. Khomeini, *Sahifeh Nur*, vol. 15, p. 142.
4. Cited in Haidari, 'Hizb-e Jumhuri Islami', *Iran*, 24 June 2002.
5. M. Sarjouei and J. Sadatian, *Entekhabat-e Majlis Panjum dar Ayeneh Matbo'at* (Tehran, 1999) p. 124.
6. Rafi'pour, *Tawse'ah va Tazadd*, p. 318.
7. *Baztab*, 1 May 2004.
8. S. Sachs, 'In Iran, More Women Leaving Nest for University', *New York Times*, 22 July 2000.
9. For some details on the different positions in this regard, see *Emrooz*. (Retrieved from www.emrooz.org/women/Archive%20Women.htm)
10. Ayatollah Sane'i webpage. (Retrieved from www.saanei.org/fa/page.php?pg=women)
11. *Iran*, 5 February 2005.
12. *ISNA*, 29 October 2004.
13. *Shargh*, 24 October 2004.
14. Yousif A. Bani-Taraf, *Qawmiyat-ha va Tuvse'ah dar Iran* (research paper, 2003). (Retrieved on 20 January 2005 from www.ahwazstudies.org/Nationalq/nationalities%20and%20development.htm)
15. Mahdi Karroubi, the former Majlis speaker, cited in *ISNA*, 2 January 2005.
16. Bani-Taraf.
17. *Shargh*, 31 January 2005.

Bibliography

Books

'Abdi, A., and Goudarzi, M., *Tahavulat-e Farhangi dar Iran*, (The Cultural Changes in Iran), Tehran: Rawsh, 1999.

'Abdi, A., and Rezaie, A., *Entekhab-e Nou*, (A New Choice), third edition, Tehran: Tarh-e Nou, 1999.

'Alavitabar, 'Alireza, *Rawshanfikri, Dindari, Mardomsalari*, (Intellectualism, Religiosity, Democracy), Tehran: Farhang va Andisheh, 2000.

'Amili, Jamal al-Din al-, *Ma'alim al-Din*, (The Religion's Signposts), Qum: al-Nashr al-Islami, 1986.

'Amili, Muhammad al-, *Al-Qawa'id wa al-Fawaed*, (The Rules and the Results), Qum: al-Mufid, n.d.

'Amili, Zayn al-Din al-, *Rasael al-Shahid al-Thani*, (The Treatises of the Second Martyr), Qum: Mar'ashi Library, 1989.

Amoli, Ayatollah Jawadi, *Biramun-e Wahi va Rahbari*, (About Revelation and Leadership), Tehran, 1998.

Amoli, Jawadi, *Wilayat-e Faqih*, (Jurist's Guardianship), Qum: Isra, 1988.

Abrahamian, Ervand, *Khomeinism: Essays on the Islamic Republic*, Berkeley: University of California Press, 1993.

Achtemeier, Paul, *An Introduction to the New Hermeneutic*, Philadelphia: The Westminster Press, 1969.

Akhavi, Shahrough, *Religion and Politics in Contemporary Iran: Clergy-State Relations in the Pahlavi Period*, Albany: SUNY Press, 1980.

Alsaif, Tawfiq, *Nazariat al-Sultah fi al-Fiqh al-Shi'i*, (Theory of Power in Shi'i Jurisprudence), Beirut: Al-Markaz al-Thaqafi al-Arabi, 2002.

Alsaif, Tawfiq, *Dhidd al-Istibdad*, (Counter-Tyranny), Beirut: Al-Markaz al-Thaqafi al-Arabi, 1999.

Amavi, Bahman, *Eqtesad-e Siasi Jumhouri Islami*, (The Political Economy of the Islamic Republic), Tehran: Gam-e Nou, 2003.

Amin, Muhsin al-, *A''yan al-Shi'ah*, (The Shi'a Notables), Beirut: al-Ta'aruf, 1986.

Amini, I., *Hukumat-e Alavi: Bunian-ha va Chalesh-ha*, (A Government Inspired by Ali bin Abi Talib: Foundations and Challenges), (e. edition, retrieved in November 2004 from www.nezam.org/persian/books/hukoomate-e_alavi_bunyan_ha_va_chalesh_ha/02.htm).

Amuzegar, Jahangir, *Iran Economy under the Islamic Republic*, London: I.B. Tauris, 1993.

Ansari, Murtada, *Kitab Al-Makasib*, (The Book of Earnings), Qum: al-Nashr al-Islami, 1999.

Ansari, Murtada, *Kitab al-Qada wa al-Shahadat*, (The Book of Judgement and Testimonies), Qum: Lajnat Tahqiq Turath al-Shaykh al-A'zam, 1993.

Ansari, Ali, *Iran, Islam and Democracy*, London: Royal Institute of International Affairs, 2000.

Apter, David, *The Politics of Modernization*, Chicago: University of Chicago Press, 1965.

Arjomand, Said, *The Turban for Crown*, New York: Oxford University Press, 1988.

Arjomand, Said, *The Shadow of God and the Hidden Imam*, Chicago: University of Chicago Press, 1984.

Ashkoari, Hassan, *Kherad dar Ziafat-e Din*, (Reason Embraced by the Religion), Tehran: Qasidah, 2000.

Ayalon, Ami (ed.), *Middle East Contemporary Survey: 1993*, Boulder: Westview, 1995.

Ayatollah Montazeri's Office, *Vaqe'iat-ha va Qazavat-ha*, (Facts and Judgements), a book in defence of Ayatollah Montazeri's positions, (Qum 1998), (e. edition, retrieved in July 2004 from www.amontazeri.com/Farsi/vageeat/FEHREST. HTM).

Bahr al-'Ulum, Muhammad, *Bulghat al-Faqih*, (Faqih's Subsistence), fourth edition, Tehran: al-Sadiq, 1984.

Baktiari, Bahman, *Parliamentary Politics in Revolutionary Iran: The Institutionalization of Factional Politics*, Gainesville: University Press of Florida, 1996.

Barzin, Said, *Jenah-bandi Siasi dar Iran*, (Political Alignment in Iran), fourth edition, Tehran: Markaz, 2000.

Bashiriyeh, Hossein, *Jame'ah Madani wa Tawse'ah Siasi dar Iran*, (Civil Society and Iran's Political Development), Tehran: 'Uloom-e Navin, 1999.

Bashiriyeh, Hossein, *Mavane' Tawse'ah Siasi dar Iran*, (The Impediments of Iran's Political Development), second edition, Tehran: Gam-e Nou, 2001.

Bashiriyeh, Hossein, *The State and Revolution in Iran*, London: Croom Helm, 1984.

Bayat, Asef, *Street Politics*, Cairo: The American University Press, 1997.

Beetham, David, *The Legitimation of Power*, London: Macmillan, 1991.

Binder, Leonard, *Islamic Liberalism*, Chicago: University of Chicago Press, 1988.

Blondel, Jean, *Comparative Government*, second edition, New York: Harvester Wheatsheaf, 1995.

Boroujerdi, Mehrzad, 'Can Islam be Secularized?', in Esfandiari, Berton and Farhi (eds), *Intellectual Change and the New Generation of Iranian Intellectuals*, (Washington 2000), p. 13, (e. edition, retrieved on 2 June 2004 from: http://faculty.maxwell.syr.edu/mborouje/Continuities.html).

Brown, Carl, *Religion and State: The Muslim Approach to Politics*, New York: Columbia University Press, 2000.

Buchta, Wilfried, *Who Rules Iran*, Washington DC: The Washington Institute for Near East Policy, 2000.

Bustani, Mahmud, (ed.), *Al-Kharajyiat* (Treatises on Public Resources), Qum: al-Nashr al-Islami, 1992.

Coker, Francis, *Readings in Political Philosophy*, New York: Macmillan, 1938.

Daftar-e Tahkim-e Vahdat, *Nezarat-e Estesvabi*, (Arbitrary Supervision), Tehran: Afkar, 2000.

Daniel, Elton, *The History of Iran*, London: Greenwood, 2001.

Dorraj, Manochehr, *From Zarathustra to Khomeini: Populism and Dissent in Iran*, London: Lynne Rienner, 1990.

Ehteshami, Anoushiravan, *After Khomeini: The Iranian Second Republic*, London: Routledge, 1995.

Eickelman, D., and Piscatori, J., *Muslim politics*, Princeton: Princeton University Press, 1996.

Elson, Ruth M., *Guardians of Tradition: American Schoolbooks of the Nineteenth Century*, Lincoln, NE: University of Nebraska Press, 1964.

Esfahani, Abu al-Faraj al-, *Maqatil al-Talebyyin*, (The History of the Killings of the Talibids), Beirut: al-A'lami, 1987.

Esfahani, Muhammad H., *Hashiat al-Makasib*, (A Comment on al-Makasib), Qum: Zakhaer House, 1984.

Esposito John and Donohue John, (eds), *Islam in Transition*, New York: Oxford University Press, 1982.

Esposito, John, and Voll. J., *Islam and Democracy*, Oxford: Oxford University Press, 1996.

Esposito, John, *Islam and Politics*, Syracuse NY: Syracuse University Press, 1987.

Euben, Roxanne, *Enemy in the Mirror*, Princeton: Princeton University Press, 1999.

Fadli, Abdulhadi al-, *Tarikh al-Tashri' al-Islami*, (The History of the Islamic Jurisprudence), London: ICIS, 1992.

Fadli, Abdulhadi al-, *Durous fi Usul Fiqh al-Imamiyah*, (Lessons on the Shi'i Principles of Jurisprudence), Beirut: Um al-Qura, 1999.

Farazmand, Ali, *The State, Bureaucracy, and Revolution in Modern Iran*, London: Praeger, 1989.

Fathi, A., (ed.), *Iranian Refugees and Exiles since Khomeini*, (1991), (e. edition, retrieved on 2 December 2004 from www.northill.demon.co.uk/relstud/Iran-patterns.htm).

Fuchs and Klingemann (eds), *Citizens and the State*, Oxford: Oxford University Press, 1995.

Ganji, Akbar, *Talaqqi Faschisti az Din wa Hukumat*, (Fascistic Perception of the Religion and State), fifth edition, Tehran: Tarh-e Nou, 1999.

Garnham, D., and Tessler, M., (ed.), *Democracy, War and Peace in the Middle East*, Indianapolis: Indiana University Press, 1995.

Golbigani, Muhammad R., *Al-Hedayah ela man lahu al-Wilaya*, (Guidance for the Holders of Authority), edited by Ahmad Saberi, Qum: Ilmiah, 1963.

Goldziher, Ignaz, *Muslim Studies,* translated by Barber, C. R. and Stern, S. M, edited by Stern, London: George Allen & Unwin, 1971.

Hajjarian, Sa'eed, *Az Shahed-e Qudsi ta Shahed-e Bazaari,* (From the Sacred Witness to the Profane Witness), Tehran: Tarh-e Nou, 2001.

Hajjarian, Sa'eed, *Jumhouriat: Afsun-zedaei az Qudrat,* (Republicanism, Demystification of Power), Tehran: Tarh-e Nou, 2000.

Hajjarian, Sa'eed, *Tavan-e Islahat,* (The Damage of the Reforms), Tehran: Tarh-e Nou, 2001.

Hakim, Muhammad Taqi al-, *Al- Usul al-'Ammah li'l-Fiqh al-Muqaran,* (The General Principles of Comparative Jurisprudence), second edition, Qum: Ahl al-Bait, 1979.

Halabi, Abu al-Salah al-, *Al-Kafi fi al-Fiqh,* (The Sufficient in Jurisprudence), Isfahan: Amir al-Mo'menin Library, 1983.

Haqiqat, S., *Tawzi'e Qudrat Dar Fiqh-e Shi'a,* (Power Distribution in Shi'i Jurisprudence), Tehran: Hasti-nama, 2002.

Hasani, Hashim M. al-, *Sirat al-Ayemmah al-Ithnai 'Ashar,* (The Twelve Imams' Biography), Beirut: al-Ta'aruf, 1990.

Hassan, Hassan, *Tarikh al-Islam,* (The History of Islam), seventh edition, Cairo: al-Nahdah al-Misriyah, 1964.

Hairi, Kazim, *Welayat al-Amr fi 'Asr al-Ghaibah,* (Government During the Occultation), Qum: Majma' al-Fikr al-Islami, 1994.

Hairi, Kazim, *Al-Marje'iah wa al-Qiadah,* (Exemplary and Leadership), Qum: 1998.

Hakimi, Muhammad, Muhammad & 'Ali, *Al-Hayat,* (Life), Beirut: al-Islamiah, 1987.

Hall, John, *Liberalism : Politics, Ideology, and the Market,* Chapel Hill: University of North Carolina Press, 1988.

Hall, S., Held, D. and McLennan, G., (eds), *The Idea of Modern State,* London: Open University Press, 1984.

Halm, Heinz, *Shi'a Islam: From Religion to Revolution,* translated by Brown, A., Princeton: Markus Weiner, 1996.

Hamadani, Agha Riza, *Misbah al-Faqih,* (The Light of the Faqih), Qum: Sadr, 1995.

Held, David, *Models of Democracy,* second edition, Cambridge: Polity, 1997.

Held, David, *Political Theory and the Modern State,* Cambridge: Polity, 1989.

Heywood, Andrew, *Political Ideologies,* second edition, New York: Palgrave, 1998.

Hilli, 'Allamah Jamal al-Din al-, *Al-Alfain,* (The Two Thousands), Kuwait: al-Alfain, 1985.

Hilli, Al-Muhaqqiq al-, *Sharie' al-Islam,* (The Rules of Islam), second edition, Tehran: Isteqlal, 1990.

Hunter, S. and Newsom, D., *Iran after Khomeini,* New York: Praeger, 1992.

Hussain, Jassim, *The Occultation of the Twelfth Imam,* (e. edition, retrieved on 1 February 2002 from www.yamahdi.com/books/pdf/occultation).

Iatridis, Demetrius, *Social Justice and the Welfare State in Central and Eastern Europe: The Impact of Privatization,* London: Praeger, 2000.

Islamic Iran Mosharekat Party, *Bayanat va Mavaze' ta Congereh Avval,* (Communiqués and Position Ahead of the First Congress), Tehran: 2001.

Jalaipour, Hamid, *Dawlat-e Penhan,* (The Hidden State), second edition, Tehran: Tarh-e Nou, 2000.

Jalaipour, Hamid, *Pas az Dovom Khordad,* (After the Second of Khordad), second edition, Tehran: Kavir, 1999.

Joyner, Christopher, T*he Persian Gulf War: Lessons for Strategy, Law, and Diplomacy,* New York: Greenwood, 1990.

Juwaini, Abo al-Ma'ali al-, *Giyath al-Umam,* (The Relief of the Peoples), Alexandria: Al-Da'wah, 1979.

Kadivar, Jamilah, *Tahavule Goftaman Siasi Shi'a dar Iran,* (The Evolution of Shi'i Political Discourse in Iran), second edition, Tehran: Tarh-e Nou, 2000.

Kadivar, Mohsen, *Daghdaghah-hye Hukumat-e Dini,* (Anxieties Regarding Religious Government), second edition, Tehran: Nashr-e Nai, 2000.

Kadivar, Mohsen, *Hukumat-e Walai-e,* (Guardianship-Based Government), fourth edition, Tehran: Nashr-e Nai, 2001.

Kalantari, 'Aliakbar, *Hukm Thanavi dar Tashri'e Islami,* (Secondary Rule in the Islamic Jurisprudence), Qum: Daftar-e-Tablighat, 1999.

Kamrava, Mehran, *Revolutionary Politics,* London: Praeger, 1992.

Kamrava, Mehran, T*he Political History of Modern Iran: From Tribalism to Theocracy,* London: Praeger, 1992.

Karaki, 'Ali al-, *Jami' al-Maqasid fi Sharh al-Qawa'id,* (The Compiler of Purposes: a Comment on al-Qawa'ed), Qum: Ahl al-Bait, 1988.

Kashif al-Ghita, 'Ali, *Al-Nur al-Sati'fi al-Fiqh al-Nafe',* (The Shining Light in Useful Jurisprudence), Najaf: al-Adab, 1961.

Kashif al-Ghita, Ja'far, *Kashf al-Ghita 'an Mubhamat al-Shari'at-e al-Gharra,* (The Unveiling of the Illusions of the Revered Shari'a), Isfahan: Mahdawi, n.d.

Katouzian, Homa, T*he Political Economy of Modern Iran,* New York: New York University Press, 1981.

Keddie, Nikki, and Cole, Juan, (ed.), *Shi'ism and Social Protest,* New Haven: Yale University Press, 1986.

Keddie, Nikki, *Religion and Politics in Iran,* New Haven: Yale University Press, 1983.

Keddie, Nikki, *Scholars, Saints and Sufis: Muslim Religious Institutions in the Middle East Since 1500,* Berkeley: University of California Press, 1972.

Khatami, Muhammad, *Ayen va Andisheh dar Dam-e Khodkamegi,* (Religion and Intellect Trapped in Tyranny), fourth edition, Tehran: Tarh-e Nou, 2001.

Khatami, Muhammad, *Az Dunia-ye Shahr ta Shahr-e Dunia,* (From the World of a Town to a Global Town), ninth edition, Tehran: Nashr-e Nai, 2000.

Khatami, Muhammad, *Beem-e Mawj,* (The Fear of the Waves), Tehran: Sima-ie Javan, 1992.

Khatami, Muhammad, *Tawse'ah Siasi, Eqtesadi, va Amniat* (Political, Economic Development and Security) Tehran: Tarh-e Nou, 2000.

Khomeini, Rohullah al-Mosavi al-, *Sahifeh Nur,* (The Paper of Light), Tehran: the

Institute for Compilation and Publication of the Works of Imam Khomeini, 2004.

Khomeini, Rohullah al-Mosavi al-, *Misbah al-Hidayah ela al-Khilafat-e wa al-Wilayah*, (The Light of Guidance to Caliphate and Guardianship), (e. edition, retrieved on 5 March 2003 from www.al-kawthar.com/kotob/mesbah.zip).

Khomeini, Rohullah al-Mosavi al-, *Islamic Government*, translated by Hamid Algar, Tehran: The Institute for Compilation and Publication of Imam Khomeini's Works, n.d., (e. edition, retrieved on 5 March 2003 from http://users.fmg.uva.nl/rsetoe/pdfs/velayat_faqeeh.pdf).

Khomeini, Rohullah al-Mosavi al-, *Kitab al-Bay'*, (The Book of Contracts), fourth edition, Qum: al-Nashr al-Islami, 1985.

Khurasani, Akhund M., *Hashiat al-Makasib*, (A Comment on al-Makasib), Tehran: Ministry of Guidance, 1986.

Kohlberg, Etan, *Belief and Law in Imami Shi'ism*, Hampshire: Variorum, 1991.

Kuhn, Thomas, *The Structure of Scientific Revolutions*, Chicago: University of Chicago Press, 1970.

Kulaini, Muhammad bin Yaqoub, *Al-Kafi*, (The Sufficient), Beirut: al-Ta'aruf, 1990.

Kymlicka, W., and Norman, W., *Citizenship in Diverse Societies*, Oxford: Oxford University Press, 2000.

Larijani, Muhammad, *Naqd-e Dindari va Modernism*, (A Critique on Religiosity and Modernism), second edition, Tehran: Ettela'at, 1997.

Lennon, A., and Eiss, C., (eds), *Reshaping Rogue States*, Cambridge: MIT, 2004.

Lerner, Daniel, *The Passing of Traditional Society*, New York: The Free Press, 1965.

Litvak, Meir, *Shi'i Scholars of 19th Century Iraq*, Cambridge: Cambridge University Press, 1988.

Locke, John, (1690), *The Second Treatise of Civil Government*, (e. edition, retrieved in March 2003 from www.constitution.org/jl/2ndtr02.htm).

Madani, Amir, *Mavane' Tavse'ah Eqtesadi Iran*, (The Impediments of Iran's Economic Development), Tehran: Shahr-e Ab, 1995.

Marsh and Stoker, (eds), *Theory and Methods in Political Science*, London: Macmillan, 1995.

Martin, Vanessa, *Creating an Islamic State: Khomeini and the Making of a New Iran*, second edition, New York: I.B. Tauris, 2003.

Mawardi, Abu al-Hassan, *Al-Ahkam al-Sultaniyyah wa al-Wilayat al-Diniyyah*, (The Principles of Kingship and the Religious Authority), second edition, Qum: Maktab al-I'lam al-Islami, 1986.

Menasheri, David, *Post-Revolutionary Politics in Iran*, London: Cass, 2001.

Miller, David; *Social Justice*, Oxford: Clarendon, 1979.

Moezzi, Mohammad, *Divine Guide in Early Shi'ism*, Albany: State University of New York Press, 1994.

Mohaddessin, Mohammad, *Islamic Fundamentalism: The New Global Threat*, Washington, D.C.: Seven Locks, 1993.

Muhajerani, 'Ata'ullah, *Hekayat Hamchenan Baqiest*, (The Case Is Still Open), Tehran: Ettela'at, 1999.

Monshipouri, Mahmood, *Islamism, Secularism and Human Rights in the Middle East*, London: Boulder, 1998.

Montazeri, Hussayn 'Ali, *Dirasat fi Wilayat al-Faqih*, (Studies in the Jurist's Guardianship), second edition, Beirut: al-Islamiah, 1988.

Montazeri, Hussayn 'Ali, *Khaterat*, (Memoirs), (e. edition, retrieved on 20 July 2004, from www.montazeri.ws).

Montazeri, Hussayn A., *Wilayat-e Faqih wa Qanoon-e Asasi*, (Jurist's Guardianship and the Constitution), (Qum 1998), (e. edition, retrieved in October 2003 from www.montazeri.com/html/books/akhar/velayat/velaya01.html).

Montazeri, Hussayn Ali, *Nezam al-Hukm fi al-Islam*, (Islam's Government System), (Qum 2004), (e. edition, retrieved on 20 July 2004, from www.montazeri.ws/Farsi/Nezam/html/0006.htm).

Moradi, Hassan, *Dar Piramun-e Khodmadari-e Iranian*, (On the Iranians' Alienated-Self), second edition, Tehran: Bakhtaran, 2001.

Morgan, David, *Medieval Persia 1040–1797*, London: Longman, 1988.

Moslem, Mehdi, *Factional Politics in Post-Khomeini Iran*, Syracuse: Syracuse University Press, 2002.

Mufid, Muhammad al-Nu'man al-'Akbari al-, *Al-Irshad*, (The Guidance), second edition, Tehran: 'Ilmiah Islamiah, n.d.

Mufid, Muhammad al-Nu'man al-'Akbari al-, *al-Muqne'ah*, (The Convincing), Qum: al-Nashr al-Islami, 1990.

Muhammad, Majid, *Jame'ah Madani Irani*, (Iran's Civil Society), Tehran: Markaz, 1999.

Murtada, al-Sharif 'Ali al-, *Rasael al-Sharif al-Murtada*, (The Treatises of al-Shareef al-Murtada), Qum: Dar al-Quran al-Karim, 1984.

Murtada, al-Sharif al-, *Tanzih al-Anbia*, (Glorifying the Prophets), second edition, Beirut: al-Adwaa, 1989.

Murtaja, Hujjat, *Jenah-hie Siasi dar Iran Emrooz*, (Political Factions of Today's Iran), fifth edition, Tehran: Naqsh va Negar, 1999.

Mutahhari, Murtaza, *'Adl-e Elahi*, (Divine Justice), Tehran: Sadra, 1993.

Najafi, Muhammad H, *Jawaher al-Kalam*, (The Best Sayings), Tehran: Dar al-Kotob al-Islamiah, 1988.

Namazi, Baquer, (ed.), Iranian NGOs: Situation Analysis, (2000), (e. edition, retrieved on 20 December 2004 from www.iranngos.org/reports/SituationAnalysis/009_10WomenPart.htm).

Naraqi, Ahmad, *'Awaid al-Ayyam*, (The Benefits of the Days), third edition, Qum: Basirati, 1988.

Nasiri, M., *Dastour-e Shahriaran*, (The Sovereigns' Order), Tehran: Buniad-e Mawqufat-e Dr. Afshar, 1994.

Nasr, H., Dabashi and Nasr, (eds), *Shi'ism: Doctrine, Thought and Spirituality*, New York: State University of New York Press, 1988.

Omid, Homa, *Islam and the Post-Revolutionary State in Iran*, New York: St. Martin's, 1994.

Parsa, Misagh, *State, Ideologies, and Social Revolutions*, Cambridge: Cambridge University Press, 2000.

Pelletiere, Stephen, *The Iran-Iraq War: Chaos in a Vacuum,* New York: Praeger, 1992.

Piscatori, James, (ed.), *Islam in the Political Process,* Cambridge: Cambridge University Press, 1983.

Plato, *The Republic,* translated by Desmond Lee, second edition, London: Penguin, 2003.

Qaemmaqami, 'Abbas, *Qudrat va Mashro'iat,* (Power and Legitimacy), Tehran: Sureh, 2000.

Qouchani, Muhammad, *Pedar Khondah va Chap-hie Javan,* (The Godfather and the Young Leftists), third edition, Tehran: Nashr-e Nai, 2000.

Quchani, M., *Yeqeh-Sefidha,* (The Bureaucrats), second edition, Tehran: Naqsh va Negar, 2000.

Qummi, 'Abbas al-, *Al-Kuna wa al-Alqab,* (Surnames and Titles), Tehran: al-Sadr, 1989.

Radi, al-Sharif al-, *Nahj al-Balaghah,* (The Speeches and Sayings of 'Ali bin Abi Talib), S. al-Saleh, (ed.), Qum: Hejrat, 1975.

Rafi'pour, Faramerz, *Tavse'ah va Tazadd,* (Development and Contradiction), second edition, Tehran: Enteshar, 1998.

Rafsanjani, 'Ali A. Hashemi, *'Ubur az Buhran,* (Overcoming the Turmoil), eighth edition, Tehran: Ma'aref Enghelab, 1999.

Rajaee, Farhang, *The Iran-Iraq War: The Politics of Aggression,* Gainesville, FL: University Press of Florida, 1997.

Rashidi, 'Ali, *Eqtesad-e Mardum-salar,* (Democratic Economy), Tehran: Awaie Nur, 1997.

Rawls, John, *Political Liberalism,* New York: Columbia University Press, 1996.

Richard, Yann, *Shi'ite Islam,* translated by Nevill, A., Oxford: Blackwell, 1995.

Robinson, M., and White G., (eds), *The Democratic Developmental State: Politics and Institutional Design,* Oxford: Oxford University Press, 1998.

Rohani, Ayatollah M. Sadiq, *Nezam-e Hukumat dar Islam,* (The System of Government in Islam), (e. edition, retrieved on 13 April 2003 from www.imamrohani.com/farisi/kotob/hokomat/01.htm).

Sachedina, Abdulaziz, *The Just Ruler in Twelver Shi'ism,* New York: Oxford University Press, 1988.

Sadr, M. Baqer, *Al-Ma'alim al-Jadidah li'l-Usul,* (The New Signposts of the Principles of Jurisprudence), third edition, Beirut: al-Ta'aruf, 1981.

Sadr, M. Baqer, *Muqaddamat fi al-Tafsir al-Mawdo'ei lil-Quran,* (Introduction to the Objective Explanation of Quran), (e. edition, retrieved on 18 February 2003 from www.rafed.net/ftp/books/moqadamat.zip).

Saduq, Muhammad bin 'Ali al-, *Kamal al-Din,* (The Completion of the Religion), Qum: al-Nashr al-Islami, 1995.

Safiri, Mas'oud, *Haqiqat-ha va Maslahat-ha,* (The Truth and the Interests: Interviews with Hashemi Rafsanjani), Tehran: Nashr-e Nai, 1999.

Salehi, M., *Insurgency through Culture and Religion: The Islamic Revolution of Iran,* New York: Praeger, 1988.

Sarjouei and Sadatian, *Entekhabat-e Majlis Panjum dar Ayeneh Matbo'at,* (The Elections of the Fifth Majlis as Narrated by the Media), Tehran: Dana, 1999.

Sayyid, Redwan al-, *Al-Jama'ah wa al-Mujtama' wa al-Dawlah,* (Community, Society, and State), Beirut: al-Kitab al-'Arabi, 1997.

Sayuri, Miqdad, *Nadhed al-Qawa'id al-Fiqhia,* (Arranging the Jurisprudential Rules), Qum: Mar'ashi Library, 1982.

Scruton, Roger, *A Dictionary of Political Thought,* London: Macmillan, 1996.

Sepah Islamic Research Centre, *Ahzab va Tashkilat-e Siasi Iran,* (Iran's Parties and Political Groups), Qum, (e. edition, retrieved on 16 August 2004, from www. tooba-ir.org/siyasi/ahzab/kargo/fehrest.htm).

Seung, T., *Semiotics and Thematics in Hermeneutics,* New York: Columbia University Press, 1982.

Shabasteri, Muhammad, *Naqdi bar Qaraat-e Rasmi az Din,* (A Critique on the Official Interpretation of the Religion), Tehran: Tarh-e Nou, 2000.

Shabestari, Muhammad, *Hermeneutic, Kitab va Sunnat,* (Hermeneutic, Quran and the Prophet's Traditions), fourth edition, Tehran: Tarh-e Nou, 2000.

Shadlo, 'Abbas, *Ettela'ati darbareh Ahzab va Jenah-haye Siasi Iran Emrooz,* (Information on the Political parties and Groups), Tehran: Gostareh, 2000.

Shalaq, Alfadl, *Al-Ummah wa al-Dawlah,* (The Community and the State), Beirut: al-Muntakhab al-'Arabi, 1993.

Shams al-Din, Muhammad, *Nizam al-Hukm wa al-Idarah fi al-Islam,* (The Islamic System of Government and Administration), second edition, Beirut: al-Dawliaah, 1991.

Shari'ati, 'Ali, *Islamology: the Basic Design for a School of Thought and Action,* (e. edition, retrieved on 11 November 2004 from http://shariati.com/islamgy2. html).

Shirazi, Makarim, *Anwar al-Faqahah,* (The Lights of Jurisprudence), Qum: Amir al-Mo'menin School, 1990.

Shirazi, Makarem, *Buhuth Fiqhiyyah Muhemmah,* (Essential Jurisprudential Issues), Qum, (e. edition, retrieved on 21 May 2002 from www.amiralmomenin.net/ books/arabic/bohos/fehrest.htm).

Skemp, J. B., *Plato's Statesman,* London: Bristol Classical Press, 1987.

Smith, Mark, *Social Science in Question,* London: Sage, 1998.

Soroush, Abdol-Karim, *Akhlagh-e Khodayan,* (The Morals of Gods), second edition, Tehran: Tarh-e Nou, 2001.

Soroush, Abdol-Karim, *Bast-e Tajrebah Nabavi,* (Expansion of Prophetic Experience), third edition, Tehran: Serat, 1999.

Soroush, Abdol-Karim, *Ferbah-tar az Ideology,* (Sturdier Than Ideology), sixth edition, Tehran: Serat, 1999.

Soroush, Abdol-Karim, *Qabz va Bast-e Theoric Shari'at,* (The Theory of Evolution of Religious Knowledge), eighth edition, Tehran: Serat, 2003.

Soroush, Abdol-Karim, *Razdani va Rawshanfikri va Dindari,* (Wisdom, Intellectualism and Religious Conviction), fifth edition, Tehran: Serat, 2000.

Subhani, Ja'far, (ed.), *Tahthib al-Usul,* (The Articulation of the Principles of Jurisprudence), Qum: Isma'ilian, 2000.

Tabari, Muhammad ibn Jarir al-, *Jame' al-Bayan*, (The Compiler of the Statements), Beirut: Dar al-Fikr, 1995.

Tabari, Muhammad ibn Jarir al-, *Tarikh al-Umam wa al-Muluk*, (The History of Nations and Kings), second edition, Beirut: Swaidan, 1967.

Tabarsi, Al-Fadl al-, *E'lam al-Wara*, (Informing the People), Najaf, n.d.

Tachau, Frank, *Political Parties of the Middle East and North Africa*, Westport: Greenwood, 1994.

Tehrani, Agha Buzurg, *Al-Thari'ah ela Tasanif al-Shi'a*, (The Guide to the Shia's Literature), second edition, Beirut: al-Adwaa, 1983.

Turabi, Hassan, *Hewarat fi al-Islam, al-Dimuqratiyya, al-Dawlah, al-Gharb*, (Dialogues on Islam, Democracy, State, and the West), Beirut: al-Jadid, 1995.

Tusi, Muhammad, *Al-Iqtisad fi ma Yata'allaq be al-I'tiqad*, (A Brief on Belief), second edition, Beirut: al-Adwa, 1986.

Tusi, Muhammad, *Al-Nehayah*, (The Conclusive), second edition, Beirut: al-Kitab al-A'rabi, 1979.

Vahdat, Farzin, *God and Juggernaut*, Syracuse, NY: Syracuse University Press, 2002.

Watt, William Montgomery, *The Formative Period of Islamic Thought*, Edinburgh: Edinburgh University, 1973.

Welhausen, J., *The Religio-Political Factions in Early Islam*, (ed.), Ostle, R., translated by Ostle, R., and Walzer, S., Amsterdam: North Holland, 1975.

Wright, Robin, *The Last Great Revolution*, New York: Alfred A. Knopf, 2000.

Ya'qubi, Ahmad, *Tarikh al-Ya'qubi*, (The Ya'qubi History), Qum: al-Sharif al-Radhi, 1994.

Yazdi, Ibrahim, *Seh Jumhouri*, (Three Republics), Tehran: Jame'ah Iranian, 2001.

Yazdi, Mesbah, *Negah-e Gozara be Welayat-e Faqih*, (A Quick Look at the Jurist's Guardianship), Qum: Mo'assaseh Imam Khomeini, 1999.

Yazdi, M., *Nazarieh Siasi Islam*, (The Islamic Political Doctrine), Qum: Mo'assaseh Imam Khomeini, 2001.

Yazdi, M., *Al-Mujtama' wa al-Tarikh min Wejhat Nazar al-Quran al-Kareem*, (History and Society Viewed by Holy Quran), translated by Khaqani, M., Tehran: Amir Kabir, 1994.

Zanjani, 'Abbas, *Fiqh Siasi*, (Political Jurisprudence), Tehran: Amir Kabir, 1998.

Zargari-Najad, G., *Rasael Mashroutiat*, (The Treatises of the Constitutional Revolution), Tehran: Kavir, 1995.

Zarifinia, Hamid, *Kalbud-shekafi Jenah-hye Siasi Iran*, (Dissecting Iran's Political Factions), third edition, Tehran: Azadi-e Andisheh, 1999.

Zibakalam, Sadiq, *Ma Chegounah Ma Shudim*, (The Orientation of Iran's Current Conditions), second edition, Tehran: Rawzanah, 1996.

Zibakalam, Sadiq, *Moqaddameh bar Enqelab-e Islami*, (An Introduction to the Islamic Revolution), third edition, Tehran: Rawzanah, 1999.

Articles and Journals

Abdo, Geneive, 'Re-Thinking The Islamic Republic: 'A "Conversation" with

Ayatollah Hussayn 'Ali Montazeri', *The Middle East Journal*, vol. 53, no. 4, (Autumn 1999).

Ackrill, John, 'Aristotle on Action', *Mind, New Series*, vol. 87, issue 348, (October 1987), pp. 595–601.

Ake, Claude, 'Charismatic Legitimation and Political Integration', *Comparative Studies in Society and History*, Vol. 9, No. 1, (October 1966), pp. 1–13.

Algar, Hamid, 'The Fusion of the Gnostic and the Political in the Personality and Life of Imam Khomeini', (e. edition: www.khomeini.com/GatewayToHeaven/Articles/PersonalityofImam.html).

Almond, Gabriel, 'A Developmental Approach to Political Systems', *World Politics*, vol. 17, issue 2, (January 1965), pp. 183–214.

Al-Sharafi, A., 'Mushkelat al-Hukm fi al-Fikr al-Islami al-Hadith', (The Problems of Government in the Modern Islamic Thought), *al-Ijtiha*d, no. 14, (Winter 1992), pp. 69–93.

Arusta, M., 'Majlis-e Khobragan az Didgah-e Nazariah Wilayat-e Faqih', (The Expert Council as Viewed by the Theory of Jurist's Guardianship), *Hukumat-e Islami*, no. 8, (Summer 1998).

Arusta, M., Ehtemam beh Aray-e 'Umumi, (The Observation of Public Opinion), *Hukumat-e Islami*, no. 17, (Autumn 2000).

Bani-Taraf, Yousif A., 'Qawmiyyat-ha va Tuvse'ah dar Iran', (Ethnicity and Development in Iran), research paper, 2003, (retrieved from www.ahwazstudies.org/Nationalq/nationalities%20and%20development.htm).

Behdad, Sohrab, 'Foreign Exchange Gap, Structural Constraints, and the Political Economy of Exchange Rate Determination in Iran', *International Journal of Middle East Studies*, vol. 20, no. 1, (February 1988), pp. 1–21.

Bendix, Reinhard, 'Reflections on Charismatic Leadership', *Asian Survey*, vol. 7, no. 6, (June 1967), pp. 341–52.

Bill, James, 'Modernization and Reform from Above: the Case of Iran', *The Journal of Politics*, vol. 32, issue 1, (February 1970), pp. 19–40.

Billings, D., and Scott, S., 'Religion and Political Legitimation', *Annual Review of Sociology*, vol. 20, (1994), pp. 173–202.

Binder, L., 'National Integration and Political Development', *The American Political Science Review*, vol. 58, issue 3, (September 1964), pp. 622–31.

Bulliet, Richard, 'Twenty Years of Islamic Politics', The Middle East Journal, vol. 53, No. 2, (Spring 1999).

Carlisle, Robert, 'The Birth of Technocracy: Science, Society, and Saint-Simonians', *Journal of the History of Ideas*, vol. 35, no. 3, (July-September 1974), pp. 445–64.

Carse, Alisa, 'The Liberal Individual: A Metaphysical or Moral Embarrassment?', *Noûs*, vol. 28, no. 2, (June 1994), pp. 84–209.

Centeno, Miguel, 'The New Leviathan: The Dynamics and Limits of Technocracy', *Theory and Society*, vol. 22, no. 3, (June 1993), pp. 307–35.

Clark, Jane, 'Fulfilling our Potential: Ibn 'Arabi's Understanding of Man in a Contemporary Context', *The Journal of the Muhyiddin Ibn Arabi Society*, vol. 30, (Autumn 2001), (www.ibnarabisociety.org/clark.html).

Dabashi, H., 'The End of Islamic Ideology', *Social Research*, vol. 67, no. 2, (Summer, 2000), (e. edition, retrieved from www.findarticles.com/p/articles/mi_m2267/is_2_67/ai_63787340).

Easton, David, 'An Approach to the Analysis of Political Systems', *World Politics*, vol. 9, issue 3, (April 1957), pp. 383–400.

Fakhr, A., 'Awamil-e Puya-ie Fiqh', (The Factors of Regenerating the Jurisprudence), *Qabasat*, no. 15–6, (Spring 2000).

Freeland, S., 'Aristotelian Actions', *Noûs*, vol.19, no. 3, (September 1985), pp. 397–414.

Geise, J. P., 'In Defence of Liberalism', *The Western Political Quarterly*, vol. 44, no. 3, (September 1991), pp. 583–604.

Gerring, J., 'Ideology: A Definitional Analysis', *Political Research Quarterly*, vol. 50, no. 4, (December 1997), pp. 957–94.

Hairi, Abdulhadi, 'The Legitimacy of Early Qajar Rule Viewed by the Shi'i Religious Leaders', *Middle Eastern Studies*, vol. 24, 1998.

Heath, Graaf, and Nieuwbeerta, 'Class Mobility and Political Preferences', *American Journal of Sociology*, vol. 100, no. 4, (January 1995), pp. 997–1027.

Heeger, Gerald, 'Bureaucracy, political Parties, and Political Development', *World Politics,* vol. 25, issue 4, (July 1973), pp. 600–7.

Hodgson, Marshall, 'How Did the Early Shi'a Become Sectarian?', *Journal of the American Oriental Society*, vol. 75, no. 1, (January-March 1995), pp. 1–13.

Huntington, S., 'Political Development and Political Decay', *World Politics*, vol. 17, issue 3, (April 1965), pp. 386–430.

Katouzian, Homa, 'Problems of Political Development in Iran', *British Journal of Middle Eastern Studies*, vol. 22, no. ½, (1995), pp. 5–20.

Katouzian, Homa, 'The Aridiosolatic Society: A Model of Long-Term Social and Economic Development in Iran', *International Journal of Middle East Studies*, vol. 15, no. 2, (May 1983), pp. 259–81.

Katouzian, Huma, 'Problems of Democracy and Public Sphere in Modern Iran', *Comparative Studies of South Asia, Africa and the Middle East*, vol. 18, no. 2, (1998), pp. 31–6.

Keddie, Nikki, 'Iran, Understanding the Enigma: A Historian's View', *Middle East Review of International Affairs Journal*, vol. 2, no. 3, (September 1998), (retrieved from www.ciaonet.org/olj/meria/meria98_keddie.html).

Kessler, Sanford, 'Tocqueville on Civil Religion and Liberal Democracy', *The Journal of Politics*, vol. 39, no. 1, (February 1977), pp. 119–46.

Khalilzad and Benard, 'Secularization, Industrialization, and Khomeini's Islamic Republic', *Political Science Quarterly*, vol. 94, issue 2, (Summer 1979), pp. 229–41.

Lankarani, M., 'Theory 'Adalat dar Hukumat-e Islami va wilayat-e Faqih', (The Theory of Justice in the Islamic Government and Jurist's Guardianship), (e. edition accessed on 14 April 2004 from www.lankarani.org/persian/najlehi/teori.html).

Larijani, M., 'Islam va Democracy', (Islam and Democracy), *Ma'refat*, no. 12, (Spring 1995).

Larijani, M., 'Hukumat-e Islami va Marz-hie Siasi', (The Islamic State and the Territorial Limits), *Hukumat-e Islami,* no. 2, (Winter 1996).

Larijani, Muhammad. J., 'Islam: Dawlat-e Qadim va Jadid', (Old and Modern Islamic State), *Hukumat-e Islami,* no. 16, (Summer 2000).

Lester, Seligman, 'Elite Recruitment and Political Development', *The Journal of Politics,* vol. 26, issue 3, (August 1964), pp. 612–26.

Ma'refat, M., 'Fiqh Jawahiri va Vijegihie unn', (The Features of Jawaheri's Jurisprudential Methodology), *Andishah Hawzah,* (Summer 1997).

Ma'refat, Muhammad. H., 'Pluralism Dini dar Boteh Naqd', (A Critique of the Religious Pluralism), *Andishah Hawzah,* no. 16, (Spring 1999).

Mahamid, 'Fiqh Mustalah Hawzah dar Dunia-ye Emrooz', (The Contemporary Challenge to the Established Jurisprudence), *Huzur,* vol. 34, (Spring 2001).

Mansfield, Harvey, 'Self-Interest Rightly Understood', *Political Theory,* vol. 23, no. 1, (February 1995), pp. 48–66.

Martin, Douglas, 'The Case of the Bahai Minority in Iran', *The Bahai World,* (1992–3), pp. 247–71.

Mehrizi, M., 'Dawlat-e Dini va Harim Khususi', (Religious State and the Private Sphere), *Hukumat-e Islami,* no. 12, (Summer 1999).

Momen, M., 'Authority and Opposition in Twelver Shi'ism', in Burrell, R. M., (ed.), 'Islamic Fundamentalism', a paper read at a seminar held at the School of Oriental and African Studies, (10 March 1988), pp. 48–66.

Momen, M., 'Din va Musharakat-e Siasi', (Religion and Political Participation), *'Ulum Siasi,* no. 7, (Winter 1999).

Muhebbi, D., 'Nazariah Din Hadde Akthar', (The Theory of Maximal Religiosity), *Naqd va Nazar,* vol. 6, issues 1 & 2, (Winter-Spring 1999).

Muhsini and Sepidrudi, 'Nabarabari-e Jensi dar mian-e Tabagheh Cargar', (April 2003), (e. edition : www.mehdis.com/tablu/print.php?sid=7801).

Nabavi, A., 'Tatavur-e Andisheh Siasi Imam Khomeini', *Faslnameh Imam Sadeq,* no. 6, (Summer and Autumn 1998), (e. edition, retrieved on 3 June 2004 from www.hawzah.net/Per/Magazine/is/006/is00604.htm).

Nikpay, A., 'Ideology, Din, va Enqelab-e Iran', *Matin,* nos. 3 & 4, (Summer 1999), (e. edition: www.hawzah.net/Per/Magazine/mt/003/mt00316.htm).

Parsa, Misagh, 'Economic Development and Political Transformation', *Theory and Society,* vol. 14, no. 5, (September 1985), pp. 623–75.

Rahman, Bodiur, 'Responsibility for Action in an Early Historical Document of Islam', *The Islamic Quarterly,* vol. 34, no. 4, (1990), pp. 235–45.

Razi, G., 'Legitimacy, Religion, and Nationalism in the Middle East', *The American Political Science Review,* vol. 84, no. 1, (March 1990), pp. 69–91.

Ringer, F., 'The Intellectual Field, Intellectual History, and the Sociology of Knowledge', *Theory and Society,* vol. 19, no. 3, (June 1990), pp. 269–94.

Rohani, Hassan, 'Daramadi bar Mashro'iat wa Karamadi', (A Comment on Legitimacy and Competency), *Rahburd,* no. 18, (Winter 2001), pp. 6–36.

Rusta, M., and Ramazani, M., 'Barrasi Vaz'iat-e Tavzi' Daramad dar Iran', (An Inquiry on the Incomes in Iran), *Ettelaat Siasi Eqtesadi,* no. 177–8, (May-June 2002) pp. 250–63.

Sadr, Muhammad B., 'Al-Ittijahat al-Mustaqbaliyah le-Harakat al-Ijtihad', (The Future Directions of the Intrepretation), *Al-Hadi*, vol. 2, no. 3, (March 1973), (e. edition retrieved on 22 August 2003 from http://209.61.210.137/uofislam/behoth/behoth_isol/06.htm).

Sadra, 'Alireza, 'Barrasi Muqayeseh-e Qanun Asasi', (Comparative Analysis in the Constitution), *Hukumat-e Islami,* no. 7, (Spring 1997).

Sadri, M., 'Sacral Defense of Secularism: The Political Theologies of Soroush, Shabestari, and Kadivar', *International Journal of Politics*, Culture and Society, vol. 15, no. 2, (Winter 2001), pp. 257–70.

Schweitzer, Arthur, 'Theory and Political Charisma', *Comparative Studies in Society and History*, vol. 16, no. 2, (March 1974), pp. 150–81.

Shah Alam, 'Conservatives, Liberals and the Struggle over Iranian Politics', *Strategic Analysis*, vol. 24, no. 3, (June 2000), (e. edition retrived www.ciaonet.org/olj/sa/sa_jun00als01.html).

Shambayati, Hootan, 'The Rentier State, Interest Groups, and the Paradox of Autonomy: State and Business in Turkey and Iran', *Comparative Politics*, vol. 26, no. 3, (April 1994), pp. 307–31.

Shils, E., 'The Intellectuals in the Political Development of the New States', *World Politics*, vol. 12, no. 3, (April 1960), pp. 329–68.

Shils, E., 'Tradition', *Comparative Studies in Society and History*, vol. 13, no. 2, (April 1971), pp. 122–159.

Shorish, M., 'The Islamic Revolution and Education in Iran', *Comparative Education Review*, (February 1988), pp. 58–75.

Somers, M., 'Narrating and Naturalizing Civil Society and Citizenship Theory: The Place of Political Culture and the Public Sphere', *Sociological Theory*, vol. 13, no. 3, (November 1995), pp. 229–74.

Steinberger, Peter, 'Ruling: Guardians and Philosopher-Kings', *The American Political Science Review*, vol. 83, issue 4, (December 1989), pp. 1207–25.

Stern, Paul, 'The Rule of Wisdom and the Rule of Law in Plato's Statesman', *The American Political Science Review*, vol. 91, issue 2, (June 1997), pp. 264–76.

Subhani, Ja'afar, 'Vijagihye Elm Fiqh', (The Peculiars of Jurisprudence), (e. edition: www.balagh.net/persian/feqh/maqalat/koliyat/29.htm).

Tabrizi, Mosavi, 'Jiegah-e Hukumat dar Andisheh Imam', (State's Posture in Imam Khomeini's Thought), Matin, (Winter 1998), (e. edition: www.hawzah.net/Per/Magazine/MT/001/mt00116.htm).

Tajbakhsh, Kian, 'Political Decentralization and the Creation of Local Government in Iran', *Social Research*, vol. 67, no. 2, (Summer 2000).

Taqavi, M., 'Sokhani dar Mafhum Jame'ah Dini', (The Concept of Religious Community), *Fiqh Ahl-e-Bait*, (Summer 1996), (e. edition accessed on 14 April 2003 from www.islamicfeqh.org/magazines/Feqh7f/taghav.htm).

Tsurutani, Taketsugu, 'Stability and Instability', *The Journal of Politics*, vol. 30, no. 4, (November 1968), pp. 910–33.

Vahdat, Farzin, Post-Revolutionary Islamic Discourses on Modernity in Iran: Expansion and Contraction of Human Subjectivity', *International Journal of Middle East Studies.*, vol. 35, issue 04, (November 2003), pp. 599–631.

243

Wa'ezi, 'Ali, 'Wilayat-e Mutlaqa az Didgah Ibn 'Arabi va Mir Haidar Amoli', *Ma'refat*, no. 49, (December 2001), (e. edition, retrieved from www.hawzah. net/Per/Magazine/mr/049/mr04915.htm).

Yazdi, M. T. Misbah, 'Hukumat va Mashro'iat', (Government and Legitimacy), *Kitab-e Naqd*, no. 7, (Summer 1998).

Yazdi, M, Qalamro-e Din, (The Religion's Jursdiction), *Kanoone Goftaman*, Qum, (2001).

Zanjani, A., 'Nizam-e Siasi-e Islam', (The Islamic Regime), *Hukumat-e Islami*, no. 1, (Autumn 1996).

Magazines and Newspapers

'Alavitabar, 'Ali., 'Mosharekat va Mojahedin Enghelab Dou Hasteh Asli Duvum Khordad', (The Parties of Mosharekat and Mojahedin Enghelab: the Cornerstone of the Seocond Khordad), *Nourooz*, (11 July 2002).

'Asifi, Muhammad M., 'Written Interview', *'Ulum-e Hadith*, (retrieved on 9 February 2004, from www.hadith.net/persian/products/magazine/olum-f/07/002.htm).

Abdo, Geneive, 'Electoral Politics in Iran', *Middle East Policy*, vol. 6, no. 4, (June 1999), (www.mepc.org/public_asp/journal_vol6/9906_abdo.asp).

Abedin, Mahan, 'The Origins of Iran's Reformist Elite', *Middle East Intelligence Bulletin*, vol. 5, no. 4, (April 2003), (www.meib.org/articles/0304_iran.htm).

Ahmedzadeh, Taher, 'Anjoman Hojjatiyeh dar Bastar-e Zaman', (Hojjatiyeh Group: the Historical Context), *Chashmandaz Iran*, vol. 5, (May 2000).

Amin, M., 'Iran Politics Turns to Right?' *The Washington Times*, (28 May 2004), (http://washingtontimes.com/upi-breaking/20040528–035422–8502r.htm).

Bahrani, Yousif al-, 'Al-Hadaeq al-Nazerah', (Flourishing Gardens), *Dar Al-Adhwa,* third edition, Beirut, (1993).

Bashiriyeh, H., 'Zawal-e Haviat-e Siasi', (The decline of Political Identity), *Iran*, (16 May 2004).

Behnoud, M., 'Mushkel-e namgozari Gurouha dar Daroun Jumhouri Islami', (The Problem of Naming the Political Groups in the Islamic Republic), *BBC*, (Farsi service), (4 April 2004), (www.bbc.co.uk/persian/iran/030317_a-mb-iran-factions.shtml).

Biran, Barviz, 'Junbush-e Ejtema'i Shahri', (The Urban Social Movement), *Aftab,* vol. 20, (October 2002), pp. 34–5.

Dayhimi, Khashayar, 'Mardomsalari-e Dini Bed'at dar 'Elm-e Siasat', (Religious Democracy, a Heresy in the Political Science), *Aftab*, no. 22, (January 2003).

Deliri, J., 'Shekl-giri Dou E'telaf va Chahar Fraxion dar Majlis Haftum', (The Shaping of Two Alliances and Four Factions in the Seventh Majlis), *Iran*, (24 May 2004), (www.iraninstitute.com/iran/1383/830304/internal.htm).

Deliri, J., 'Farzandan-e 'Asr-e Enghelab va Islahat dar Reqabati Tazah', (The Sons of the Revolutionary Age and Reforms in a Fresh Contest), *Iran*, (11 January 2004).

Eta'at, J., 'Shekafhay-e Ejtema'i va Gurouh-bandi Siasi dar Iran', (Social Fraction and Political Alignment in Iran), *Aftab*, vol. 19, (September 2002).

Ghulami, F., 'Kalbud-shekafi Mo'talefeh', (Dissection of Mo'talefah Party), *Baztab,* (4 & 8 February 2003).

Haidari, Muhammad, 'Hezb-e Jumhuri Islami: Tashakul-e Siasi dar Rohaniat', (The Islamic Republic Party, a Clerical-based political Group), *Iran,* (24 June 2002).

Haidari, M., 'Matbo'at Siasi az 57 ta 80', (Political Publication From 1979 to 2001), *Iran,* (27 May 2002).

Haidari, M., 'Enqelab-e Islami dar 'Asr-e Ma', (The Islamic Revolution Viewed by Asre-ma [paper]), *Iran,* (20 May 2002).

Hajari, Mohsen, 'Muqaddamah bar Sinkh-shenasi Rast dar Iran', (Introductory to the Typology of the Right-Wing), *Chashmandaz Iran,* vol.9, (June 2001), 59–66.

Hajjarian, Sa'eed, 'Henjar-hye bi-Arzesh, Arzeshye bi-Henjar', (The Interchange between Values and Custom), *Nourooz,* (7 March 2002).

Hashemian, Hussayn, 'Zarorat-e Tahqiq va Tafahus Majlis dar Umur Keshwar', (The Necessity of Majlis's Scrutiny of the Public Affairs), *Hamshahri,* (26 June 2000).

Ibrahimi, N., 'Unha Sherkat Kardand', (Those who Participated), *Shargh,* (17 February 2004), (www.sharghnewspaper.com/821128/polit.htm).

Ibrahimi, N., 'Purojeh Yak-dast Shodan', (The Project of Power Consolidation), *Shargh,* (18 April 2004), (www.sharghnewspaper.com/830130/polit.htm).

Ibrahimi, Z., 'Janah-bandi-hye Siasi Majlis Sheshum', (The Sixth Majlis's Factional Structure), *Hamshahri,* (9 September 2000).

'Iran-Iraq Ceasefire: UN Conducts Peace Talks in Geneva, New York', *UN Chronicle,* vol. 25, issue 4, (December 1988).

Jalaipour, Hamid., 'Democracy Dini Mohafeze-caranah va Islah-talaban', (The Reformists and the Conservatives' Perception of Religious Democracy), *Yas-e No,* (5 February 2004).

Jalali, Gholamreza, 'Nazariah Insan-e Kamil az 'Erfan Ibn 'Arabi ta 'Erfan Imam Khomeini', (The Doctrine of Perfect Man from Ibn 'Arabi Gnosis to Imam Khomeini Gnosis), *Hawzah,* no. 94–5.

Jenan-Sefat, M., 'Sun'at-e Iran pas az Bahman 57', (Iran's Industry after February 1979), *Hamshahri,* (20 May 2002).

Jenan-Sefat, M., 'Sun'at-e Khodro', (Iran's Car Industry), *Hamshahri,* (10 December 2002).

Kadivar, Muhsen, 'Mardomsalari-e Dini', (Religious Democracy), *Tabarestan Sabz,* vol. 15, (22 September 2001), pp. 5–7.

Khiyati, Hassan, 'Siasatgorizi va Tarvij Jedayi din az Siasat', (Apathy and the Propagation of the Religion-Politics Diversion), *Jumhuri Islami,* (31 October 2002).

Kiyan, 'Alireza, 'Ustad wa Shagerdanesh', *Hamshahri,* (20 March 2003).

Larijani, M. J., 'Zohd-e Siasi', (Political Selflessness), *Jam-Jam,* (6 September 2004), (www.jamejamdaily.net/shownews2.asp?n=63602&t=pol).

Mahmoudi, F., 'Mafarre Jadid', (A New Escape), *Hamshahri,* (8 August 2002), (e. edition www.hamshahri.org/hamnews/1381/810517/intep.htm).

McCarthy, Rory, 'Rise of the Cleric with all the Answers', *The Guardian*, (16 January 2004), (e. edition www.guardian.co.uk/Iraq/Story/0,2763,1124233,00.html).

Quchani, M., 'Dou Jenah-e Rast', (Two Right-Wings), *Shargh*, (8 April 2004), (www.sharghnewspaper.com/830120/index.htm).

Rafsanjani, 'Ali A. Hashemi, 'Diaries of 1362 (1983)', *Jam-e Jam*, (28 October 2002), (www.jamejamdaily.net/shownews2.asp?n=23061&t=book).

Rahimi, R., 'Congereh Haftum ya Congereh Aval', (The Seventh or the First Congress), *Shargh*, (1 May 2004), (www.sharghnewspaper.com/830212/polit. htm).

Razavi, H., 'Saff-aray-e Tazeh', (A Fresh Alignment), *Hamshahri*, (12 May 2003), (www.hamshahri.org/hamnews/1382/820222/world/intep.htm).

Razavi, Hussayn, 'Bazkhani Parvandeh Anjoman Hojjatiyeh', (The Case of Hojjatiyeh Revisited), *Hamshahri*, (23 October 2002).

Renani, 'Tathir-e Qanun-e Asasi bar Sakhtar-e Eqtesad-e Siasi-e Iran', *Iran*, (5 May 2004).

Rezaie, A., 'Technocrat-hye Muhafezeh-kar', (Conservative Technocrats), *Shargh*, (10 April 2004), (www.sharghnewspaper.com/830122/econom.htm).

Roh, M., 'Mo'talefeh Hezb Shod', (Mo'talefeh Becomes a Party), *Shargh*, (10 January 2004), (www.sharghnewspaper.com/821020/index.htm).

Roh, M. J., 'Moze'e Mosharekat darbareh Namzadi Mosavi', (Mosharekat's Position Regarding the Nomination of Mosavi), *Shargh*, (22 July 2004), (www.sharghnewspaper.com/830503/index.htm).

Sachs, S., 'In Iran, More Women Leaving Nest for University', *New York Times*, (22 July 2000).

Sadri, M., 'Dastan-e Degarguni dar Iran-2', (The Story of the Change of Iran's Economy), *Donya-e Eqtesad*, (19 September 2004), (e. edition www.donya-e-eqtesad.com/83-06-29/070629.htm).

Samii, A. W., 'Sisyphus' Newsstand: the Iranian Press under Khatami', *MERIA*, vol. 5, no. 3, (September 2001), (e. edition http://meria.idc.ac.il/journal/2001/issue3/jv5n3a1.html).

Shabestari, Muhammad, 'Mardomsalari Dini Cheest?', (What is Democracy), *Aftab*, vol. 7, (August 2001), pp. 4–9.

Tajbakhsh, Kian, 'The Fate of Local Democracy in the Islamic Republic', *Iran Analysis Quarterly*, vol. 1, issue 2, (Autumn 2003), pp. 5–8.

Tajik, Muhammad Reza, 'Ahzab: Furobashi Haviat-e Sunnati', (Political Parties and the Vanishing of the Traditional Identity), *Baztab*, (5 January 2003).

Tawakkul, Muhammad, 'Bazaar Sunnati Iran dar Seh Dawreh', (Iran's Traditional Market in Three Epochs), *Chashmandaz Iran*, no. 16, (October 2002), pp. 34–45.

Aftab monthly, vol. 22, (February 2002).

BBC News, (25 January 2000).

Emrooz, (4 August 2004).

Hamshahri, (11 July 1999).

Hamshahri, (3 September, 2000).

Hamshahri, (2 July 2001).

Hamshahri, (27 June 2002).
Hamshahri, (22 August 2002).
Hamshahri, (14 September 2002).
Hamshahri, (18 February 2004).
Hamshahri, (7 September 2004).
Hawzah, no. 23, (December 1987).
 Iran, (3 June 2002).
Iran, (22 July 2002).
Iran, (20 January 2003).
Iran, (25 February 2004).
Iran, (22 August 2004).
Iran, (10 January 2005).
Iran, (5 February 2005).
ILNA, (9 July 2004).
IRIB News, (11 December 2004).
IRNA, (6 February 2003).
ISNA, (9 July 2002).
ISNA, (1 October 2003).
ISNA, (4–7 December 2003).
ISNA, (2 January 2004).
ISNA, (12 January 2004).
ISNA, (24 January 2004).
ISNA, (8 February 2004).
ISNA, (18 May 2004).
ISNA, (23 July 2004).
ISNA, (29 October 2004).
ISNA, (3 November 2004).
ISNA, (17 November 2004).
ISNA, (2 January 2005).
Jomhuri Islami, (20 October 2003).
Jomhuri Islami, (6 April 2004).
Kayhan, (8 February 2000).
Kayhan, (2 December 2002).
Kayhan, (25 February 2004).
Kayhan, (27 June 2004).
Khorassan, (30 July 2000).
Mehr News Agency, (9 February 2004).
Nourooz, (2,10, 11, 12, 13 & 20 June 2002).
Quds, (12 May 2001).
Resalat, (31 March 1998).
Resalat, (23 December 2002).
Shargh, (3 January 2004).
Shargh, (12 June 2004).
Shargh, (24 October 2004).
Shargh, (31 January 2005).

Websites

Ayatollah Sane'i webpage: www.saanei.org/fa/page.php?pg=women
Council for the Maintenance of the Constitution: www.irisn.com
Emrooz: www.emrooz.org
Faith: http://ilrs.org/faith/aghajaritext.html
Gooya: http://news.gooya.com
Iran NGO Resource Centre (Hamyaran): www.hamyaran.org
Ministry of Jihad-e Keshavarzi (Agriculture): www.frw.org.ir/fa/saruquz/darbure_
    suzmun/majmooe_qavunin/1359.htm
Mohsen Kadivar: www.kadivar.com
Mosharekat Party's Unofficial Website: www.ardekan.com
MOSNAD: www.mosnad.com/News/telexu.htm
Salam Iran: www.salamiran.org

Documents

Reporters without Borders, (organisation), 'Iran Annual Report 2003', (www.rsf.
    org/article.php3?id_article=5382&var_recherche=iran).
Statistical Centre of Iran, Statistical Year Book, (1382), Tehran, 2003.
UN Human Development Report 2004, (http://hdr.undp.org/statistics/data/
    indic/indic_10_1_1.html).
United Nations & IRI Plan and Budget Organisation, Human Development Report
    of the Islamic Republic of Iran, 1992.
World Bank, Islamic Republic of Iran: An Agricultural Policy Note, Report no.
    29428–IR, 22 June 2004.

Index